Future Fame in the *Iliad*

Also available from Bloomsbury

A Homeric Catalogue of Shapes, Charlayn von Solms
Homer's Iliad and the Trojan War, Jan Haywood and Naoise Mac Sweeney
The Materialities of Greek Tragedy, edited by Mario Telò and Melissa Mueller

Future Fame in the *Iliad*

Epic Time and Homeric Studies

Yukai Li

BLOOMSBURY ACADEMIC
LONDON • NEW YORK • OXFORD • NEW DELHI • SYDNEY

BLOOMSBURY ACADEMIC
Bloomsbury Publishing Plc
50 Bedford Square, London, WC1B 3DP, UK
1385 Broadway, New York, NY 10018, USA
29 Earlsfort Terrace, Dublin 2, Ireland

BLOOMSBURY, BLOOMSBURY ACADEMIC and the Diana logo are trademarks of
Bloomsbury Publishing Plc

First published in Great Britain 2022
Paperback edition published 2023

Copyright © Yukai Li, 2022

Yukai Li has asserted his right under the Copyright, Designs and
Patents Act, 1988, to be identified as Author of this work.

For legal purposes the Acknowledgements on p. viii constitute an extension
of this copyright page.

Cover design: Terry Woodley
Cover image: Les Salins d'Hyères, Provence Alpes Côte d'Azur,
France. Alexandre FP/Getty

All rights reserved. No part of this publication may be reproduced or transmitted
in any form or by any means, electronic or mechanical, including photocopying,
recording, or any information storage or retrieval system, without
prior permission in writing from the publishers.

Bloomsbury Publishing Plc does not have any control over, or responsibility for, any
third-party websites referred to or in this book. All internet addresses given in this book
were correct at the time of going to press. The author and publisher regret any
inconvenience caused if addresses have changed or sites have ceased to exist,
but can accept no responsibility for any such changes.

A catalogue record for this book is available from the British Library.

Library of Congress Cataloging-in-Publication Data
Names: Li, Yukai (Classicist), author.
Title: Future fame in the Iliad : epic time and Homeric studies / Yukai Li.
Description: New York : Bloomsbury Academic, 2022. |
Includes bibliographical references and index.
Identifiers: LCCN 2021033204 (print) | LCCN 2021033205 (ebook) |
ISBN 9781350239197 (hardback) | ISBN 9781350239210 (ebook) |
ISBN 9781350239227 (epub)
Subjects: LCSH: Homer. Iliad. | Fame in literature. | Epic poetry,
Greek–History and criticism.
Classification: LCC PA4037 .L5726 2022 (print) | LCC PA4037 (ebook) | DDC 883/.01—dc23
LC record available at https://lccn.loc.gov/2021033204
LC ebook record available at https://lccn.loc.gov/2021033205

ISBN:	HB:	978-1-3502-3919-7
	PB:	978-1-3502-3920-3
	ePDF:	978-1-3502-3921-0
	eBook:	978-1-3502-3922-7

Typeset by RefineCatch Limited, Bungay, Suffolk

To find out more about our authors and books visit www.bloomsbury.com
and sign up for our newsletters.

青山依旧在
几度夕阳红

Contents

Acknowledgements		viii
Introduction		1
1	A Different Poet of the Same Name	19
2	The Breaking of the Present	41
	I. From local to generalized division	43
	II. Presentiment and memory	50
	III. The neoanalytic difference	61
3	The Dream of the Instant	71
	I. The instant from Parry to Nagy	72
	II. History and diachrony	83
	III. Difference and multiformity	97
4	Sutures	101
	I. Suture in speech	102
	II. Objecthood and meaning	108
	III. Vignette and simile	115
	IV. The doom of Troy	120
5	Three Syntheses of Time	131
	I. The living present	132
	II. The pure past	140
	III. Time out of joint	149
	IV. Conclusion	157
Notes		163
Bibliography		215
Index		225

Acknowledgements

This book is based on a doctoral dissertation, extensively revised and substantially rewritten, but the ideas and preoccupations it develops reach back to my earliest encounter with the *Iliad* in sophomore Greek, which is to say that I have incurred a whole variety of debts over its long gestation. Let me record my gratitude, first of all, to my dissertation supervisors, Egbert Bakker and Moira Fradinger, whose generosity and guidance extended long past the completion of that project. I am also grateful for the advice and kindness of Pauline LeVen, as well as of David Quint, Irene Peirano Garrison, Joshua Billings and Jay Fisher.

I have been fortunate to have received tremendously helpful feedback on chapters and drafts of the manuscript in various states of revision and incompletion. I am therefore grateful to Justin Arft, Emily Austin, Jonathan Burgess, Thomas Nelson, James Porter, Ruth Scodel and Matthew Ward. I must especially thank Emily Austin and Matthew Ward, who went above and beyond in reading and commenting on versions of the whole manuscript in its earliest and latest states, respectively, as well as James Porter, who had been subjected – not always intentionally – to several early revisions in very rough shape. Let me also record my thanks here to the anonymous reviewers, whose suggestions have been invaluable.

For their comments, questions and patience, I am grateful to the audiences before whom I was able to test out my ideas and arguments, hosted by classics or literature departments at Whitman College, Michigan (Ann Arbor), Toronto, Guelph, Yale and the City University of New York, as well as at meetings of the Society for Classical Studies and the Classical Association of the Middle West and South. I have also benefited from the scholarly and practical advice of my colleagues in the College of the Humanities at Carleton University.

I must record the contribution of Mark Buchan, Andrew Ford, Andrew Feldherr, Sheila Murnaghan and Armand D'Angour to the first inklings of this book. And I thank Justin Arft, Ahuvia Kahane and Matthew Ward for the latest contributions to it, in making available to me their forthcoming work.

At Bloomsbury, my gratitude goes to Alice Wright, Lily Mac Mahon and Georgina Leighton, as well as to other editorial and production staff, who have been wonderful to work with at every stage.

I had previously found rather repetitive – formulaic, even – the way authors absolve the people thanked in these contexts of responsibility for 'all remaining errors', but now I find myself feeling most acutely aware of all the excellent advice and suggestions that I have not been able to put into practice, or could only implement ineptly. There may be a universe in which this book is as good as it can be, but in this one, all remaining errors and infelicities are indeed mine alone.

Introduction

This book results from the meeting of two motivating preoccupations: the temporality of the *Iliad*, and the relationship between scholarship and poetry. Let me first introduce these motivations separately and describe how they combine, before moving on to discuss three figures drawn from the *Iliad* and Homeric scholarship to illustrate the approach that will have been outlined. I will then offer a summary tour of the chapters which follow this introduction.

My fascination with time in the *Iliad* is closely connected with a central concept in Homeric poetics, that of *kleos*, etymologically meaning 'something that is heard' and used to designate the 'fame' or 'glory' that is so important for the Homeric heroes and the singers of epic.[1] For the heroes, the song of their *kleos* provides the meaning of their actions and judgement of their lives, while for the singers, *kleos* is the glorious story which they hear, passed down through tradition, and which they themselves spread in their songs and pass on in turn. A basic observation follows from this initial sketch: that *kleos* is a temporal concept. It is temporal for the heroes because the fame they anticipate will only come in the future, while, for the poets, *kleos* arrives along the chain of tradition from the distant past.[2] Given that *kleos* is at once the future fame of the heroes and the propagating tale of the singers, how can we characterize the form of time that is implicit in the functioning of *kleos*? It would seem intuitive to consider *kleos* a concept of connection, and to characterize the time of *kleos* as a continuous one in which meaning and memory are preserved and transmitted. Indeed, as we will see, this is a common supposition in conceptions of the Homeric tradition and in interpretations of the poems' temporality.

In place of the image of the Homeric tradition as continuous and self-identical, I would like to shift the emphasis to those aspects of the Homeric poems which show us the breaks in continuity and the failures of anticipation and memory, in particular in the *Iliad*. Instead of seeing *kleos* as the bearer of identity through time, I would like to see it instead as expressing difference. What might such a reading of this central concept reveal, and what concepts and figures might be connected through this shift from continuity to interruption, from identity to difference? By putting the emphasis on the futurity of the heroes' future fame and the gap it imposes between an action or event and its meaning, we will be able to explore the effects of different forms of time in the Homeric poems.

At stake in my argument is not so much the epic's own words and concepts for time and related notions, but rather the forms of time presupposed in the poems. These forms might be expressed, for example, in the question of whether the continuity of time allows the memory of a hero's life to survive into future song, or if the poem presupposes a bar between the 'now' of action and the 'other time' of song that either prevents such a survival or transforms the transmitted meaning.[3] My approach is more hermeneutic than ontological. This also then raises the possibility of differences between the two Homeric poems in what they presuppose about time. I focus in this book for the most part on the *Iliad*, with only rare mentions of the *Odyssey*, because I find a different image of time and a different concept of *kleos* in the *Odyssey*.[4] This dependence on interpretations of the *Iliad* makes this book in part a literary investigation of that poem, as opposed to a purely philological or philosophical investigation of archaic Greek concepts of time.

Beside my preoccupation with Iliadic time, a second impetus for this study comes from considerations of the relationship between the Homeric poems and the scholarship deployed in explaining them. It is customary to take the Homeric poems – along with the variously oral and literate traditions which produced them – as the literary objects to be explained or interpreted, while considering Homeric scholarship as explanations or interpretations which do a better or worse job of illuminating these literary objects. I propose to suspend this kind of approach, and instead look for the ways in which Homeric scholarship can be considered fully part of the Homeric tradition and as part of the reception history of the Homeric poems. What might result if we tried to understand the philological and historical hypotheses of Homeric scholarship – I have in mind the school of oral theory in particular, although by no means exclusively – as responses to what might otherwise be considered 'literary' aspects of the Homeric poems? Behind my readings of the Homeric poems and Homeric scholarship in this book lies the assumption that they can be treated on the same plane, both at the level of phenomena rather than hierarchized into phenomena and explanation.

What are the reasons for expecting that such an approach would be appropriate or productive? We can think of this as a question of the relationship between literary interpretation – addressed at the poems – and literary history – the scholarship on the nature and genesis of the poems. For the Homeric poems, in particular, history and interpretation are closely intertwined. We see this clearly in, for instance, the debates over 'particularized epithets', whether a formulaic phrase can ever gain a meaning from the context in which it occurs, as opposed to only from its typical use in the formulaic system. Does the phrase 'laughter-loving Aphrodite' take on any extra meaning – irony, perhaps – when it is used in the context of Aphrodite wounded and complaining (v. 376)? Does a repeated phrase call attention to and ask us to compare the different contexts in which it occurs, or not? Does a phrase 'remember' its 'earlier' uses and thereby carry with it a memory of its own history – and who can say which occurrences of a phrase are 'earlier' and which are later? Even to begin to address this cluster of basic questions about the possibilities of interpretation is already to be knee-deep in debates concerning the history and compositional context of the Homeric poems. And because so much is uncertain about the early history of these poems, the possibilities for reconstructing their history are less constrained than for most other literary works, and are therefore especially responsive and potentially dependent on interpretive needs. Put more directly, the Homeric poems offer the scope for historical hypotheses to be constructed to suit certain ways of interpreting the poems, as opposed to the more common notion in which 'objective' historical hypotheses constrain the forms of interpretation. In raising this possibility, I do not mean to impeach the scientific impartiality of the historical hypotheses of, say, oral theory or neoanalysis, but rather to shift the emphasis to their literary potential.[5]

I hope in this way to sidestep the contentious polemic that has not infrequently accompanied the history of Homeric studies, which often arises over questions of historical correctness. If, as a consequence, I sometimes 'misuse' scholarly arguments in reinterpreting them in a way that is most likely unintended, then that is entirely the point.[6] And even though there will sometimes be occasion to point out the impasses, blind spots and contradictions within, for instance, oral theory, the goal is not refutation. I am not arguing that oral theory does or does not adequately reflect the truth of its object, the Homeric poems or oral tradition. The goal of this book is not so much critique or evaluation, but rather experimentation by putting heterogeneous texts and discourses next to each other and seeing what new relations they produce.

All this may already have been clear enough from the stipulation that we will be putting scholarship and poetry on the same plane, a process in which the philological and historical theses of scholarship *about* the poems might shed light on literary and philosophical stakes *of* the poems. I propose treating scholarship as part of the reception of the Homeric poems, and, as the mantra goes, meaning is always produced at the moment of reception.[7] The concept of reception allows me to address a methodological consequence of my approach, the problem of anachronism. Am I arguing that, for instance, a sixth-century rhapsode would recognize or endorse the readings I will be proposing? On the one hand, the answer is clearly no, given that the rhapsode would not have the experience of the history of reception and scholarship which gives context to the readings proposed here, nor the philosophical questions which give them meaning and cogency. On the other hand, if we were to grant the rhapsode experience of all of those things, then he might well agree, but he would no longer be a sixth-century rhapsode. In line with the methodological gambit of placing poetry and scholarship on the same plane, the primary site where the concept of *kleos* is produced is in the interaction between the Homeric poems as we have them and the scholarship that they have provoked.

My understanding of the dynamics of reception can be clarified with reference to recent scholarship on 'deep classics'. When we say that meaning is produced at the moment of reception, it is all too often tempting to assume that the 'moment of reception' is an encounter between antiquity and a later moment that, under the conditions and constraints of its own time, imposes its own meanings onto the ancient texts or situations. But it is not so easy to disentangle what is supposed to be authentically *within* antiquity and what is added to it by modernity, not least because modernity itself is shaped in that very encounter. The question raised in the previous paragraph is recapitulated here: where does the product of a 'reception encounter' reside or where does it come from, the ancient text or the modern reader? Shane Butler highlights this problem in his discussion of the reception of Achilles and Patroclus' relationship. On the one side, he notes 'the ordinary principles by which the reception of classical antiquity has come to be studied': under these principles, a scholar seeks an 'aha!' moment in which 'a thoroughly modern impulse has just been detected making of antiquity what it wills'.[8] In Butler's example, John Addington Symonds seems to project a Victorian conception of equality onto the 'relatively blank slate' of 'the enigma of a distant Homeric "friendship"' between Achilles and Patroclus, and a scholar of reception would be satisfied with noting how the modern Symonds has imposed his values onto antiquity.[9] In contrast, Butler reminds us to pay attention to the unspoken anticipations of that modern impulse within antiquity. In the case of Symonds, the 'ordinary principles' of reception studies would have missed the hints of equality in a series of discourses about Achilles and Patroclus that can be traced back from the Italian Renaissance, through Aristotle and Plato, to the *Iliad* itself, in which these two heroes are engaged in various relations of substitutability and exchange. Symonds is thus not simply imposing his own meanings, but rather expressing something that might be present *in nuce* in antiquity. But even this still does not escape the dichotomy of 'in antiquity' and 'in modernity'. It is necessary to also note that, whatever the *something* Symonds finds and expresses, that *something* is changed in being expressed in modernity, and cannot therefore be said to remain the same in expression.[10] What Symonds expresses may have been expressed differently by a rhapsode, or may not have been expressible at all. Butler asks, 'How, in other words, should we describe the temporality of a process in which the past, even if in retrospect, seems so pointedly to anticipate the future?'[11] The key phrase in this question is 'in retrospect': it is only with a backward glance, after *something* has been expressed, that we can recognize its presence. There is often no way of making a solid distinction between the past and its future. Thus, returning to the context of this book, the concepts which we are after are not so much *latent* or *anticipated* in the past and *revealed* or *fulfilled* in the present, but are instead properly produced in the encounter itself between Homeric poem and modern scholarship.

This study, then, is the result of these two motivations, Iliadic time and the encounter of poetry and scholarship: I examine in this book the encounter of the *Iliad* and its modern scholarship *via the various images of time that they presuppose, express or produce*. Through this examination, we will gain not only a closer understanding of time in the *Iliad*, but also a clearer view of how major schools of Homeric scholarship – most significantly oral theory, neoanalysis and traditional referentiality – differ from and relate to each other and to the Homeric poems in terms of their temporalities of poetic composition and interpretation. In particular, we will find an important divide in relation to whether time is continuous and enables the self-identity of meaning and memory through tradition, or if there is an irreducible divide or difference in and through time. I explain the ways in which the former, the ideal of continuity and self-identity, dominates and is promoted by oral theory. Meanwhile, the figures of discontinuity and difference are relatively isolated, and it will therefore be necessary to gather them and progressively describe a structure or logic that can make sense of them. This logic is that of *kleos*, as I have hinted earlier, a concept of *kleos*-as-difference which will need to be derived from readings and interpretations, as an alternative to the more common conceptualizations of *kleos*-as-identity. Let us turn now to some concrete figures to see how *kleos* and difference can manifest across poetry and scholarship. There will be three of these figures, exemplifying, respectively, the motivation of the Homeric hero, the position of the epic poet and the perspective of oral theory. Individually, these figures of *kleos*-as-difference will seem tenuously connected at this stage. We might think of them as vignettes or motivating questions, and it will be the task of the following chapters to provide the structure proper to them.

Let us begin with the moment when Hector challenges the Greek heroes to single combat and imagines his future fame.[12] His speech reveals a specific temporal structure to the fame that he anticipates:

> And some day one of the lateborn men will say [καί ποτέ τις εἴπῃσι καὶ ὀψιγόνων ἀνθρώπων], sailing in his benched ship on the wine-blue water: 'This is the mound of a man who died long ago, one of the bravest, and glorious Hektor killed him.' So will he speak some day [ὥς ποτέ τις ἐρέει], and my glory [κλέος] will never perish.[13]

One way to read this passage is offered by Irene de Jong, who briefly considers it in a discussion of speeches in the *Iliad* which are attributed to an indefinite 'someone', *tis*.[14] De Jong calls it an 'oral epitaph', one which 'reveals more about the character speaking than about the person it is supposed to talk about'.[15] The point of this speech, placed into the mouth of an anonymous future speaker, is for de Jong contained in self-praise: 'Hector, under the guise of praising his opponent, in fact makes an *a fortiori* compliment to himself as victor of this excellent warrior. In his own comment on this tis-speech he makes the compliment explicit: τὸ δ' ἐμὸν κλέος οὔ ποτ' ὀλεῖται [and my glory will never perish].'[16] De Jong's analysis of the figure of the anonymous future speaker is founded on a psychology in which the form of expression can be stripped away to reveal a truer meaning: '[T]he fictitious speaker is used to give expression to the *inner* voice of the real speaker. This transposition of the character's own inner thoughts to some outward voice fits in very well with the general picture of Homeric psychology.'[17] In this reading, then, Hector means to praise and glorify himself, while the fact that this self-praise is attributed to someone else is merely a feature of Homeric psychology and does not affect its essential meaning.

While this reading produces a cogent interpretation, I would like to dwell further on the fact that what Hector performs here is not simply self-praise. His *kleos* is projected out of his present, and the words of praise are indirect and put in the mouth of another. Nor does Hector put his words in the mouth of just any other, but the imagined speaker is 'one of the lateborn men' speaking in an indefinite future, set adrift in time by the repetition of *pote*, 'some day'. The indefiniteness of the qualification *pote* is not merely a negative attribute, the lack of definiteness, but has a positive consistency of its own. Hector's glory, *kleos*, is not of his present, but one that will arrive through a series of intermediaries. Before arriving at Hector's glory, we must pass through his opponent, the grave mound of his opponent, the recognition of this grave mound by one of the lateborn men, and finally the speech inspired by this recognition. Is there a logic of identity and continuity or of difference and interruption here? On the one hand, Hector expects that the *kleos* preserved by the grave mound will combine with the *kleos* of the story of Hector's duel in order to produce a link between himself and the glory due to him in the future; in this reading, *kleos* connects the epic past and the poetic present. But on the other hand, Hector's expectations are not fulfilled: he will not in fact kill his opponent, Ajax, whose own death will tell a very different story in very different contexts to what Hector is expecting. How can we navigate the interrelation of these two different readings of *kleos* and the different images of the epic that they project? As we will come to see, the reading of *kleos* as an expression of identity and continuity has been a productive one in oral theory. Can we also make the reading of *kleos*-as-difference productive, and in which directions might that lead?[18]

The second preliminary figure has to do with the position of the poet. The contrast between identity and difference we noted in the context of Hector's *kleos* also manifests as different ways of conceiving the connection between the present of Homeric song and the epic past. Does the figure of the poet in the *Iliad* believe that he preserves the continuity and self-identity of tradition through *kleos*, or is there something that interrupts that continuity and imposes difference? Gregory Nagy reflects the oral theoretical perspective in which *kleos* links the poet to the hero in a relationship of continuity: '"That which is heard," *kleos*, comes to mean "glory" because it is the poet himself who uses the word to designate what he hears from the Muses and what he tells the audience. Poetry confers glory.'[19] In this reading, *kleos* is what the poet receives from the muse and preserves in poetry, as an allegory of transmission through an oral tradition. But what must give us pause is that the most direct invocation of the notion of *kleos* as a poetological concept in the *Iliad* is also the most direct refutation of the notion that *kleos* offers a guarantee of continuity. I mean the well-known invocation of the muses from the introduction to the catalogue of ships: 'You are goddesses; you are always present, and you know everything; but we [poets] only hear the *kleos* and know nothing.'[20] Nagy reads this passage as an assertion that 'the Hellenic poet is the master of *kleos*', and as evidence of 'the pride of the Hellenic poet through the ages', yet this passage is in fact where the *Iliad* presents most explicitly the stark difference between the knowledge and presence of the muses and the ignorance of the poets who only hear *kleos*, which is thus strongly contrasted to and distinguished from certain knowledge.[21] On the one hand, the poet calls upon the muse as the authority which guarantees the truth of his song, but on the other hand, that call to the muse is only ever just that, an invocation that receives no answer. While it is of course pedantically facile to note that the mythological figure of the muse never actually sings, and hence cannot actually guarantee anything, let us not neglect to ask what it means for our understanding of *kleos* that the appeal of the poet is addressed to such an inaccessible figure. Just as in the case of Hector's projection of his *kleos* to the hypothetical speech of a radically indefinite future speaker, we can ask what productive use can be made of the fact that the poet also projects his certainty to the position of the silent muse. We begin to see here that the two senses of *kleos* – as the glory of the hero and as the rumour of the poet – could be connected in a structural logic of separation and difference that works its way through both.

Our third figure is that of oral theory itself and the changes it introduced into the way we conceive the Homeric poems. Through a study of the system of formulaic epithets in the Homeric poems – the repeated descriptive tags appended to the names of people and things, like '*fleet-footed* Achilles' or '*rosy-fingered* Dawn' – Milman Parry argued that the complex yet elegantly parsimonious system of epithets could not have been created by a single poet, but was part of a traditional poetic language designed to help preliterate singers compose verses and songs on the spot, using the metrical building blocks that the formulaic epithets provided.[22] Parry's argument shook up preconceived notions about the activity of the poet or singer: no longer a creative genius crafting his poems in isolation, but rather a performer responding to a live audience, half-improvising, half-repeating the songs and stories handed down from time immemorial, using a special poetic language designed to help him fit his ideas into metre. This change in the nature of the poet of course affected the nature of the poem: how to interpret an oral poem composed in this way? Since the poet is no longer the creative origin of the poem, to whom can we attribute responsibility for the poem when we make a literary interpretation or judgement? Oral theory seems to have dispersed the unity of authorship and intention irrevocably into the anonymous series of innumerable singers and audiences in a centuries-long tradition.

But curiously, the loss of the creative poet as an original site of unity has prompted all the more stringent assumptions of unity, continuity and self-identity elsewhere in the oral theoretical approach to the Homeric tradition. Unity, continuity and self-identity are the ideals of what I will call the dominant or 'major' image of the Homeric tradition in oral theory, in contrast to which we will develop a 'minor' series of figures which challenge the major image by operating on a different logic.[23] We will be working through these issues in greater detail, but, for now, let us take the work of John Miles Foley as an illustrative example. Foley is most helpful for our understanding because he expressed most explicitly the demand for unity in the major, oral theoretical approach. Foley proposed a theory of Homeric language, called traditional referentiality, in which a traditional phrase evokes a whole set of traditional meanings and implications immediately and epiphanically. A traditional reference is thus a signifier that is directly unified with its signified, and the particular performance of song directly manifests the authoritative, eternal and self-identical Song of tradition.

Against the background of the major image of the Homeric tradition as unified, continuous and self-identical, it is possible to detect, in its margins, figures and objects which seem to work by a different logic. In the case of Foley, for instance, he preserves stories from Parry's fieldwork in 1930s Yugoslavia on South Slavic oral traditions. One figure, that of a legendary singer or *guslar*, stands out. This legendary *guslar* goes by several different names, and represents for South Slavic singers the figure of an exemplary master singer, one who was responsible for many of the songs in their tradition. Foley uses the legendary *guslar* as a figure of the unity of present performance and total tradition, in which 'individual and tradition coalesce, the tangible instance standing *pars pro toto* for the larger, intangible whole of the poetic tradition'.[24] The legendary *guslar* is thus part of the major image, operating by the logic of unity, continuity and self-identity. Yet Foley also preserves a story in which a young and self-confident singer meets the legendary *guslar* at an inn, but without recognizing him. The brash young singer challenges the incognito master to a singing contest and is humbled. The young man asks the master: from whom did he learn to sing so well? The master does not reveal himself, but replies that he learnt from 'Isak', which was his own name. In this story, the exemplary figure of unity, the legendary *guslar* in whom individual and tradition are supposed to coalesce, is divided against himself. He separates himself from the great 'Isak', as if even he himself is not up to the task of assuming the unity of instance and tradition that the legendary *guslar* is supposed to embody. Here is a disturbance in the way an oral tradition is supposed to make sense in oral theory, an interruption in the continuity of meaning that the oral tradition is supposed to guarantee. It is from a series of these kinds of discordant and marginal figures that we will pull together possibilities for an alternative to the major image presented by oral theory. These figures will include, from the *Iliad*, the great wall of the Achaeans that seems to spring up overnight and then disappears without a trace, but also the reading practices and presuppositions of the neoanalytic school of Homeric scholarship. In this way – reading and comparing Homeric scholarship and Homeric poems, asking questions of them and making them ask questions of each other – we will trace the play of difference and identity through the hybrid object composed of poetry and scholarship.

Through these preliminary figures, I have illustrated the kind of arguments I will be making in connecting poetry and scholarship through the time of *kleos*. While the initial connection is made via a parallel or a porousness between *kleos* as a heroic concept of future fame and *kleos* as a poetic concept of transmission, the choice of whether to emphasize *kleos* as a guarantor of sameness or as a mark of difference will have wider consequences. Before moving on to an overview of chapters, let me address two points which may arise later in the book, but which can best be addressed in this introduction. First, because my arguments will sometimes be based on readings of the whole story of the *Iliad*, the question may arise of whether it is necessary to be a 'unitarian' in order to find these arguments convincing. I do not believe this is necessary. My argument presupposes that there is a pre-understanding of time that is expressed in the *Iliad*, and this does not require a single author crafting a unitary story. The term 'pre-understanding' itself implies a structured way of thinking about time that is nevertheless not expressed explicitly or conceptually in the poem or in the consciousness of anyone who takes part in producing or receiving it, and thus does not require a single responsible individual.[25] Conversely, there is no necessity for a single individual to be bound to a single pre-understanding of time; hence my suggestion that the *Iliad* and the *Odyssey* differ on this point does not necessarily mean that they must have been produced by different people or different traditions. My investigation is thus relatively agnostic with respect to the various proposals regarding the origins and development of the poems that have been transmitted to us. I do not therefore try to judge whether, for instance, an evolutionary or a dictation model is more likely, and where I do discuss such models, it is in order to examine the temporality of meaning-making or interpretation that they imply.[26]

Second, and related to the previous point, is the question of how the scholarship I have closely engaged with were chosen. Since this book seeks to read scholarship for their images of time, I engage in most detail with those works which form the most striking connections with the contrast of continuity and difference that I find in the concept of *kleos*. Thus, even though the fortunes of Nagy's evolutionary model may wax and wane with respect to its acceptance as a historical theory, it remains strikingly innovative in its assertions about, for instance, the possibility of synchronic meaning.[27] I also focus on John Miles Foley's formulations, even as others have followed his methods more recently, but do so without, I will argue, affecting the fundamental innovations he introduced about where meaning resides in an oral tradition.[28] Similarly, I will emphasize the earlier, 'unreconstructed' neoanalysts rather than more recent versions of the approach which aim at a rapprochement with oral theory. Where the search for the 'truth' of the Homeric tradition tends to round off the less plausible edges of theories about Homer, I am instead fascinated by what might be condemned as 'unreasonable': those aspects which do not have the alibi of likelihood.[29]

* * *

This section will outline the chapters to follow and describe their organization with respect to the overall aims of the book. There are five chapters. The first four work between the Homeric poems and Homeric scholarship and aim to, first, bring out the contrast between the ideals of continuity and self-identity, and a series of figures which undermine those ideals; second, work out a temporal reading of *kleos* that can account for these figures and show the importance of this concept in the *Iliad*; and third, use the concept of *kleos* and the structure of time expressed by it to connect aspects of poetry and scholarship which may initially seem distant. These chapters thus bounce between poetry and scholarship, as well as between *deriving* a concept for difference and discontinuity and *applying* it. The last chapter is somewhat different. Where the first four chapters follow closely the concerns and contours of the Homeric poems and scholarship, the last chapter organizes the various images of time that have appeared throughout the book and structures them using Deleuze's philosophy of time. The different images of time are not isolated from each other, nor are they accidental and indifferent, but instead form a structured sequence. This last chapter thus also functions as a recapitulation and conclusion.

The first chapter begins to derive a contrast between the concepts of continuity and identity, on the one hand, and interruption and difference, on the other. The focus is on John Miles Foley's account of how traditional oral poetry works, a form of meaning-making that he called 'traditional referentiality'. Why take Foley as a starting point? There are two reasons: first, as previously noted, because traditional referentiality states explicitly the ideals of continuity and self-identity which govern oral theory; and second, because the way in which signs work in traditional referentiality allows us to begin to straddle poetry and scholarship by comparing the relation between signs and meaning in oral theory and in the Homeric poems. We will see that traditional referentiality conceives the particular occurrence of a sign – whether that be a word, a structural pattern or the epic *Kunstsprache* as such – as directly and epiphanically manifesting the meaning it bears in the tradition. A sign – which Foley often calls *sēma* – therefore bears meaning because of a continuity between present performance and past tradition, and the meaning it bears is self-identical across time. In contrast, the *sēmata* in the Homeric poems are often marked by the loss of meaning and the failure of memory. We will examine a prominent example of these *sēmata*, the strange object that is the Achaean wall. Between its foundations in an anonymous mass grave and its proleptically narrated utter destruction at the hands of the gods, the Achaean wall is a potent expression of what Andrew Ford called an 'antifuneral, the symbolic opposite of commemoration'.[30] The Achaean wall not only testifies to a logic of signs and meaning different from the continuity and self-identity of traditional referentiality, it also parallels the figure of the legendary *guslar* which Foley himself highlights as an avatar of traditional referentiality, and who, as discussed earlier, is also divided from his own identity. These links show that oral theory is not monolithic in agreement with itself, but instead contains the seeds of further development contrary to its explicit commitments. Between the Homeric figure of the Achaean wall and Foley's development of the legendary *guslar*, we find the first elements of a series of expressions of a counter-logic of discontinuity and difference. Foley's traditional referentiality therefore provides a useful point of entry to the discussions in this book because it captures, within a concrete and constrained set of references, both the concepts that we are interested in deriving and the method of reading the mutual refractions of poetry and scholarship.

Chapter two is a key chapter in this book. This chapter picks up the counter-logic of discontinuity and difference – which were only exemplified in individual figures in the first chapter – and develops a more precise account of how it functions through the *Iliad*. I introduce *kleos* at this point as the central concept that expresses discontinuity and difference in the Homeric tradition. The way *kleos* fulfils this role is through its effect on time: because the Homeric heroes understand that the meaning of their actions will be found in the form of their *kleos* or 'fame' that will come into being in a song to be sung in their relative future, every present moment is no longer whole or contained in itself, but is instead opened onto the prospect of a meaning that will only arrive in the future. Each present is split or divided between the 'now' – what the hero understands and intends in the present moment of action – and another time that is yet to come. We have already seen something of this logic of *kleos* at work in the brief discussion of how Hector projects his fame into the mouth of 'one of the lateborn men' (VII. 87) in the future, but in the context of the fuller discussion in chapter two, Hector's speech is only a first, localized form of the logic that will be generalized and superseded. Hector's speech is 'local' because it concerns a particular moment at which future fame has become narratively important and thematically explicit; in this case, the occasion is that of the impending duel between Hector and Ajax. Other, more ordinary moments are unaffected by the local division of the present. What I will go on to argue, however, is that the *Iliad* also contains a more fundamental, 'generalized' form of this division, in which every moment is affected. The generalized division is expressed succinctly in Helen's words to Hector: 'Zeus set a vile destiny upon us so that hereafter we shall be made into things of song for the men of the future.'[31] Here, the future song is called upon to explain their *kakon moron*, 'vile destiny', in general, as opposed to any particular event.

A fuller demonstration of the generalized division of the present will be developed in the context of Achilles' changing relation to *kleos*. For Achilles, his *kleos* is closely connected to his death, as demonstrated by the choice he faces between long life without future glory and early death with unwithering fame. Before the death of Patroclus, Achilles acted as if *kleos* were knowable and controllable through his plans and actions, but after Patroclus dies, Achilles realizes that *kleos* is radically unknowable. Achilles expresses the unknowability of *kleos* through the definite indefiniteness of his own death, which he imagines will arrive on 'a dawn or an afternoon or a noontime when some man in the fighting will take the life from me also either with a spearcast or an arrow flown from the bowstring.'[32] The meaning of Achilles' *kleos* will not be sealed before his death, and because he does not know the circumstances of his death, he also does not know which events will turn out to have been significant. Hence, in contrast to the localized divisions of the present in which a specific occasion prompts the division of the now by a future meaning in the future song of *kleos*, the unknowability of *kleos* means that the meaning of every moment could change and become significant. Meaning is always open to retroactive modification in the Homeric poems – we will see this in connection with Agamemnon's response to the wounding of Menelaus (IV. 155–7), and Patroclus' response to the defeat of the Danaans (XI. 816–18) – and this openness is caused by the fact that *kleos* is never accessible in the present.

In addition to defining discontinuity and difference by tracing the function of *kleos* from localized to generalized forms of the division of the present, chapter two also demonstrates the same progress from local to general in the logic of the neoanalytic school of Homeric scholarship. Neoanalysis, I will argue, is essentially based on reading the difference between a Homeric text present and available in front of us and another, often lost or absent text against which the Homeric text makes sense. For neoanalysis, the genius of Homer is precisely in the way that difference is made meaningful. Using the distinction we have derived between the local and the general in the context of the Homeric poems, we will be able to see that much of neoanalytic scholarship is dedicated to demonstrating local differences, in the sense that it tries to prove that specific – local – passages or aspects of the Homeric poems are made meaningful if read in their difference from other specific passages or aspects; the classic example is the way in which the Achilles–Patroclus–Hector triad in the *Iliad* is a repetition-with-difference of an Achilles–Antilochus–Memnon triad in a hypothetical *Achilleis* or *Aethiopis*.[33] In contrast to the localized difference between two actual *comparanda*, we will also see a generalized difference in an argument by Ken Dowden.[34] Dowden asks us to consider Homer's silence to be as potentially allusive as Homer's references, a step that leads, we will argue, to making the whole of the Homeric poems allusive in the sense of being made meaningful by its difference from an absent and unknown text.

Where the second chapter works through a temporal logic of difference that organizes and connects significant aspects of Homeric poetics, chapter three asks how this logic might interact with the developments of oral theory in the work of Gregory Nagy. Nagy's work initially appears to have close points of similarity to the interests of this study: his evolutionary theory of the Homeric poems places great emphasis on the function of time, and his conception of the *Iliad* and the *Odyssey* as a form of poetry which 'cannot belong to any one time, any one place' but instead 'defies synchronic analysis' seems to parallel the division of the present.[35] But the situation is more complex. This chapter will therefore first track the influence on Nagy of Parry's formulation of oral theoretical principles and the arguments of his critics, and second, work out the relation between Nagy's concepts of time and his distinctions between synchrony, diachrony and history. Through these investigations, I will demonstrate that Nagy's system incorporates conflicting forces: on the one hand, the legacy of Parry's conceptions which valorize an undivided present in which meaning is instantaneous, and on the other hand, the results of Nagy's own contributions which pull in a different and often opposing direction. In particular, we will see that in the figure of a Panhellenic poet who must contend with the contradictions between various local traditions, Nagy presents a form of poetry marked by its unspoken difference from other texts and other stories. The structured set of concepts we derived in earlier chapters – continuity or discontinuity, identity or difference – allows us to see the tensions which produce Nagy's system, and provides lines of communication between the often polemically opposed schools of oral theory and neoanalysis without reducing either one to the other.[36]

The fourth chapter extends the second in another direction. One result of the discussions in the second chapter is a general statement about the form of meaning in the Homeric poems: the fact that meaning is projected out of the present and into an unknowable *kleos* produces a general *formal* rule that accompanies the appearance of any particular meaning *content*. Whenever any specific meaning appears – for instance, the oaths of truce Agamemnon swore which seemed to mean peace (III. 259–309) – it appears under the formal condition that it is not final and remains subject to retroactive change – the meaning of the oaths turns out to be death for Menelaus (IV. 155–7). Chapter two left things here, at a formal level that is empty of content. Chapter four picks up and extends this discussion by examining figures in which the formal rule comes to be thematized as content, an operation which we will call suture.[37] In what ways does the formal principle that meaning is subject to revision and never final manifest as content in the Homeric poems? We will consider various different kinds of manifestation. First, sutures in speech, that is, situations in which a character borrows the force or truth of the formal principle in order to support a particular decision or attitude. For instance, when Hector rejects Polydamas' interpretation of a bird sign with the striking statement, 'One bird sign is best: to fight in defence of the fatherland',[38] we will see how this rejection of the principle of basing action upon a calculating divination of the future borrows its rhetorical power from an awareness that the potential for meaning to change persists beyond all calculation. Then, we move onto sutures which manifest in the poem as either objects or as aspects of objecthood. The retroactive revision of meaning implies the failure of one meaning and the installation of another, and we will see that the first part of this operation, the failure of meaning, is often expressed in terms of a mute and unsignifying objecthood. Objects and objecthood, in these cases, are used for their resistance to meaning. A series of such figures are associated with Achilles: a brightness, *selas*, which cannot be looked at; the wordless scream of a trumpet; and Achilles' description of himself as a 'useless burden on the good land'.[39] This is because the death of Patroclus produces in Achilles the most dramatic failure of meaning in the *Iliad*, and figures of objecthood cluster around Achilles in this loss.[40] The last section considers a suturing operation that gives content to *kleos* itself. While the logic of *kleos* requires that *kleos* remain formally unknowable and therefore without content, it can become identified with specific meanings. In this final section, then, we examine one such suturing in which the final meaning of heroic action is given as the doom of Troy.[41] By tracing the effects of giving *kleos* a specific content on the structure of time, we will be able to connect and explain two oddities about Hector's meeting with Andromache at the end of book VI: why do Hector's speeches contradict themselves in first assuming the destruction of Troy and then imagining the triumph of Astyanax as if Troy were to be still standing; and why does Hector's path to Andromache take a narratively inconsequential detour in which he initially fails to find her at home? This chapter thus demonstrates that our preoccupation with the formal nature of time and meaning in the logic of *kleos* is not empty and sterile, but closely entwined with and implicated in the thematic richness of the Homeric poems.

The fifth and final chapter performs two functions. First, it serves as a conclusion because it recapitulates the concepts and relations which have been worked through in the previous chapters. But what makes this chapter more substantial than only a conclusion is the fact that the recapitulation does not retread the same ground, nor does it go through the concepts in the same order. The progression of the first four chapters is, to a large extent, determined by the existing contours of Homeric scholarship, and the logic of *kleos* that we have derived from the poetic and scholarly material appears, in a sense, as an empirical feature of that material, without considering whether there is any particular reason for the logic of *kleos* to have the form that it does. Even if we can say, based on our interpretations, that *kleos* divides the present, we have not considered what necessity there is for the present to be divided. The second function of this last chapter is therefore to provide at least the beginnings of an answer to such questions. This is done by rebuilding and reorganizing the various moments in the logic of *kleos* according to Deleuze's philosophy of time.[42] Deleuze organizes the philosophy of time into three stages or syntheses in which the syntheses focus on, respectively, the present, the past and the future. Moreover, the three syntheses are connected in a series in which the deficiencies of the one motivates the production of the next, and thereby offers a dynamic framework that provides the impulse for the development of the logic of *kleos* through its various moments. The discussion will begin by correlating the first Deleuzian synthesis, that of the living present, with versions of the present in Homeric scholarship from Parry and Auerbach to Norman Austin and Nagy. The inability of the living present to account for its own conditions then propels us to a second synthesis of the pure past, which we will discuss in relation, again, to Nagy, as well as to various scholars' contributions to the question of the plan of Zeus, *Dios boulē*, and also to the Odyssean episode of the encounter with the sirens. In the discussions of the second synthesis, we will identify the notion of a pure past – which will receive a precise description – with forms of *kleos* which are understood to be fixed and known. The transition from an interpretation of *kleos* as fixed and known to one that is open because unknowable brings us from the second to the third synthesis. We will discuss the third synthesis mostly in connection with one of its aspects, Deleuze's Shakespearean motif that 'time is out of joint'. The distinction between time that is 'in joint' and 'out of joint' will be connected to Aristotelian and non-Aristotelian ways of conceiving the epic plot, in particular the term *eusynoptos*, 'easily seen in a single glance'. The epic plot would be 'in joint' if there is a figure – such as Zeus, the poet or the muse – who is able to see or control all of it and thereby occupy an eusynoptic position, but I will make the case that none of them actually do occupy the eusynoptic position, thereby freeing the epic and disjointing time.

1

A Different Poet of the Same Name

If we are to consider the Homeric poems and Homeric scholarship on the same plane, as I promised, we quickly run into the obvious problem that these are very different kinds of texts and discourses. We can state this problem more specifically in the following way: if a particular problematic logic of *kleos*-as-difference can connect Homeric poetry and scholarship, as I am arguing, it is still the case that this logic of *kleos* is not expressed in the same figures, objects or images in the different kinds of texts with which we are working. The Homeric poems expresses *kleos*-as-difference in various figures of fame and rumour, as well as, we will come to see, in its forms of meaning-making; these are very different from the problems of oral tradition, historical transmission and social and performance conditions that are the preoccupations of scholarship. This presentational problem of the heterogeneity of the texts might be overcome if we already had a clear and strong conception of what *kleos*-as-difference is and how it functions, but this is precisely the goal of these initial chapters, and not a starting point; *kleos* is not yet a well-defined concept for us at this stage.

One point of convergence offers a place to begin weaving together the heterogeneous concerns of poetry and scholarship. John Miles Foley, through his theory of traditional referentiality, presents a version of signs and signification in traditional oral poetry. The traditional reference is, for Foley, a special type of sign that links, for instance, the naming or description of a hero directly to the full weight of the traditional stories and attributes of that hero. The traditional reference is thus the way in which a particular instance of performance, in the here and now, is able to epiphanically evoke the timeless authority and plenitude of tradition. Foley often calls these oral signs or traditional references by the Homeric word *sēma*, and by putting Foley's traditionally referential *sēmata* next to the Homeric instances of the *sēma*, we can produce a first concrete confrontation of oral theory and the Homeric poems. The *sēma* as a special kind of sign presupposes a specific kind of linguistics. Is the linguistics of traditional reference adequate to that of the Homeric *sēma*? We begin with Foley, then, because traditional referentiality offers us the link between poetry and oral theory in the form of the *sēma*, as well as because his work develops the assumptions of oral theory with a particular rigour and explicitness and carries those assumptions to a certain logical terminus. We will see that Foley presents in clear and bold strokes the ideals of continuity and identity that inform oral theory in general.

One further reason for beginning with Foley is the fact that, while he espouses the oral theoretical ideals of continuity and identity – what I will sometimes call the major image – he also supplies us with the figure of the legendary *guslar* which we described in the introduction, and which begins to chip away at the explicit ideals of continuity and identity. This figure, let us recall, is reputed to be the creator of the songs in the South Slavic oral singers' repertoire, but is frustratingly elusive for anyone who hopes to meet him; he is always in the next village, or has just left, or is otherwise inaccessible.[1] The elusiveness of the legendary *guslar* reflects something of our difficulties with Homer: after oral theory, any notion of 'Homer' as the origin of the Homeric poems is something that we displace and disavow but cannot quite exorcize. This is the logic behind the joke of this chapter's title, which, in its most common version, claims that Shakespeare was not the author of Shakespeare's plays – they were by a different poet of the same name. The joke makes us aware that, although we usually assume that proper names are 'rigid designators' tied to a specific, substantial object, in the case of the Homeric tradition, the name 'Homer' covers a shifting, self-differing conception of origin, while still naming *something*.[2] The joke would be defused if we were perfect nominalists who are entirely happy with the conception of names as mere convention and if we did not still, on some level, believe in 'Shakespeare' or 'Homer' or the legendary *guslar*. Something that we cannot yet identify escapes nominalism here. What remains, what survives the shifts and displacements that can no longer be covered by the notion of 'Homer the monumental poet'? I will suggest that what survives is a logic of *kleos* as difference itself, as an essential *dérive* or *mouvance*.[3]

The legendary *guslar* is thus a figure of an internal resistance to continuity and identity in the major image of oral theory. The legendary *guslar* is not simply the name corresponding to some empirical person or object, but instead implies a whole set of questions and assumptions for how we think about oral tradition: the figure of the legendary *guslar* corresponds to a structured problematic. These kinds of figures and objects which imply specifically structured ways of thinking about problems are important for our discussions of both the Homeric poems and Homeric scholarship. They are objective correlates, that is, objects which correlate to or express an implied structure. The legendary *guslar* who is never where you look for him, for instance, helps us talk about and make palpable the sense of elusiveness and displacement we feel when encountering oral traditions, even though we cannot yet isolate that feeling in a definite concept. He is one of a minor series of such figures, which can be extended into the Homeric poems themselves, which is where we rejoin the nodal figure of the *sēma*: whereas Foley's traditionally referential *sēma* expresses an ideal of continuity and identity, the Homeric *sēmata* link up with the figure of the legendary *guslar* in a minor series that resists such an ideal.

This chapter will begin by describing Foley's notion of traditional referentiality as a response to problems within Milman Parry's theory of orality. We will then examine the nature of the *sēma* in Foley and in the Homeric poems, in particular the enigmatic wall of the Achaeans which is built overnight and ends up disappearing without a trace. By reading traditional referentiality and its implicit linguistics in contrast to the way signs, *sēmata*, work in Homer, we can begin to see how Foley's understanding of Homeric poetics contrasts with how Homeric poetics understands itself. We will also see internal tensions within Foley's work, which coalesce in the figure of the legendary *guslar* who plays an exemplary role in traditional referentiality, and yet can be read against traditional referentiality itself. The *guslar*, the Achaean wall and the *sēma* are the conceptual figures of a form of a failure of memory and an interruption of tradition which will lead the discussion here into the following chapters.[4]

* * *

Foley traces the origin of traditional referentiality to the aftermath of Milman Parry's theory about the traditionality of Homeric language, and the assertion that such traditionality must imply that the Homeric poems were composed orally rather than with the use of writing. Parry's original insight was that the Homeric poems were *traditional*, in the sense that they were the product of a long tradition rather than the creation of a creative individual poet. Parry supported his claim by demonstrating the systematic nature of Homeric language. A major part of this demonstration was the fact that the repeated noun–epithet combinations found in the Homeric poems, which provided ways of fitting names in various grammatical cases into different positions of a hexameter verse, were so distributed that, in most situations, there existed at least one noun–epithet combination for the requirements of case and metre. Parry called this the property of extension: the noun–epithet combinations formed a system that extended over all the needs of a poet. Parry further demonstrated that, in most situations, there did not exist more than one noun–epithet combination for each situation. This was the property of economy or thrift: the system did not have much redundancy. On the basis of the extension and economy of the system of noun–epithet combinations, Parry argued that it was beyond the ability of any one poet to create in its entirety, hence a long succession of poets must have been at work, which therefore merits the name of tradition. Parry gave the noun–epithet combination the name 'formula', defined as 'a group of words which is regularly employed under the same metrical conditions to express a given essential idea'.[5]

To this point, Parry's demonstration of Homeric traditionality met no resistance.[6] It was the next step Parry took that became crucial in the critical divisions which followed, and out of which Foley developed his theory of traditional referentiality. Taking further the results obtained from the demonstration of traditionality, Parry sought to show in addition that Homeric traditionality necessarily entailed that the Homeric poems were the result of oral composition, composed and performed in the same moment, the moment of composition-in-performance.[7] As the centrepiece of this demonstration, Parry presented the openings of the *Iliad* and the *Odyssey* with all the formulaic sections underlined.[8] Since the use of formulaic phrases was taken to have the function of making fast composition easier during performance, the density of formula was taken to demonstrate that the poems were composed under the duress of time and therefore orally, during performance.

Going even further, Parry argued that the oral composition of the poems meant that the singer lacked time for thinking, which must therefore be a decisive consideration in how we read and interpret the poems. Thus, along with the belief that he had discovered in the formulaic system the psychological mechanism of oral composition, Parry also laid out a set of interpretive strategies for recreating what the oral poet must have intended in the moment of composition-in-performance, a moment in which the lack of time was thought to have excluded significant conscious deliberation. In the study of noun–epithet formulas, for instance, there arose the question of whether some epithets can be particularized: can a particular occurrence of an epithet carry meaning specific to a situation, such as irony when the epithet 'smiling' accompanies Aphrodite in pain? Parry advises that no such particularized interpretations should be entertained, and that one should 'firmly exclude any interpretation which does not instantly and easily come to mind'.[9] This position rules out a large part of what is usually thought of as literary interpretation, and sets off a series of controversies, on which we will not dwell in detail.[10] We can briefly observe that, in this strong form, Parry's theory of orality uses the quantitative determination of the oral nature of Homeric poetry – the systematicity of extension and economy – in order to decide qualitative interpretive questions of how we read. Parry's theory also strongly alienates the poet from his language, in the sense that the poet as an individual is, in performance, bound to the essential ideas and instantaneous interpretations which the epic language makes available.

This, then, was the general state of the question. The problem, for Foley, is contained in an opposition between 'mechanism and art', between the seemingly intentionless technical utility of Parry's conception of Homeric language and the particular artistic intention that is thought, by Parry's critics, to be required for the consummation of great poetry.[11] Foley is committed, on the one hand, to the scientific rationality of Parry's analysis, which brought the study of oral poetry out of Romantic conceptions of folk or popular poetry and into the modernity of structural linguistics.[12] At the same time, he is also committed to a firm belief in an aesthetic category of great art. Between the two seemingly irreconcilable forces, Foley saw his task as the reconciliation of utility and aesthetics. In his desire for 'both a fully analysed and an aesthetically pleasing oral poem', Foley demanded nothing less than an entirely rational theory of art, to be realized on the field of traditional oral poetry.[13] What was his answer, and what useful articulations does it introduce into oral theory and the study of Homeric poetics?

* * *

Traditional referentiality describes the way oral poetics bridges the gap between what takes place during an actual, individual performance and the totality of the tradition that performance is thought to incarnate. The privileged units of traditional referentiality are called traditional references, linguistic elements which occur within performance but which establish a continuity with the totality of meaning found in the tradition. The traditional reference, as a concept, is thus that which mediates and harmonizes between the particular appearance of a repeated traditional element – be that a word or a phrase or some larger unit – and the meaning that, for Foley, is inherent in a tradition. Against the accusation that Parry's mechanistic conceptualization of repetition in traditional language reduces the singer to a mere mouthpiece of tradition with no possible claim to artistic value, Foley mounts an affirmative defence: the language of traditional poetry may on the surface be conventional and repetitive and utilitarian to the eyes of literate readers, but that very conventionality and repetition serve an artistic purpose in bringing to life a richness or plenitude that is found in tradition:

> [S]tructural elements are not simply compositionally useful … rather they command fields of reference much larger than the single line, passage, or even text in which they occur. Traditional elements reach out of the immediate instance in which they appear to the fecund totality of the entire tradition, defined synchronically and diachronically, and they bear meanings as wide and deep as the tradition they encode.[14]

Traditional references can therefore manifest at every level of linguistic organization, from a word to an entire poem, as long as they perform the function of marking or referring to the totality of tradition.[15] Thus, a formula like 'swift-footed Achilles' is a traditional reference. It transcends its local context and refers to the entire, multivariant mythological career of Achilles. But similarly, larger units like repeated scenes can be a traditional reference. The significance of Agamemnon arming himself is an instance of the 'arming scene' as such, which brings in all the different expectations of what happens in and around arming scenes. To go even larger, the form of the 'return song', as found in the *Odyssey*, is also a traditional reference, because it sets up expectations for the contents and values traditionally expected from a return song. Tradition, Foley tells us again and again, is like a language, '*only more so*'.[16] It is like a language insofar as each element bears with it connotations which can be exploited by a poem, and it is more like a language than language in that these connotations can be much more specific than 'natural languages' in what they point to, such as in the case of a character who carries with him a traditional reputation, or a seemingly innocent repeated phrase that turns out to prime an entire sequence of narrative expectations.

What interests us here is not so much the specific interpretations Foley offers, but how his concept of traditional referentiality affects the ways in which we can arrive at meanings and interpretations within the context of oral theory. To start, we can see that the concept of traditional reference breaks literary interpretation out of Parry's insistence on meanings which come 'instantly and easily to mind'. This is not because Foley refutes Parry's notion of the poet who lacks time to compose and therefore has to make do with what is immediately at hand, but rather because the traditional reference expands the possibilities of what is immediately at hand. In understanding the traditional reference as being like a language, '*only more so*', Foley implicitly historicizes the field of what comes instantly to mind. What comes instantly to mind for the poet and audience of a traditional oral performance is not the same as what comes instantly for us: through the instantaneous, epiphanic power of the traditional reference, oral poets and audiences can bring to mind much more than what we have access to. It is therefore the task of the modern reader and scholar to reconstruct the field of what the oral tradition places at the instantaneous disposal of its participants – and how can we do this but by using our literate methods of interpretation? The traditional reference is thus a blank cheque or a form of alibi through which, within certain constraints, Foley reauthorizes the kinds of literate reading banished by strict forms of Parryism. It would be easy to point out the circularity of a logic that places literate interpretations in the *tabula rasa* of a tradition reference, and thereby allowing us to rediscover it there as an oral traditional interpretation. But be that as it may, traditional referentiality does at least free interpretation from Parry's straitjacket.[17]

Let us consider instead the nature of the tradition that traditional referentiality presupposes, and the kind of linguistics that underlies such a tradition. In linking the present performance to 'the fecund totality of the entire tradition', traditional referentiality is a system of allusion in which the text alluded to is a hypothetically complete corpus of all traditional song. In positing the conceptual importance to traditional poetry of an ideal and ideally complete song that contains all of tradition, Foley is anticipated by Lord.[18] Outside of the direct Parry-Lord tradition, it is also found in Paul Zumthor's work.[19] Not just in Foley, then, but in theories of orality more generally, the notion of a total song occupies an important position. Even if this total song is never conceived as ever actually existing or possible, it is a conceptual image that correlates to a way of thinking the relationship between a particular song and the totality of tradition.[20] Just as Parry's conception of composition-in-performance presupposed a particular kind of traditional language and led to a particular kind of interpretation, we can examine the linguistics and interpretive goals and strategies entailed by traditional referentiality and its form of allusion.

The term 'allusion' is avoided in traditional referentiality, as it is in oral theory more broadly. This is because it is too closely associated with the conscious act of referring to the fixed words of an already-existing text in another text by a creative individual – thereby implying a written poetics – and, at the same time, with an old-fashioned philology of tracking down sources.[21] In using the term here, I do not intend to bring back that kind of philology, but I am instead interested in describing the nature of allusiveness in traditional referentiality and the kinds of readings and interpretations it entails. The direct, epiphanic link between present instance and total tradition in a traditional reference allows much broader fields of allusion than from one text to another.[22] The traditional reference always refers its particular instances to ever larger wholes:

> Such a process of generating meaning I call *metonymy*, designating a mode of signification wherein the part stands for the whole ... in this case we are speaking about a situation in which a text or version is enriched by an unspoken context that dwarfs the textual artifact, in which the experience is filled out – and made traditional – by what the conventionality attracts to itself from that context. The phrase or scene or tale as a whole commands its meaning by synecdoche.[23]

What is the upper limit to the expanding circle of synecdochic, part-to-whole relations? There is no limit, and we have already seen that the traditional reference reaches all the way to 'the fecund totality of the entire tradition'. The system of allusion of traditional referentiality becomes a single mood of generalized allusiveness.[24] Foley has broken interpretation from Parry's constraints, but this freedom is bought at the price of a totalizing conception of tradition. In contrast to Parry's interpretations which must come 'instantly and easily' – a limitation upon the *content* of interpretation imposed by the oral traditional *form* of song – traditional referentiality as a form of meaning no longer limits what can be accepted as the content of an interpretation. But the meaning of an individual performance is nevertheless still constrained by its specific kind of formal relation to the image of a total tradition. It is through this conception of a total tradition which subsumes individual performances and poems that Foley gives us a particularly clear version of the major image of oral theory.

Foley's image of tradition authorizes an aesthetic theory in which 'great art' is the subjective experience of the unity and harmony of local performance and total tradition. A traditional poem must convey meaning, and convey it perfectly, with no gaps. The duty of the audience is thus to recreate the gapless experience of unity. Foley reintroduces at this level the strong opposition between oral and written poetics of oralist orthodoxy. He thus warns us against 'an uncompromisingly *literary* reading of such texts [which] will create indeterminacy where, according to a *faithful* reception of the work, it does not exist, thus doing further *damage* to the aesthetic experience'.[25] In keeping with oral theory's tendency to shift focus from texts to performances, reading in traditional referentiality is reconceived as an aesthetic experience of performance, where the goal is 'the reinvestiture of traditional structures with their inherent meaning', a meaning which is conceived as a mass or quantity that one is able to 'tap' from 'the traditional reservoir'.[26] The rhetoric of a wholeness of aesthetic experience that is to be reconstituted is clear enough to require no further comment, but it is worth noting that in place of a triple relation of poet, text and reader, traditional referentiality is structured as an imaginary duality between man – without differentiation, at this level, between poet and reader, singer and audience[27] – and the totality of tradition.[28] Oral theory achieves here an apotheosis of sorts, and becomes man's literal *theōrein* of the Idea of Tradition, in which success is measured by how closely he is able to approach the original Form, which can be reached only 'if we are a good and faithful audience'.

In the account of traditional referentiality, formula and theme from the Parry-Lord conception of traditional language emerge as a fiat currency, laden with the value of meaning, issued by the central bank of art, and accepted as legal tender in the marketplace where aesthetic experience may be obtained.[29] The position of Treasurer, whose signature legitimizes this currency, is occupied by the figure of the legendary *guslar* and his alter ego, Homer. It is true that, for Foley, the legendary *guslar* and his Homeric counterpart are only the metaphorical retrojections of an entire tradition onto a single ancestral figure.[30] Nevertheless, a rhetoric of wholeness and epiphany enters whenever the legendary *guslar* is invoked: 'When a real-life *guslar* performs, he appropriates the *Guslar* [the legendary *guslar*] as a direct ancestor and makes himself the present-day embodiment of the greatest of all bards. In the process, individual and tradition coalesce, the tangible instance standing *pars pro toto* for the larger, intangible whole of the poetic tradition.'[31] Foley makes explicit the paradoxical relationship between 'songs and the Song' found already in Lord, but goes on to directly assert the harmony between individual and tradition as an aesthetic value. The stringency with which this harmony is enforced is not supported by argumentation, but through fiat. As we just saw in the language that elevates a faithful reception over a literary one, the proper aesthetic appreciation of traditional poetry is made into a moral imperative, the truth of which is ineffable and must be directly experienced through participation in that form of performance-as-ritual towards which oral theory, in its more vatic modes, has always inclined.[32]

What makes Foley's traditional referentiality exemplary of oral theory is that it makes entirely explicit the continuity between the linguistic elements of the performance – the traditional reference – and the total tradition. In structuralist terms, this is a short circuit between the levels of the *parole* and *langue*.[33] Putting aside all other critiques of oral theory more broadly, the crucial aspect of orality that Foley brings to the surface is the assumption of continuity between performance and tradition, the notion that the individual poem is able to access what Karl Reinhardt called 'a heaven of forms and ideas' from which it can draw meaning and authority.[34]

Foley's traditional referentiality is a specific inversion of Parry's conception of traditional poetry. Where Parry was concerned with limiting the assignment of possible meaning to traditional language and so was accused of taking away the traditional poet's capacity for artist expression, Foley conceives of a traditional language that is filled with meaning to excess, to the breaking of every instance into the superabundance of tradition.[35] And yet, within the paean to ideal, uninterrupted continuity between tradition and performance that is traditional referentiality, the receding figure of the legendary *guslar* stands out. The elusiveness and inaccessibility of the legendary *guslar*, the avatar of the plenitude of tradition itself, acts as an internal figure of interruption or failure of transmission within the ideal of total continuity. Foley never manages to quite fit the legendary *guslar* within the logic of traditional referentiality except through a kind of short circuit, which we can now examine.

To what use does Foley put the figure of this *guslar*? To be sure, no one mistakes the legendary *guslar* for a real figure. Foley himself argues that the absolute ambiguity about the legendary *guslar*'s biographical details is what enables him to become a mythical figure: 'The core of the master singer's identity is his very rootlessness or, more precisely for present purposes, his ubiquitousness.'[36] A crucial shift happens over the course of this sentence, which opens with the lack of definition of the master singer. Foley is drawn to the inaccessibility and endless deferral that strongly marks the figure of the legendary *guslar*, in conflict with the ideal image of continuity that rules traditional referentiality. The conflict is resolved in favour of the latter, and, by the end of the sentence, this figure has passed from the negative pole of his absence everywhere to the positive pole of presence everywhere. The absent centre has become a positive principle, and the ever-receding figure of the legendary *guslar* comes to be the avatar of the unmediated presence of total tradition, a short circuit from rootlessness to ubiquity.[37] The positive principle governs reading and reception just as mechanically as Parry's traditional language had governed composition, and is able to distinguish 'good and faithful audiences' from bad and apostate ones – that is, literate readers.[38]

Having seen the essential thrust of traditional referentiality as the direct connection between the particular word, phrase or performance and the totality of tradition, we can now ask: what might the Homeric poems think about traditional referentiality? In order to begin to answer this question, we need a common ground between the Homeric poems and traditional referentiality in order that one may confront the other. We find this common ground in Foley's identification of the traditional reference and the Homeric *sēma*, 'sign'. In contrast to Parry's conception of traditional language, Foley's sign or *sēma* is not restricted to the lexical level of particular words or phrases. In addition to individual formulas, a *sēma* can be any perceivable aspect of traditional language, up to and including the epic *Kunstsprache* as such:

> The mere invocation of the hexameter rhythm and diction, in addition to whatever particular phrases or scenes command more specific attention, opens a channel for reception of the performance text ... The very act of designating such a specialized idiom brings the world of heroic epic within the significative reach of poet and audience with great efficiency. The most important *sēma* is the register as a whole.[39]

The various levels of what may be found in the work of other scholars as formula, generative formulaic pattern and theme are subsumed here under a series of synonymous terms: 'word', South Slavic *reč*, 'sign', *sēma*. Again, what all of these terms express is the conception of tradition as a totality accessible through the traditional reference: 'Although superficially diverse, each of these signs has a common thrust: it signals an emergent reality that would otherwise remain hidden.'[40]

The tradition, in order to remain whole, requires that traditional language become *sēmata*; this is the injunction of traditional referentiality upon language. Traditional referentiality commands the legendary *guslar*: 'He must assume the double identity of finite instance and ongoing tradition. He must, in short, serve as a *sēma*.'[41] Only by making traditional language the domain of signs which immediately join the linguistic element – from words and formulas to rhythm and diction – to its traditional meaning is Foley's goal possible, the notion of a tradition that is both 'fully analysed' and 'aesthetically pleasing'.

Traditional referentiality is not wrong in positing an intimate relationship between the *sēma* and tradition, but whereas it unites the *sēma* and tradition as avatars of an ideal continuity, we will see in reading the Homeric poems that the Homeric conception of the *sēma* is one of interruption, which thereby makes interruption an essential aspect of Homeric poetics. We have already seen an example of a figure of interruption internal to a concept of tradition in the legendary *guslar*. The exemplarity of the legendary *guslar* lies, after all, not in the positing of his mere existence, but in his absence as the condition of his existence. He is always elsewhere, always separated temporally or geographically, or mistaken for another because of a failure of recognition. He is still Homer, but Homer is not himself, but a different poet, the two connected only by the tenuous thread of a name. Likewise, the legendary *guslar* is also absent from himself: when, at the end of the story, the humbled youth asked the great Isak from whom he had learnt such wondrous songs – 'from Isak', came the reply. As a figure of the absent and the inaccessible, the legendary *guslar* is no less a *sēma* and no less an image of tradition, but of a tradition shorn of its magnificent veil of pure immanence.

To confront traditional referentiality with the Homeric poems on the same ground, it is necessary to probe the structure of the *sēma* more closely. The *sēma*, as Nagy notes, is not only sign, signal and symbol, but also a tomb or a grave mound.[42] In place of the all too meaning-laden loquacity of that which can only repeatedly signify the presence of a 'monotonous' tradition, the silence of death descends over the *sēma* as tomb, a silence that marks a space within which other voices can sound.[43] Of such a kind is the great defensive wall that the Achaeans build in front of their ships across the Trojan plain, in the last year of the war. In its function as an absent centre that holds open a space of and for narrative, we will see that the great wall of the Achaeans parallels the figure of the legendary *guslar*, but with the exception that the great Achaean wall is absolutely unable to function as a traditionally referential sign of a tradition that is whole in its totality and that can be made epiphanically present in the moment of performance. It does not lend itself to the same short circuit as the legendary *guslar*. In the remainder of this chapter, we will examine the *sēma* of the Achaean wall as another instance in the series of figures which resist oral theory's major image of identity and continuity.

* * *

The ambiguities and contradictions that attend the construction, destruction and afterlife of the Achaean wall have been noted since antiquity. Two passages, in books VII and XII, describe how the wall was proposed and built upon the funerary pyre of dead Achaeans in a few hours and how, after the Trojan war was over and the Greeks had departed, Poseidon and Apollo loosed the obliterating force of rivers upon it to wipe it from memory. The lateness of the wall's construction in the last year of the war, the speed with which it was built, and the traumatic, seemingly disproportionate force of its divine destruction mirror in some ways the experience of encountering the *Iliad* itself in the wake of oral theory, in which the monumentality of the poem can seem to come from nowhere and vanish into insubstantiality. In a discussion most relevant for the present discussion, James Porter addresses directly the ambiguities and contradictions of the Achaean wall.[44] Let us use this as a guide in fitting the Achaean wall into the contrast between the image of continuity and identity, on the one hand, and figures of interruption and difference, on the other. We have said that the legendary *guslar* – fundamentally an image of the poet as origin – is a figure which corresponds to different conceptions of oral poetry and its tradition. Where does the Achaean wall sit in relation to the different readings of the legendary *guslar*: as the manifestation and guarantee of a total tradition, or as the expression of self-difference instead of self-identity? Can we see playing out in Porter's argument the same dynamics of interaction between figure and concept, where the interpretations on offer of poetic figures like the legendary *guslar* or the Achaean wall imply specific conceptions of poetry and tradition?

Porter's interests parallel our own concerns here, in that he, too, wants to think through what the Achaean wall as a figure might say about how poetry is conceived, that is, what the content can tell us about the form.[45] The status of the wall and its effacement, Porter argues, implies that Homeric poetry is in some sense, on a formal level, fictional:

> Of greater interest to me ... is the status of the Achaean wall itself as an object and as a critical obstacle – less the authenticity of the wall as an *episode* than the claims the wall makes to carrying a certain ontological status as a Homeric *object*, which is to say, first as a poetic object in its own right, and then as an object of criticism. For at stake in the wall, I believe, and underlying all the debates around it, is its basic status as a fictional object.[46]

Fiction and fictionality form central categories in Porter's understanding of the status of the Achaean wall. The irreconcilability of the wall's contradictions – the wall is implausibly big for an ad hoc construction and is described in contradictory ways in the poem – finds its purpose and resolution in the power of fiction. The very implausibility and contradiction of the wall is read as the flaunting of the licence that fictionality as a governing principle grants to the creative artist: 'But what if the solution to the problem of the Achaean wall is to be sought for not in its embarrassing presence but in its very status as an object and in its *arbitrary character* – that is, as an object that can be made and unmade *at will*?'[47] In a gesture parallel to Foley's assumption of a positive poetic and interpretive principle directly from the negativity of the legendary *guslar*'s constitutive absence, arbitrariness – the strictly negative property of that for which no rational motivation can be found and no coherent account given – is here raised to the level of a positive principle that accounts for its own negativity. Like the person of Homer, the arbitrary and the fictional gain a self-consistency through being named:

> One can speak of the poet's modesty if one so wishes. But there is nothing [im]modest[48] about this gesture. Is he marking his invention with a temporal *sphragis*? If so, he is pulling out all the stops – literally so. We have already seen how central

to the action of the *Iliad* the Achaean wall is. Here, Homer is pointing to the centrality of the wall in a most remarkable way, by pointing to its absence.[49]

There is perhaps a gentle irony in how the image of Homer as a creative poet who wished to show off the freedom of his creativity enters the argument of the same critic who so penetratingly identified Homer as an idea that persists through the history of scholarship.[50] And yet this is not so much a fault of the writer, but rather points to a certain substitutive logic at work. The hypostatized image of a creative Homer is exchanged, in another instance of the short circuit that we have already encountered, for the fictional and arbitrary object. The elusive Achaean wall, like the legendary *guslar*, makes visible a gap or interruption that hides under positive images. In the explanation that the strangeness of the wall serves as the sign of a poet exercising the creative freedom of fiction, that gap slips out from under the cover of the image of the wall and to the cover of the creative poet.

Porter concludes his article with the idea that the great wall of the Achaeans is not only a 'fictional' or 'metapoetic' object that demonstrates the full range of the poet's powers of arbitrary invention, but also a 'sublime object', which does not receive further definition except as something 'that is endowed with an indelible *kleos*, a lasting fame that lives on, not even if the wall vanishes, but precisely *because* the wall vanishes – for as long as the memory that recalls it persists, wanted or not'.[51] Porter refers us to Slavoj Žižek for the notion of a sublime object; let us pursue this thread for only a short distance, because we are close to an important distinction.[52] Žižek, in the cited work, explicates Hegel's critique of the Kantian sublime. For Kant, the sublime is an object in which we find the experience of an 'impossibility, this permanent failure of the representation to reach after the Thing[-in-itself]'. Through the sublime, we experience, 'within the domain of phenomenality, this transcendent dimension of the Thing which persists in itself beyond phenomenality'. For Hegel, in contrast:

> [the Kantian] negative experience of the Thing must change into the experience of the Thing-in-itself as radical negativity. The experience of the Sublime thus remains the same: all we have to do is to subtract its transcendent presupposition . . . that this experience indicates, in a negative way, some transcendent Thing-in-itself persisting in its positivity beyond [the experience].[53]

Both the Kantian and Hegelian conceptions of the sublime describe an experience of negativity. The distinction between the two, in Žižek's account, is between the Kantian experience of negativity as the sign of a transcendent, positive Thing and the Hegelian elimination of the transcendent beyond in an experience of negativity as such. The sublimity of the Achaean wall could, in Porter's account, be referred to either the Kantian or the Hegelian sublime, depending on how fictionality – to which the Achaean wall as sublime object offers access – is itself conceived. Porter does not pursue the choice between the two, but the choice is crucial for our discussions here. Does the sublime object that is the wall refer to a Kantian transcendent beyond, which in this case would be the fictive power of the creative poet, or does it make the negativity of a gap or interruption appear as such? And if the Achaean wall is a sublime object insofar as it is 'endowed with an indelible *kleos*', the same question can be asked of *kleos*: is it a positive principle of a transcendent tradition, or something else? Does *kleos* express identity or difference? With these questions, we arrive at a direct choice between Foley's reading of the *sēma* within the major image of oral theory, and the figures of interruption – the elusiveness of the legendary *guslar* and the contradictions of the Achaean wall – which resist it.

This choice was not urgent for Porter's article, which turns instead towards the question of fictionality and its pleasures:

> Fictionality was not openly allowed in the ancient critical traditions, and therefore the pleasures it afforded had to be stolen, displaced, and disputed as well ... It was also that the Achaean wall was something that came from nothing, and that bore the signs of this negation in itself – a terrifying prospect no matter how one looked at it. Homer was both traumatic *and* pleasurable.[54]

For our purposes, however, it is necessary to go beyond simply demonstrating the presence of fictionality, because we can tease out more connections between the fictional or sublime object and the nature of the Achaean wall itself. We would like to answer the following questions: if the poet could have invented and destroyed anything, if 'it only takes a second breath to draw the last bit of implication from this insight, and to leap to the conclusion that Homer fabricated Troy, in other words that the whole myth of Troy is a monumental falsehood', then why was it the great wall of the Achaeans that he chose to invent and to destroy as the sublime object?[55] How is possible to reconcile the generality of the poet's infinite imagination with the particularity of the Achaean wall, which 'cannot help but have this claim to interest just by virtue of being an object that *once* so magnificently and palpably and *uniquely* – but also, so curiously and suddenly – was and then so utterly is no more'?[56] Why is it significant that the sublime object is a wall and a grave mound, as the *Iliad* tells us, a wall built upon a tomb? If the poet's subjectivity is taken as the sovereign creative power that wields its fictions, then of course no answers are possible, because the question itself would be lost in a meaningless abyss of freedom. But more can be said if we follow oral theory in putting aside the figure of the poet and his creative subjectivity.

In ways that we will presently work out, the Achaean wall functions as *sēma*, and the *sēma* takes the form of a gap. The crucial question is whether we are able to say something about this gap that does not immediately make it into the sign of a totality or a continuity: 'To make the wall vanish is to conceal, not so much the evidence for its former existence, as the absence of any such evidence. But it is, at the same time, to produce this absence and to make it palpable in the text.'[57] The *sēma* is a gap or a palpable absence, but the temptation is always to either turn this gap into an object with positive consistency, like Foley's traditional sign which acts like an object of the Kantian sublime, or to make it the signifying mark of a creative subject, as in Porter's fiction-wielding poet.[58] With the intimate connections between the *sēma*, the poet and the tradition,[59] it is only a short step from giving the *sēma* a positive consistency to giving the same positivity to the poet and the tradition, along a path at the end of which lies traditional referentiality.[60]

How does the Achaean wall act as interruption? One answer can be given from the perspective of narrative. The wall interrupts Hector and the Trojans as they seek to set fire to the Greek ships beached on the shore. The wall interrupts the progress of the – traditional – narrative, that it may not come too soon, and protects, for a while, the conditions for the end of Achilles' withdrawal from battle when fire threatens the homecoming of the Greeks. The withdrawal of Achilles constitutes itself an interruption in the narrative, and insofar as it is about the withdrawal of Achilles, the *Iliad* as a whole constitutes an interruption.[61] The Achaean wall, as an objective representation of the interruption that is the poem, keeps the Greeks and the Trojans apart and interrupts their consummation in battle.

But the wall intervenes in more than this rather abstract conception of the narrative. The Achaean wall can be seen as a *sēma* both in Foley's sense and literally, since it also marks a grave mound:

> But when it was not yet dawn, but still the night in half light, a chosen body of the Achaians formed by the pyre; and they gathered together and piled one single mound [*tumbon*] above it indiscriminately [*akriton*] from the plain, and built a fort on it with towered ramparts, to be a defence for themselves and their vessels.[62]

This is a paradoxical grave mound. The function of a grave mound as *sēma* is to be a conspicuous and lasting sign of the hero who has died and is buried there, as the soul of Agamemnon describes the tomb of Achilles: 'We piled up a great and perfect grave mound over the bones, on a jutting promontory, by the wide Hellespont, so that it can be seen from afar, out on the water, by men now alive and those yet to be born hereafter' (xxiv. 80–4).[63] The pyre upon which the Greeks built their wall, on the other hand, was a mass grave, in which neither the fame nor even the identity of its occupants can be preserved. G. S. Kirk, in his commentary, concurs with Aristarchus as to the impossibility of separating the bones left on the pyre, in contradiction to Nestor's initial proposal that they be individually carried back to the children of the dead.[64] Kirk reads *tumbon akriton* as meaning '"one communal mound in the plain" ... for *tumbon akriton* must mean "undiscriminated" in relation to individual corpses, not "indistinguishable from the plain"'.[65] The Achaean wall is thus a *sēma* that confers no fame, *kleos*, to those buried under it. It does not represent the continuity of a tradition that preserves fame, but rather embodies an interruption of the function of memory that we would expect from a *sēma*.[66]

The function of the wall against fame and memory does not stop there. The *Iliad*, in a conspicuous prolepsis, describes how the wall is eventually destroyed by Poseidon and Apollo through the medium of water. 'When in the tenth year the city of Priam was taken and the Argives gone in their ships to the beloved land of their fathers, then at last Poseidon and Apollo took counsel to crush the wall, letting loose the strength of rivers upon it, all the rivers that run to the sea from the mountains of Ida' (xii. 15–19).[67] Citing James Redfield's concept of an 'antifuneral, the symbolic opposite of commemoration', Ford compares Achilles' battle with the river Scamander to emphasize the power of water to obliterate, in direct opposition to the commemorative function usually attributed to the *sēma*:

> His splendid arms somewhere below the water will lie covered with mud; and his body I will bury in the sands, piling on a great heap of pebbles, numberless, and the Achaeans will not know how to collect his bones ... There will his *sēma* be shaped, and there will be no need of heaping a tomb over him for his burial, when the Achaeans bury him.[68]

The Achaean wall's death by water is thus, as Porter notes, a paradoxical 'monumental obliteration', that is, a memorable, unforgettable forgetting.[69] But, as we saw above, the Achaean wall is already itself a *sēma* that can preserve nothing of the dead for epic memory and already a forgetting rather than a remembering. Its destruction becomes the destruction of a forgetting, the compounding of obliteration upon obliteration.

The Achaean wall as *sēma* is thus an interruption in the tradition of traditional referentiality. It interrupts the processes of fame, memory and commemoration usually attributed to epic, and it refuses the signifying, referential function of the traditional reference. The Achaean wall as a sublime figure of interruption almost demands the invocation of a creative poet and the category of fiction to cover up its abyssal, traumatic nature. It is a point of vulnerability at which oral theory's assumptions of an ideally continuous tradition can no longer hold without paradox. The wall's explicit and ostentatious opposition to every form of continuity within the epic tradition demands a different conception of Homeric poetics.[70]

* * *

Traditional referentiality's paradoxical gesture of covering over gaps in favour of continuity is illustrated in its interpretive strategy and its implicit linguistics, which, like much else about traditional referentiality, can be seen as a response to Parry's linguistics of traditional language. Parry imposed a stringent distinction between the formula as a signifier and the 'essential idea' it expresses as signified, in which the arbitrariness of the signifier is expressed in the assertion that the formula can only carry its essential idea, without concessions to context. In response to the stringency of Parry's distinction, Foley's traditional reference acts as a signifier immediately and ideally combined with its signified in the form of a natural sign.[71] As Rainer Nägele observes, 'The more clearly the rupture [between signifier and signified] manifests itself, the more intensely the luring image of a natural sign, immanently endowed with significance, counters the allegorical split of the sign.'[72] The intensity with which Foley's traditional referentiality pursues the traditional sign, the *sēma* that guarantees the aesthetic value and immanent meaning of traditional poetry, is no accident, but is conditioned by the uninhibited procedural reductiveness of Parry's conception of traditional oral poetry. 'It is a frequent phenomenon ... that the more reductive the procedure is, the more pious is the expression of aesthetic appreciation. The more effusively the critic assures us of the incommensurability and sublimity of the work of art, the less inhibited he is to pursue the work of reduction.'[73] In the case of traditional referentiality, the reductiveness was not due to Foley himself, but was inherited from Parry's linguistics of orality. In some senses, Parry's influence was all the more inescapable inasmuch as Foley saw his project as a continuation or justification of Parry's rather than, as I would suggest, its inverse or recoil.

Traditional referentiality's implicit linguistics of the natural sign has interpretive consequences. Foley devotes a chapter of *Immanent Art* to reformulating traditional referentiality in terms of the reception theory, and the same gesture of refusing interruption appears again – strikingly, in its treatment of *gaps* in interpretation.[74] Gaps in reception which invite the reader's participation are exchanged for an ideal continuity, so that Foley ends up on the other side of a reception theory that is initially introduced with approval: 'Receptionalism reminds us that we cannot settle for the distortion of dynamic activity into stasis, of ever-contingent reception into known and appropriated fact, of the implied reader's continuing responsibility into the kind of textual archaeology that converts our living literary tradition into a museum filled with dusty artifacts.'[75] The openness of the living tradition and the reader's active role in interpretation is first asserted, and a passage from Wolfgang Iser is cited on the importance of sites of 'indeterminacy' for the literary value of the text:

> [E]very literary text invites some form of participation on the part of the reader. A text which lays things out before the reader in such a way that he can either accept or reject them will lessen the degree of participation as it allows it nothing but a yes or no. Texts with such minimal indeterminacy tend to be tedious.[76]

Initially, as in this quoted passage, the interpretive participation of a reader faced with gaps of indeterminacy is welcomed. But soon, Foley changes the values of gaps and indeterminacy. Where the figure of the Achaean wall embodies a *sēma* that expresses the interruption of memory and the failure of meaning, Foley turns the gap of indeterminacy – introduced as the freedom of the reader – into a gap always already filled by tradition:

> For if we understand that a *literary* reception of an *oral traditional* text ... must by its very nature fail to bridge all of the gaps of indeterminacy in anything approaching a way faithful to the aesthetic reality of the work, then we shall see that calling these gaps 'flaws' is itself a mistake ... Indeed, an uncompromisingly literary reading of such texts will create indeterminacy where, according to a faithful reception of the work, it does not exist, thus doing further damage to the aesthetic experience.[77]

Traditional referentiality bridges gaps in a way that 'literary' readings do not. The very image of the bridging of gaps already conceives of the proper meaning as something that pre-exists on the farther side, the side that it is the task to interpretation to reach. By insisting that the goal and virtue of traditional referentiality is to explain away flaws and to bridge gaps of indeterminacy, Foley's interpretation of reception theory turns into something of an anti-reception theory, insofar as the gaps which are left open to the reader in reception theory turn out to be gaps prefilled by the oral tradition. Traditional referentiality not only becomes a way of smoothing over the gaps in the text, but, more fundamentally, it is an insistence that the gaps never existed in the first place. The 'successful interpreter', 'a worthy co-creator' of the work and one who does not impair 'its ability to convey meaning', is the one retrojected back to a world in which all the references of traditional referentiality are known, a world that 'remains immune to the ravages of time'.[78]

The time that ravages the ideal world of traditional referentiality is that which ruptures the traditional reference and introduces the allegorical split of the sign into signifier into signified, hence the ideal world of traditional referentiality is also the prelapsarian Eden of language. Keenly aware of the fallen nature of man in the world of written works and literate criticism, Foley resists this awareness in the large-scale structure of *Homer's Traditional Art* by repeatedly asserting and performing immanently meaningful natural signs, which *are* immediately what they *mean*, unmarked by the split between signifier and signified. This is a work which states its conclusions at the beginning, and it is notable that these conclusions take the form of proverbs and work like the very traditional signs and traditional references they are meant to explicate: 'For the moment I will explain each proverb only telegraphically, preferring to let its full meaning emerge in the context of usage and discussion throughout the subsequent chapters.'[79] The proverbs demonstrate a conservation of form each time they recur. The first proverb, '*Oral tradition works like language, only more so*', can be found in the same form ten times at the end of paragraphs – in the way of punctuation or of the *quod erat demonstrandum* at the end of a mathematical proof – in the first third of the book alone, varying only in its grammatical subject, which may be, interchangeably: oral tradition, *sēmata*, living idiom or a combination of special/specialized traditional/poetic/South Slavic epic/Homer's register/language/*koinē*.[80] The key to all of these concepts working 'like language, only more so' is the immanent meaning and coherence of the natural sign as distinguished from the Saussurean sign, split between signified and signifier. In explicitly using traditional formulas to expound the doctrine of traditional referentiality, Foley explains traditional poetry through performing it.

* * *

> *Thus, afterwards, Poseidon and Apollo were to put things in place; but at this time the clamour of battle still blazed about the strong-founded wall...*[81]

In this chapter, we have described the major image of the Homeric tradition in oral theory, one that emphasizes continuity, wholeness and self-identity. This emphasis is apparent on a number of levels: poetically, as the harmony of the individual performance and the total tradition; in interpretation, as an ideal seamlessness that brooks no gaps; and linguistically, as the unity of signifier and signified. We have also started to develop a minor series of figures and conceptual images that inhere within both Homeric poems and oral theory, and undermine the major image: the legendary *guslar*, the wall, the *sēma*. What use can we make of these ideas? The figures of the minor series seem relatively peripheral – so what connections can we make to link these marginal figures to the more central figures and problems of the Homeric poems and scholarship? We will address these questions in the following chapters, but let us anticipate slightly and return to the consideration of the Achaean wall.

When the Trojan war was finished, with Troy destroyed and the Greeks gone in their ships, gone back to their homeland, the Achaean wall remained, it was said, on the field of battle, to be a sign of the events that had taken place there. But Zeus sent nine days of rain, and Poseidon and Apollo let loose the power of rivers upon it, until the Trojan plain was smooth again and bore no more sign of the war and the *Iliad*. Porter, without addressing the question directly, seems to be aware of some significance in the historicity of the Achaean wall, the fact that the event had to have a certain duration at all: 'The Achaean wall cannot help but have this claim to interest just by virtue of being an object that once so magnificently and palpably and uniquely – but also, so curiously and suddenly – *was* and then so utterly is *no more*.'[82] He diagnoses the same preoccupation with duration in concerns of the 'literal-minded' parts of the scholia: 'It is as though Homer was keen to disarm the worry that the wall, built in an *ad hoc* fashion though it was (αὐτοσχεδῶς ᾠκοδομημένον), would not have had a chance to appear to collapse with historical time and so to vanish from sight: there wasn't time enough for it to collapse on its own.'[83] What is the significance of the Achaean wall's historicity, the fact that it is not merely a symbol that represents metaphorically, but had to have taken place within the metonymy of narration between the *was* and the *is no more*?

What emerges strongly here is a preoccupation with time, which the Achaean wall makes visible in an image. How does the wall make us – scholiasts, scholars, audiences – so keenly aware of time, of the passage of time between the *was* and the *is*? The place of the episode of the wall's destruction within the narrative structure of the *Iliad* as a whole is significant. The destruction of the wall is placed in the 'very center' of the poem, as an audacious prolepsis.[84] The temporal contrast is emphasized at the end of the passage – 'Thus, *afterwards*, [ὣς ἄρ' ἔμελλον ὄπισθε] Poseidon and Apollo were minded to put things in place, but *at that time* battle and clamour were blazing' – and with verbs in a vertiginous imperfect at the beginning: 'nor was the Danaans' ditch going [οὐδ' ἄρ' ἔμελλε] to hold them back … it was [ἦεν] not to stand firm for a long time.'[85] We will dwell further on the temporality of these imperfects and the semantics of *mellō* in particular, but, for now, let us simply note that the proleptic narration of the wall's destruction makes its appearances in the rest of the book take on the character of a double vision. Whenever we see the wall in its solidity at the centre of the fighting, we also recall its later effacement. Our vision of the wall is divided between the two times, and thus the wall makes visible the difference between them, and that difference is time itself. In this sense, the Achaean wall offers us an image of time.[86]

Making visible difference as time: this is the thread that will allow us to say more than that the marginal figures of the *guslar* and the wall merely resist the ideals of continuity and identity. Rather, they connect to problems in the work of Nagy and the neoanalytic school, on the side of scholarship, and, on the side of poetry, to the central tragedy of Achilles itself. What is the question of the Homeric *sēma* as tomb and sign but the problematic of bearing meaning through time? The Achaean wall, a phantasmatic materialization of the failure of commemoration that nevertheless obtrudes so memorably within our experience of the *Iliad*, is one of the objects that precipitate from this problem, and might be considered a response or a form of solution. Traditional referentiality is another solution, one that, compared to the wall, responds in exactly the opposite way. Instead of the wall's materialization of oblivion, traditional referentiality is powerfully governed by the image of an eternal tradition that is immediately evoked within the particular performance. How to more precisely define the problem and trace its various paths and effects throughout the Homeric poems and scholarship? The essential relationship between meaning in the Homeric tradition and forms of time will be the theme of the next chapters.

2

The Breaking of the Present

In the previous chapter, I drew from the relation between John Miles Foley's traditional referentiality and the Iliadic figure of the Achaean wall a resistance to the ideal of continuity and self-identity governing oral theory. Where the sign conceived as a traditional reference guarantees continuity between the poetic tradition and the individual poem, the Homeric *sēma*, meaning at once 'sign' and 'grave-mound', inserts a gap or interruption between the poem and its tradition. The *sēma* in Homer, like the forgotten grave marker with which Achilles marks the course of the chariot race or the great wall of the Achaeans destined to disappear in flood, marks places where the work of memory and the continuity of meaning are radically threatened.[1] There were also hints that the resistance to the harmonious fullness of tradition may subsist at a fundamental level, as shown by the way that the ever-receding figure of the legendary *guslar* inheres even within the desire of traditional referentiality for a poetic tradition that becomes epiphanically present in each performance.

The first chapter focused on Foley and the Achaean wall because they demonstrated within a compact set of reference points the tension between the ideal of a continuous, whole tradition and the figures of interruption, but this compactness also meant that the discussions there remained limited in both scope and generality; the figures of the wall and the *guslar*, however suggestive, were minor and relatively peripheral to the *Iliad* and oral theoretical scholarship, respectively. In this chapter, I will argue that the marginal is in fact essential, extending the significance of discontinuity and difference to major themes of both the Homeric poems and Homeric scholarship. I will also further substantiate the methodological gambit of placing poetry and scholarship on the same plane, because we will see how the concept of difference so far exemplified in the series of minor figures is in fact capable of connecting the preoccupations of the Homeric poems and of the scholarly discourses about them.

I have been using a somewhat unwieldy set of terms – 'discontinuity', 'difference', 'resistance' – to designate that which undermines the ideal of continuity and identity. In particular, 'difference' is an especially portentous and inconveniently resonant term. We will be able to be more precise from now on, because the first thing to be demonstrated in this chapter is that the Homeric concept of *kleos* expresses the specific kind of difference that our discussions have been seeking. This chapter will thus go some way towards the goal outlined in the introduction of shifting the emphasis of *kleos* from identity to difference. By the end of this chapter, we will be able to approach this thesis with a fuller appreciation of its position between poetry and scholarship.

One last piece of the conceptual apparatus remains to be introduced, and this is the link between difference and time which we saw briefly at the end of the last chapter. The bold prolepsis of the description of the Achaean wall's destruction makes time visible as the difference between the wall that stands at the heart of the fighting and the wall as it will be, effaced from the world except in its *kleos* within the Homeric poem. A fuller statement of the agenda for this chapter, then, runs thus: the series of minor figures joining poetry and scholarship, described in the previous chapter, are correlates of a concept of time as difference, and this concept is expressed in the Homeric tradition as *kleos*.[2]

Having placed *kleos* in its context within the broader architectonics of the book's argument, let me present a brief overview of what the present chapter will look like. The logic of *kleos*, we will find, splits or divides every present moment in the *Iliad*, so that it is no longer complete or whole in itself, but includes another time that cannot be contained in the present. We will consider the division of the present in two forms, the first a local form, followed by an extension to the generalized form. The local form of the division is seen in moments in the epic in which a hero thinks explicitly about his future fame or reputation; it is local because a particular narrative situation prompts this reflection. As instances of the local form, we will consider Hector's anticipation of his *kleos* which we already saw in the introduction, as well as, on the lexical level, the word *essomenoisi*, 'for those to come'. These local divisions give us only a relatively superficial form of the splitting of the present, since my present anticipation of the future is still a part of my present moment, and the difference that we see is still only the difference between two chronological presents. But we will find a radical breaking of the present in the generalized form of the division. In the generalized form, we are no longer limited to specific narrative moments in which the questions of future fame are explicitly considered: every moment can be divided. The transition from local to generalized division is dramatized in Achilles' career through the *Iliad*; we will see how, through the course of the poem, Achilles learns that *kleos* cannot be mastered and it thereby divides every moment.³ We will see this logic in several instances where Homeric heroes reveal how they think about change through time, such as when Agamemnon sees Menelaus wounded by an arrow. Lastly, the splitting of the present in its two forms of local and generalized division applies not only to the *Iliad*, but also enables us to link poetry to scholarship. In this connection, we will see how a parallel development from local to general can be seen in the neoanalytic school of Homeric interpretation.⁴

I. From local to generalized division

Let us begin with some basic propositions about *kleos*. Turning to linguistics, we find that the noun *kleos* is related to the verb *kluō*, 'I hear'.⁵ So *kleos* can be understood as 'something heard', and both rumour and fame are essentially things that we hear, in particular in the preliterate context of the early Homeric tradition. It occupies a central place in epic because it plays three major roles: first, *kleos* as fame and glory motivates the hero; second, *kleos* as the 'things heard' in oral performances links the poet to epic tradition; third, the circulation of *kleos* connects the performance of epic song to its social contexts, in which the glory of particular heroes can be bound up with the civic self-identities of the societies in which heroic song was performed. Hero, poet, audience – these elements of epic performance are linked through the concept of *kleos*.⁶

I want to create some space between these linked elements, and to do this by prising open a gap internal to the concept of *kleos* itself.⁷ We will focus for now on the role of *kleos* in the motivation of the epic heroes, or, more broadly, in how the heroes understand themselves and their actions and decisions. The heroes are motivated by the prospect of *kleos* as the future glory that will come into being in heroic song, but how do the heroes conceptualize this *kleos*? It is a commonplace to note that the claims of epic song about its ability to keep *kleos* alive are performatively self-fulfilling, in the sense that, as long as the song is performed and an audience hears it, the song fulfils its role in perpetuating the *kleos* of its heroes.⁸ In other words, the performance of the *kleos* is simultaneous with and identified as the performance of the *claim*. Thus the epic song never lies about its ability to perpetuate *kleos*, because if it ever stopped perpetuating *kleos* – that is, if epic song ever stopped being performed – the *claim* that the song perpetuates *kleos* will also be silenced. This logic seems at first unimpeachable: since the *kleos* of the hero consists in stories about the hero being performed, *kleos* necessarily comes with performance, and the hero obtains or retains his *kleos* as long as the performance tradition persists.

But let us pause here and consider if this is the way that the epic hero sees things. Would the epic hero – say, Hector – consider his expectations about his future glory fulfilled as long as *some* or *any* story is told about him? This is plainly not the case, since the heroes often have very particular ideas about precisely what story his actions and sufferings will amount to, and what meaning can be drawn from that story. In the example discussed in the introduction, Hector imagines what will be said about him over the tomb of his vanquished opponent.[9] The *kleos* that Hector projects into the future has a particular content. To be sure, he cares *that* his *kleos* will endure, but he is not indifferent to *what* endures as his *kleos*.

Even as this point – that the content of *kleos* matters, and is not interchangeable – significantly complicates the commonplace understanding of just what is perpetuated when epic song claims to perpetuate *kleos*, it is quite obvious when stated explicitly, so let us not belabour it with excessive examples.[10] We can instead observe that in Hector's claim to future fame, the preoccupation with *kleos* means that the heroes act in their present as if they are under observation by the eye of the poetic tradition in their future. The logic of *kleos* contains an inner temporality, in which the context of action does not entirely exist in the heroic present but lies in conditions which are still to come. These conditions, as projected from within heroic ideology – as the heroes conceive – are the future traditions of heroic song. There is thus both a content of *kleos* – what will be sung – and also a form – *that* a song will come to bestow meaning to the decisions and acts of the heroes. If this sounds very close to the commonplace understanding, we must still observe that, unlike the commonplace in which the formal aspect of *kleos* does not affect the decisions and actions of the heroes, who are supposed to be complacent in their assurance that they will be sung about, what we are after here are the ways in which the expectation of future song affects what the heroes do, that is, the ways in which the form affects the content.

The link between *kleos* and a 'song to come' is indexed in the heroic world by the word *essomenoisi*, 'for those who are still to come'. The word is a sign of the form left in the content. When Agamemnon tests the resolve of his army by calling on them to retreat in defeat from the war, he adopts the perspective of a future audience: 'And this shall be a thing of shame for the men hereafter [ἐσσομένοισι] to be told, that so strong, so great a host of Achaians carried on and fought in vain a war that was useless.'[11] Here, again, we can observe that, on the level of form, Agamemnon's thinking about his current situation presupposes the perspective of a future audience of heroic song, and, on the level of content, the meaning of and judgement upon his actions from that perspective is significant for him. The fact that here, as with Hector in the previous example, Agamemnon has to consider a future perspective is what breaks him out of his present moment of action, hence it is an instance of what I am calling a splitting or breaking of the present. But insofar as the motivation for both Agamemnon's and Hector's explicit considerations of the future perspective lies in specific narrative situations – the duel for Hector and the prospect of failure for Agamemnon – these divisions in the present remain local divisions, and do not generalize to every moment.

How might it be possible for us to move beyond local divisions and to think a generalized division, an image of time in which every moment is divided between now and another time? The key is a crucial, formal feature of *kleos* we have not yet mentioned, which is the fact that the future perspective of the song to come is always inaccessible to the heroes themselves, even as their motivation and self-understanding depend so much upon it. What is generalized in the generalized division of the present is precisely the unknowability of *kleos*.[12] Already, in the example of Hector, we know that Hector's projection of his fame into the mouth of the future speaker will be in vain, since events do not turn out in the way he anticipates. A bar is interposed between the hero and his future fame, and we will be able to see the barred structure of *kleos* at work in figures which, unlike those already considered, do not depend on local situations to call upon the concept of *kleos* explicitly. Instead of a futurity that matters only at specific, narratively motivated moments, every moment comes to be divided. A transitional figure leads us from merely local divisions to the generalized splitting of the present, and this figure is the trajectory or tragedy of Achilles in the *Iliad*. The career of Achilles stages the imposition of the prohibition that bars the hero from his own *kleos*, as Achilles learns the condition or logic of the inaccessibility of *kleos* through what he does and suffers in the *Iliad*, and thereby recognizes the division of every moment.

The distinction between the form and content of *kleos* – between *kleos* understood as the formal structure in which meaning is deferred to a song to come, and *kleos* understood as the contents of that song – is crucial to understanding what Achilles undergoes over the course of the *Iliad*. We can outline briefly the stages in Achilles' career: he starts off acting as if he is able to know and manipulate his future *kleos*, as if the hero in his contemporaneous context can arrange events in such a way as to produce a specific meaning or content of *kleos* in the future. The death of Patroclus makes Achilles understand that the unexpected upends even the best-laid plans, and that *kleos* arrives in the form of an inaccessible and unknowable future song.[13] This realization is of course of a piece with what is usually called Greek pessimism as we might encounter in Herodotus, but what makes Achilles' case interesting for our interest in the form of time is what he does with this realization; in Achilles' speech to Lykaon, he generalizes the unknowability of *kleos* in a way that will lead us to another image of time.

In the opening dialogue between Achilles and Thetis in which Achilles asks his mother to persuade Zeus to arrange events so that the Greeks suffer in his absence, the stakes seem at first glance to be set at the level of *timē*, honour among the peer group, rather than that of *kleos*, fame from the perspective of future song. These two related terms are often conflated, often for good reason, but let us note the temporal difference between these terms.[14] Charles Segal, for instance, readily runs *kleos* into 'how one is viewed and talked of by one's peers … a measure of one's value to others and to oneself', which is more properly designated by *timē*.[15] In the context of our interest in the image of time, however, we need to distinguish *timē*, a synchronic social concept fully realized in the hero's present, from *kleos*, which properly includes an irreducibly temporal displacement.

As Achilles frames his request, Zeus is asked to 'pin the Achaians back against the ships and the water, dying, so that thus they may all have profit of their own king, that Atreus' son wide-ruling Agamemnon may recognize his madness, that he did no honour [οὐδὲν ἔτισεν] to the best of the Achaians'.[16] Thetis herself, in conversation with Zeus, also frames Achilles' request in terms of honour: 'Zeus of the counsels, lord of Olympos, now do him honour [τῖσον]. So long put strength into the Trojans, until the Achaians give my son his rights, and his honour is increased among them [ὄφρ' ἂν Ἀχαιοὶ / υἱὸν ἐμὸν τίσωσιν ὀφέλλωσίν τέ ἑ τιμῇ].'[17] The stakes of *timē* and *kleos* are not well distinguished here; *timē*, rather than *kleos*, seems to be the ultimate horizon against which value is judged. But we can see the level of *kleos* in the sense of the meaning of a life, as distinct from the social value of *timē*, introduced in Thetis' perspective on Achilles' destiny: 'How bitterly I gave birth to you and raised you. If only you could sit by your ships untroubled, not weeping, since indeed your lifetime is to be short, of no length. Now it has befallen that your life must be brief and bitter beyond all men's. To a bad destiny I bore you in my chambers.'[18] Thetis here understands the stakes of Achilles' request not only on the level of the honour he might obtain from his heroic peers, but also in the perspective of the meaning of the *kleos* of his whole lifetime, brief and bitter as it must be.

What kind of act is Achilles' request to Zeus, and what understanding of *kleos* is presupposed by it? By asking for the death of the other Achaians in his narrative present, Achilles hopes to produce a particular meaning – say, 'Achilles was the best of the Achaians' – in the site of *kleos*, which is the future of the song to come. In the opening of the *Iliad*, then, Achilles takes up a particular position with respect to *kleos* in which, through his request to Zeus, he thinks that he can actively and deliberately manipulate the meaning of his *kleos*.

Achilles' position implies a particular conception of time and action. Achilles acts as if he is able to shape the narrative of his own life by asking for the death of the other Achaians in order to produce the meaning, 'Achilles was the best of the Achaians', without the fact that he asked for the death of the other Achaeans affecting the desired meaning. It is as if Achilles believes he can act without acting, in the sense that the act of asking for the death of the other Achaeans is an act that Achilles tries to perform behind the back of what we might call history, without its becoming inscribed as part of his *kleos*.[19] Thus Achilles, at the beginning of his story in the *Iliad*, believes that he can see all the elements that will form part of his *kleos* and thereby manipulate *kleos* from outside history, as if his very manipulation can escape judgement and not form part of the meaning to be found in *kleos*.[20]

Achilles places himself in the same position, or meta-position, outside time or history when he appears again during the Embassy, describing the choice he has between dying young in Troy and living out a long but obscure life at home:

> For my mother Thetis the goddess of the silver feet tells me I carry two sorts of destiny towards the day of my death. Either, if I stay here and fight beside the city of the Trojans, my return home is gone, but my glory shall be everlasting; but if I return home to the beloved land of my fathers, the excellence of my glory is gone, but there will be a long life left for me, and my end in death will not come to me quickly.[21]

Here, we can see why Achilles acts as if he can manipulate *kleos* – because he thinks he can choose his death.[22] The treatments of the death of Achilles are at least superficially inconsistent in the *Iliad*, but lead to the same result.[23] On the one hand, Achilles is represented as having a choice between fame and long life as in the Embassy. On the other hand, Thetis also says that Achilles would always be short-lived, as previous quoted (1. 414–18). This inconsistency reflects the double perspective of the epic present, in which the outcome of events is supposed to be still in flux, and the retroactive view upon the epic from the time of song. We should note here two further points: first, the ambiguity of the fate of Achilles is yet another aspect of epic in which we can see the splitting of the present – the epic present is divided between its own now and the view of a song to come; second, this doubled perspective is dramatized in Achilles' career, which moves from that of someone who attempts to determine the future song outside the epic present, to the realization, as we will see, that such an attempt is impossible because he is necessarily within time. In either case, whether Achilles is destined to be short-lived or if he has a choice, Achilles' knowledge of his own death is more complete and more certain than that of any other mortal. This is why he comes to believe that he could will death, and thereby control the meaning of his death and, with it, his *kleos*. Achilles will be fatally and decisively shaken from his initial position by the death of Patroclus, when he discovers that the progress of narrative can produce a retroactive re-evaluation of all the values that informed his initial choice.

Throughout his absence from the action between the Embassy and the *aristeia* of Patroclus, Achilles occupies a liminal position at the end of the Greek lines. Just as he is a spectator of the battle as it flows between the Greeks and Trojans, Achilles is also a spectator in relation to his own *kleos*, watching the progress of his plot – in both secretive and narrative senses of the word – and waiting for the most dramatically effective moment to make his entrance.[24] The language of drama here is no accident as Achilles turns his liminal position into one external to the action, the position of the Aristotelian spectator, the better to judge from the outside the effect of the plot. Mark Buchan notes that Achilles sends Patroclus to find out the identity of the wounded Machaon because he 'sustains Achilles's desire to find out more about himself and his own relative social worth', which is true, though we should also emphasize here a more basic point that, as architect and spectator *of* the plot, Achilles needs to find out what is going on *in* it.[25] Achilles sends Patroclus to gauge the plight of the Greeks as his eyes and ears, like a spectator who raises his opera glasses, distant and unaffected by the action.

The progress of the *Iliad* shows Achilles' attempt to orchestrate his own *kleos* to be fallacious. Where the spectator at the theatre risks nothing in maintaining only a visual relation to the action onstage, it is precisely through Patroclus, Achilles' surrogate eyes on the action, that the narrative disabuses Achilles of the notion that he can manipulate the plot from the outside. The death of Patroclus while Achilles is still putting off the decision of whether to return to battle shows that the choice that was apparently available for Achilles to make was always a false choice. With the death of Patroclus, Achilles' choice is made for him, behind his back and without his knowledge; far from Achilles choosing to have his undying fame over a long life, *kleos* comes for him in an unexpected way, from an unseen quarter. All that remains for Achilles is to recognize that, even when he chooses *kleos*, *kleos* will not arrive in the way he expects.[26] And it is precisely the *way* that Achilles chose to orchestrate his imagined *kleos* – through the suffering of the Achaeans – that forms the unimagined *kleos* he in fact obtains. Insofar as the career of Achilles in the *Iliad* is tragic, it is precisely because Achilles does get the fame that he wants, through the very events that he set in motion to get it, but its meaning is completely different; the content of *kleos* is not heroic but tragic.²⁷ It is notable that, when Thetis confronts Achilles with a second prophecy, 'it is decreed your death must come soon after Hektor's', Achilles now sees it not as a contingent choice to be made in the future – to kill or not kill Hector – but as the mere expression of a result of a decision made in the past, before he knew he was making a decision: 'I must die soon, then; since I was not to stand by my companion when he was killed.'²⁸ Achilles' attempt to remedy his ignorance of what is happening in the Greek camp turns out to be the mechanism through which Achilles' greater ignorance of his own *kleos*, which he thought he could manipulate, comes to be revealed.²⁹ It is this lesson, learnt through devastation, that Achilles now assumes.

Achilles began by acting as if he can actively control his *kleos*, but a two-stage change happens with the death of Patroclus. The first change is that he learns that *kleos* is beyond his control – he aimed for one kind of content or one intended meaning at the site of *kleos*, and the progress of time has instead produced an entirely different meaning or content. The second change is that the inaccessibility of *kleos* does not remain merely a negative principle of what Achilles cannot know, but, we will see, he comes to occupy a particular relation to it and uses it as an ethical principle. The inaccessibility of *kleos* is in the first stage a formal principle of how meaning is produced in the time of epic: whatever meaning will come of the epic hero's actions, it will come in a song to come that is unknown to that hero at the moment of his acting.³⁰ In the second stage, however, the formal principle comes to be thematized as content. And it is the positive thematization of the negative formal principle of unknowability that extends into a generalized division of the present. I will demonstrate this generalization first in Achilles after the death of Patroclus, and then in other figures.

Achilles assumes the ignorance of *kleos*, the ignorance of the meaning his life will have come to take on in the song to come. In this assumption is the affirmation of death, in accordance with the Greek wisdom that the meaning of a man's life is not revealed until his death, or, in another idiom, that death is the ownmost possibility of his being.³¹ Death is affirmed not only as that which one cannot outrun, but also as that which one cannot run after or actively choose; the active choice of death was the basis of Achilles' self-delusion in thinking he could choose death in return for unfailing fame. Death is now assumed as essentially unknown and unknowable. The key passage for our concern with the image of time is found in Achilles' encounter with Lykaon. In Achilles' reply to Lykaon's supplication, we see that he has come to understand death as incorporating a radical uncertainty:

> Do you not see what a man I am, how huge, how splendid and born of a great father, and the mother who bore me immortal? Yet even I have also my death and my strong destiny, and there shall be a dawn or an afternoon or a noontime when some man in the fighting will take the life from me also either with a spearcast or an arrow flown from the bowstring.[32]

Like Oedipus when he takes upon himself the title of *paida tēs tukhēs*, 'child of Fortune', Achilles accepts the radical openness of a death that is elsewhere, beyond his ken, in the other scene of the song to come.[33] The two-stage change in Achilles' position can be seen here. First, the negative stage: Achilles does not know when or in what form death will come, and does not know how the story of his *kleos* will end. Second, the positive stage: the uncertainty about the circumstances of death, along with the meaning of *kleos* which attends upon it, infiltrates every moment, whether it be 'a dawn or an afternoon or a noontime'.[34] This stage is positive because Achilles makes it part of his ethical system; the passage occurs in the context of Achilles considering or explaining whether he will spare Lykaon or kill him. Achilles feels that the radically indefinite certainty of death, as the condition of mortality, unites Lykaon to himself. Mortality means here the fact of being within a time split between the present and the site of *kleos* in an inaccessible song to come. Achilles' position provides a succinct statement of a generalized rather than local division of the present: because we do not know *which* moments will turn out to have been significant in the time of *kleos*, *every* moment becomes divided between its present and an unknowable future retroaction that may upend its meaning – the division of the present is thus generalized.[35]

II. Presentiment and memory

The next two sections of this chapter will take the generalized division of time, which we have so far only seen in the context of Achilles, and explore the ways in which we might use it to connect other figures from Homeric poetry and scholarship. Let us recap and restate the transition from local forms of the division of the present to the generalized division. We first saw the local form of the division of the present, the moments in which Hector and Agamemnon consider how their present actions will appear to audiences of epic song in the future, *essomenoisi*. These instances were 'local' because the considerations of the perspective of the song to come are prompted by the particular contexts in which Hector and Agamemnon found themselves, and hence were still motivated by the individual present moment in those particular cases. Achilles' position at the beginning of the *Iliad* represents this attitude writ large: not only is Achilles concerned with what *kleos* will come to him in the future song, he thinks he can actively produce it. Achilles' position changes dramatically with the death of Patroclus, as the unknowability of *kleos* enters every moment, and no longer only moments of explicit reflection.

Another, more precise way of conceiving this transition is to consider what image of time itself is implied in each of the two cases, local and generalized. The local instances imply a chronological conception of time, in which time is understood as a sequence of presents. We can furnish a more precise philosophical context to these discussions by referring to Paul Ricoeur's aporetic synthesis of the history of understandings of time in the context of the representations of time in narrative. Ricoeur distinguishes between chronological and phenomenological understandings of time.[36] The chronological and phenomenological conceptions are represented in the first place by Aristotle in book four of the *Physics* and by Augustine in book eleven of the *Confessions*, respectively.[37] Where Augustine presents a time constituted through the distention of the soul, Aristotle's conception is a time of the world and of physical movements independent of the soul. The latter corresponds to what we have been calling the chronological conception of time, which Ricoeur also calls 'ordinary' time, with reference to Heidegger, 'conceived of as a succession of abstract instants': '[O]rdinary time can be characterized as a series of point-like "nows", whose intervals are measured by our clocks. Like the hand moving across the face of the clock, time runs from one now to another.'[38] In contrast to chronological or ordinary time, Augustine inaugurates a series of phenomenological understandings of time, also represented by Husserl's contention that time is constituted through the inner consciousness of the human subject, which is not a series of instantaneous 'nows' but a duration stretched between the retention of past perception and the anticipation of future perception.[39] The series of phenomenological understandings culminates in Heidegger's analysis of Dasein's ecstases in thrownness, projection and fallenness, and how ordinary conceptions of time arise, as secondary misapprehensions, from these fundamental or 'authentic' structures.[40] Ricoeur's thesis, which I will not examine in detail here, is that the chronological and phenomenological understandings cannot do without each covertly borrowing from the other, even as they try to distinguish themselves from each other, resulting in aporias to which narrative – Ricoeur predominantly analyses history and fiction – responds by poetically and performatively interweaving and, to some extent, reconciling the two understandings of time.

The local division of the present implies a chronological understanding of time as a sequence of indifferent nows. The situation in the now of Hector or Agamemnon leads them to consider the meaning their actions will take on in a future now. What does Achilles' story add? What liberates time from its anchoring in the local situation of the indifferent now? The missing ingredient is the function of the unexpected and the unknowable, *Schicksalskontingenz* in Jonas Grethlein's analysis, which intervenes to remove the prospect that any now can put an end to the possibility for change.[41] In contrast to the particular moments which Hector and Agamemnon assume will be significant for their *kleos*, Achilles, by the time he meets Lykaon, no longer knows which dawn or afternoon or noontime will turn out to be the critical points of his *kleos*. It is this contingency – the unknowability of *kleos* and the inaccessibility of the song to come – that breaks time out of the sequence of indifferent presents, instead dividing each moment between a now and an indefinite, unfulfilled locus of what its meaning will have turned out to be.

Let us now consider three connections which will flesh out the discussion of the transition from local to generalized forms of the splitting of the present. These three connections link the three levels of poetry, Homeric scholarship and further philosophical reflections on time and memory. Taking these in reverse order, we can address an obvious question that arises from the correlation of the local form of division with the chronological understanding of time: does this therefore imply that the generalized division correlates to the phenomenological understanding of time? Perhaps.[42] But a closer comparison can be made with Bergson's discussions of memory and perception. Bergson investigates the nature of memory and asks the pointed question of *when* memory is formed in relation to the perception to which it is connected. After demonstrating the contradictions entailed by the notion that the memory of an event is formed *after* the perception of it, Bergson argues that memory must be formed at the same time as perception. 'The memory will be seen to duplicate the perception at every moment, to arise with it, to be developed at the same time, and to survive it precisely because it is of a quite different nature.'[43] If memory and perception are formed simultaneously at every moment, then our experience of the present must be continually divided:

Each moment of life is split up as and when it is posited. Or rather, it consists in this very splitting, for the present moment, always going forward, fleeting limit between the immediate past which is now no more and the immediate future which is not yet, would be a mere abstraction were it not the moving mirror which continually reflects perception as a memory.[44]

An objection may arise at this point, as we try to draw a comparison between the splitting of the present by the contingency of *kleos* and the splitting of the present in Bergson's memory: how do we reconcile the fact that *kleos* for the Homeric hero is projected into a *future*, while Bergson's memory seems necessarily to concern the *past*? This objection pushes us to realize that what is expressed as future *kleos* in the Homeric context is not a chronological future, and what Bergson calls memory or the past is not the chronological past. For Bergson, memory is not the memory of a past in the sense of 'something that was present' – the succession of presents is the chronological or 'ordinary' understanding of time from which we are attempting to distinguish Homeric time – but rather a 'past *in general*' that 'has no date and can have none'.[45] The need to abandon the chronological understanding of time in this context becomes clear when we consider Bergson's explanation of the feeling of déjà vu as those moments in which we become consciously aware of the constant splitting of the present, in which we experience the duplication of our present as memory:

> As we are becoming conscious of this duplication, it is the entirety of our present which must appear to us at once as perception and as memory. And yet we know full well that no life goes twice through the same moment of its history, that time does not remount its course. What is to be done? The case is most extraordinary and bewildering. It contradicts everything that we have been accustomed to. We feel that we are confronted with a recollection: a recollection it must be, for it bears the characteristic mark of states we usually call by this name and which only appear when their object has disappeared. And yet it does not present to us something which has been, but simply something which is; it advances *pari passu* with the perception which it reproduces. It is a recollection of the present moment in that actual moment itself. It is of the past in its form and of the present in its matter. It is *a memory of the present*.[46]

Just as, for Bergsonian memory, the memory of the present cannot be assimilated to the chronological past, so, too, Homeric *kleos*, which is expressed as projected to a future song to come, is independent of any actual fulfilment in a chronological future.[47] Achilles' awareness of his definite, indefinite death is effective in the present context of his encounter with Lykaon, and the division is 'of the present' just as Bergsonian memory is 'of the present'.[48]

A second connection, this time to Homeric scholarship and specifically to Grethlein's reading of Achilles, allows us to further clarify the relation of *kleos* to time. Grethlein, as mentioned, demonstrates how the experiences of the heroes in the *Iliad* as well as the narrative of the poem itself are marked by unexpected interventions of contingency, *Schicksalskontingenz*, which splits expectation from experience. What clarifies the reading of *kleos* I advocate here is in its contrast to Grethlein's interpretation. Grethlein understands *kleos* as a way of *overcoming* the temporality he describes, time divided by contingency:

> The experience of *Schicksalskontingenz*, represented for [Achilles] by the death of Patroclus, becomes the reason for exposing himself to chance in its most acute form. Furthermore, heroic action becomes for Achilles the opportunity for overcoming *Schicksalskontingenz*. As the reward for his action, he obtains *kleos aphthiton*. The immortality which 'the best of the Achaeans' achieves with his early death supersedes [*hebt auf*] the power of chance and makes possible a life beyond contingency.[49]

According to this reading, which commands wide consensus, *kleos* or poetic fame is a form of immortality that overcomes the contingency of the course of a hero's life, represented in the highest degree by Achilles both through his claim to fame as 'the best of the Achaeans' and to his great suffering. However, in the analysis of the splitting of the present in this chapter, *kleos* plays the role of *cause* or *agent* of that splitting: it is the anticipation or projection of an unknowable *kleos* into an inaccessible song to come that divides the present, just as contingency divides expectation from experience. Thus, *kleos* cannot be the overcoming of contingency, but is instead the most essential *affirmation* of contingency.[50] It is Grethlein's analyses of *Schicksalskontingenz*, pushed a little way further, that enable this insight.[51]

One more connection can be made from the generalized division of the present to our previous discussions of the Homeric *sēma*. We have seen how, in contrast to the ideal of a continuous and self-identical tradition exemplified by Foley's traditional referentiality, figures like the Achaean wall and the legendary *guslar* express the lack of such continuity and self-identity. Instead of a memorial that links the time of the epic heroes to the poetic performance, the wall is an anti-memorial, a grave marker, *sēma*, that fails to preserve the identity of those buried inside, and is emphatically destroyed so that no sign of its presence remained. On the one hand, we can say that the wall bears no *kleos*, if we understood *kleos* as the glue that guarantees the continuity of epic tradition. But on the other hand, if we understand *kleos* as we do now as that which divides every moment and which liberates time from the chronological sequence of presents, the wall as *sēma* becomes an emphatic sign of *kleos* in its resistance to the preservation of any self-identity or unchanging Same through a homogeneous, chronological time.

In the previous chapter, the proleptic description of the wall's destruction was described as making time visible as the difference between the wall standing in the midst of battle and the wall destroyed. Let us reconsider this notion of difference. Conventionally, difference is the difference between two identities: two states of affairs are compared and difference is extracted from them, and indeed this is the way difference works in the first sentence of this paragraph. But it is significant here that one of the *comparanda* is the wall after its effacement, after all was smooth again. Instead of one positive, self-identical state of affairs being compared to another, the destroyed wall begins to approach a nothing or a lack of any identity. In proleptically describing the destruction of the wall, the *Iliad* invites us to compare the standing wall and the future wall, but in taking away in the same gesture the future wall as a geographical marker of where the Trojan war took place, the *Iliad* is really inviting us to compare its story in the time of myth with no definite state. Just as, for Achilles, each moment is divided between the present and the radical unknowability of *kleos*, so the wall in the *Iliad* is divided between the time of heroic battle and an effaced nothing. The work of comparison which conventionally extracts difference from two self-identical *comparanda* finds that one *comparandum* is missing – we are no longer working with conventional comparisons in which difference comes after and from identities, but instead we are dealing with a form of difference that comes first.[52] How can we think through this concept of a pure difference, how is it to be related to the generalized division of the present, and how do these problems manifest within the Homeric context? We will address these questions via the poem once again.

Let us return to the perspective of the heroes, and this time consider some instances from the *Iliad* in which we can now recognize the signs that every moment in the heroes' experience is divided between the now and another time. Recall that our analysis of the divided present started by looking at how the preoccupation with *kleos* and the heroic song to come enters into the heroes' present and thus opens it up to another time. The most general yet succinct statement of this relation is found in Helen's words to Hector, in which she posits an explanation for heroic suffering. 'Zeus set a vile destiny upon us,' she says, 'so that hereafter we shall be made into things of song for the men of the future [*essomenoisi*].'[53] We quickly note the formal features of *kleos* that we have seen before: first, the perspective of the future embodied in heroic song, indexed again by the word *essomenoisi*; second, the fact that the future song, while inaccessible, is supposed to pass judgement or give meaning to the events of the present;[54] and third, how the anticipated meaning that *kleos* will bring splits every moment into a present of action and its anticipated but unknowable meaning that is projected to the site of a song to come. In these two verses is compressed the logic of a generalized division of the present, which we are now able to parse out.[55]

Building on these propositions, let us consider what use Helen makes of this logic of *kleos*. What meaning does Helen make out of the absence of meaning, what sense does she make of a sense that is only available elsewhere? Helen's answer to a hypothetical question of the kind, 'what is the meaning of our suffering', is 'to be made into future song'. Future song looks at first glance like an explanation for suffering, but is in fact a non-explanation: Helen has no idea *what* that future song will be or what meanings and judgements it will retroactively endow. The explanation thus leaves Helen none the wiser about *why* they suffer. She is only able to project her ignorance of the meaning of heroic suffering into a future song to which she has no access, to exchange one ignorance for another. In the previous chapter, we discussed how the structuralist analysis of the concept of *mana* interprets it as a signifier that represents the failure or incompleteness of signifiers, the fact that the order of signifiers cannot correspond perfectly to the world.[56] In parallel to this analysis of *mana*, the song to come is an expression, within the heroic present, of the structural inadequacy of the heroic present to produce its own meanings. The anticipated song is a formal principle of Homeric epic realized or incarnated in the content of the poem, a veil of meaning that hides the failure of meaning-making.

Moving beyond passages which explicitly make reference to the notion of future song, the proposition that the inaccessibility of *kleos* splits every present moment frees us from the chronological limitation of the 'future' and allows us to recognize other figures of the divided present. A first instance is found in a speech of Agamemnon. Agamemnon and Priam swore oaths (III. 259–309) to allow the war to be settled by a duel between Menelaus and Paris, in which Menelaus emerged victorious and the war seemed to be over. But the Trojan Pandarus is persuaded to break the truce by shooting Menelaus, and when Agamemnon sees the blood from Menelaus' wound, he first thinks that it would be fatal, saying: 'Dear brother, it was your death I sealed in the oaths of friendship, setting you alone before the Achaians to fight with the Trojans. So, the Trojans have struck you down and trampled on the oaths sworn.'[57] What interests us in this passage is the image of time that is expressed in how Agamemnon understands the meaning of the oaths which sealed the truce. Understood literally, Agamemnon is saying here that the oaths sealed the death of Menelaus directly.[58] This compressed expression retrojects the later or true outcome of 'death' back to the time of the oath-taking, when the oaths would have had the apparent meaning of 'peace'. It is not the case that the oaths, when sworn, meant peace, but subsequently, after the Trojans broke the truce and seemingly killed Menelaus, mean death. This would be a chronological image of time. Instead, the shooting of Menelaus does not *change* the meaning of the oaths, but rather *reveals* the meaning that the oaths have always held from the first, even though those meanings were initially concealed. The peace that the oaths seemed to augur did not first come into existence and subsequently come to be lost in a chronological sequence of events, but was always illusory. The only time taken is the time for the realization of this fact. The logic of *kleos* entails that the meaning of an event is never knowable at one moment for all time, nor can an event have one meaning at one point in time and another meaning later, when circumstances change. Rather, the entire meaning of the event throughout time is projected beyond the time of *kleos* into the song to come. In other words, every moment is always already divided between what it seems to mean in the known, existing and intended context of the present, and what it actually means in another time. In Agamemnon's speech, we see the same formal structure of the projection of *kleos* into future song, but from the reverse direction: instead of projecting meaning into a future, Agamemnon retrojects meaning into a past event. Of course, we should take care to note here that the meaning that Agamemnon retrojects into the oath-taking is not the final meaning either. Indeed, it is not even the meaning of a couple of dozen verses later, when Menelaus assures him that the wound is not fatal (IV. 184–7). The important point here is the division of the moment of oath-taking that Agamemnon presupposes.

If this particular example puts too much weight on a form of expression that might be explained as merely rhetorical[59] – Agamemnon could simply be indulging in some histrionic self-blame – we can furnish others. Egbert Bakker offers an analysis of Homeric tenses that supports our analyses of a generalized division of the present. The analysis turns on the semantics of the verb *mellein*, to be about to or to be likely to do something. Bakker considers the words of Patroclus when he sees the wounded Eurypylos and takes pity upon the Greeks:

'Ah, you poor leaders and rulers of the Danaans. So in this way, <I see now [*ar*']>, you were going [*emellete*], far from your friends and your fatherland, to glut the swift dogs of Troy with your shining fat.'[60] Arguing against an interpretation that would reduce the phrase 'you were going/were about to' to an objective statement of fact or a 'purely temporal' statement set in the chronological past about its chronological future, Bakker proposes a different emphasis: 'Such notions as "destiny (future) in the past", however, do not seem to be entirely appropriate for this use of Homeric *mellein*; they imply a temporal, chronological, relationship, whereas what seems to be the central feature is consciousness, present and past, with a crucial difference in knowledge between the two.'[61]

Let us unpack Bakker's interpretation. In ordinary chronological order, there is a sequence of two events: first, the Danaan heroes leave home and go on the expedition to Troy; second, Patroclus observes the misfortunes of those heroes and makes the observation quoted here. As with Agamemnon's speech, the crucial question is how Patroclus understands time, or what image of time is expressed in Patroclus' words, in particular the word *emellete*, 'you were going to'. Bakker argues emphatically that 'you were going to' does not express a merely chronological relationship of objective fact, something that would fit into a sequence like 'you were going to do X', 'you did X', 'you have done X'. Instead, *emellete* emphasizes the difference between what the Danaan heroes *thought* they were doing in embarking on the Trojan expedition and what they *actually turned out* to be doing, given what Patroclus now knows about the misfortunes of the expedition. Just as with Agamemnon's speech, then, what is expressed is the gap between the meaning that was intended or available at the time of the embarking, and a meaning that has subsequently been revealed. And, again, repeating the analysis of Agamemnon's speech, the meaning subsequently revealed to Patroclus is not the final meaning of the song to come either – this latter is strictly inaccessible – because it will turn out that the Danaans do not in fact 'glut the swift dogs of Troy', or at least not all of them. Thus the significance of the expression is not that it turned out to be true, but that it expresses the division of that present.[62]

Extending the analysis from the syntax of speech and tense to the field of Homeric concepts, Bakker offers an interpretation of the word *nēpios*, literally 'foolish' or 'naive', as used when the poem comments on Patroclus' request to be allowed to fight against the Trojans in Achilles' armour: 'So he spoke pleading, greatly *nēpios*; yes, for he was begging for ugly death and destruction to himself.'[63] Again, what is at stake is the way *nēpios* expresses a split in time rather than pick out a character trait, as a literal interpretation might conclude. '[The character who is *nēpios*] is no more silly or out of touch than other humans. Rather his fundamental condition is that he is out of touch with poetic truth ... [T]his means that he is explicitly presented as *not in the future*, and since he is not in the future, *he is no poet*.'[64] The hero who is called *nēpios* is marked as not being in a position to see the full consequences of his present actions, which will only unfold in his future. Like the notion of the song to come, *nēpios* expresses the formal condition of *kleos* – meaning does not come except in an inaccessible site – as part of the poem's content.

The Homeric hero, always open to the time of *kleos*, does not skip a beat in registering the gap that separates his knowledge from what is subsequently revealed, because his openness to the time of *kleos* means that this gap is always already anticipated. 'The imperfect is our paradise', they might say with Stevens. But it will be noticed that the instances we have examined so far in the speech of Agamemnon and Patroclus are quite special and localized in that they are instances in which the availability of a later, fuller – though still not final – understanding of a past event enables the retroactive reinterpretation of that event. If we claim that a *generalized* form of the splitting of the present divides *every* moment, how can we account for all of the other moments which do not correspond to a belated realization, all those moments and acts which bear contemporaneously understood meanings and intentions unchallenged by the emergence of later understanding? We can answer this question in two ways, with reference first to a more literary interpretation, and second to the encounter of poetry with scholarship.

If we take the literary interpretive route, we are faced with two possible answers. Either we choose to consider that all the 'ordinary' moments which do not become the occasion for later, retroactive reinterpretation are exempt from the logic just demonstrated in the cases of Agamemnon and Patroclus, or we can insist on the general applicability of that logic even in those 'ordinary' moments. If we choose the former, then we would also be giving up the results of the analysis of Helen's position earlier in this section, as well as the entire arc of the argument in the first section of this chapter, culminating in the central story of Achilles, because all of these analyses lead to the conclusion that the heroes' ignorance about what their *kleos* will be divides every moment. This is especially clear in Helen's case, because if the meaning of misfortune will be given in a future song inaccessible to the heroes, they also do not know which moments – which actions, sufferings or minute events that go unremarked at the time in which they happened – will turn out to have been significant.[65] Similarly, Achilles can affirm the significance of the moment of death, but which moment will turn out to be the moment of death and which moments will turn out to have been significant in relation to it are all unknown. There is therefore compelling reason to choose the latter answer to this question of 'ordinary' moments, and to affirm that even these 'ordinary' moments which do not correspond to later re-evaluation are constitutively split.[66]

What would this mean? Let us recall the discussion of comparisons and difference at the end of the first section of this chapter. There, we described conventional comparisons in which a difference is drawn out through comparing two pre-existing states of affairs. This is the situation of Agamemnon looking at Menelaus' arrow wound and of Patroclus looking at the suffering Danaans. Agamemnon is able to compare his hopes for peace and his fears of his brother's death, and he sees both in his retroactive view of the oaths that he swore. Patroclus is able to compare the expectations of the Danaans on their way to Troy – presumably expectations of glory, wealth and victory – with what he later finds to be their actual destination in death and ignominy. More interesting are the cases in which conventional comparison breaks down, cases where only one of the terms to be compared is given. This is precisely the situation of 'ordinary' moments if we insist that they are still to be thought of as divided. There is the meaning of the ordinary moment as it was intended or experienced at the time, but we have no later re-evaluation against which to compare the initial meaning, or to draw a difference from the comparison. Nevertheless, if there is to be a splitting of the moment, there must still be a difference even if there is no positive description of what the initial meaning is to be different *from*. We would thus have to assert that difference in this case must be first, it must be prior to the terms which differ. Difference would therefore be a pure difference, a formal difference prior to content and prior to the act of comparison which only extracts difference from previously established identities.

We thus have arrived at a notion of pure difference which is difficult to envision. We can see the path that took us here, but we are not entirely sure where here is or where to go next. We can clarify our situation by backtracking to the point where we chose to answer the question of 'ordinary' moments by a literary interpretive tack, and now pursue the other option, that of the encounter between poetry and scholarship. My argument will be that the notion of pure difference arrived at here, via the path of interpretation, has already been at work in the school of Homeric scholarship called neoanalysis. What we have made explicit here as pure difference has already been expressed – in different figures, to be sure, and with different goals – and we need only to refind its traces.

III. The neoanalytic difference

In this section, I seek to demonstrate how neoanalysis tends towards expressing pure difference implicitly, in its method. I will then describe an extension of the neoanalytic method of relating the Homeric poems and their mythological background that reaches an almost explicit statement of pure difference. As is perhaps already evident from the implicit nature of what I am arguing about neoanalysis, my position is not that neoanalytic scholars intended to produce an interpretive method that resonates with the themes we are most interested in here. Instead, the resonant image of neoanalysis I am proposing arises from the encounter of poetry and scholarship, the themes of one with the method of the other.[67] We will begin with an overview of the neoanalytic method, before connecting it with our themes of the splitting of the present and pure difference.

Neoanalysis is a school of Homeric scholarship active for the most part in German-speaking countries in the period approximately contemporaneous with the development of oral theory in anglophone scholarship.[68] The core of neoanalysis is its method of interpretation, one in which a passage from the Homeric poems, often one that – a neoanalytic scholar would argue – does not quite fit in its existing context, is read as a repetition of themes and phraseology from another context. This repetition is understood as a conscious allusion from one to the other context – the deliberateness of repetition is what crucially differentiates neoanalysis from the oral theoretical repetition of formulas – and interpretations are based on the connections between the alluding passage and the context alluded to. Neoanalysis offers a radically different set of presuppositions about how to approach the Homeric poems, in contrast to the versions of oral theory which we saw in the case of traditional referentiality earlier and which we will see in more detailed discussions of Parry and Nagy in the next chapter. Where oral theory is governed by an ideal of continuity and self-identity, the distinctiveness of neoanalysis is the breaking of the present, since to consider the passage in front of us as only explicable in relation to another context is always to interrupt the present with a different time.[69]

The fundamental claim of neoanalytic scholarship is intertextual: what makes the Homeric poems artistic and distinct is in the way they modify, reuse and repurpose traditional language, themes and stories.[70] Therefore, what ought to be appreciated as 'the Homeric in Homer' is the artful difference between the Homeric use of a traditional element and its prior uses. This claim rests on the presupposition that the audience of the Homeric poems knows the prior poems in the epic tradition and is therefore able to recognize when and how the

Homeric reworking of a traditional element differs from its prior appearances. A typical neoanalytic reading seeks to demonstrate a parallel between a Homeric – typically Iliadic – linguistic or narrative element and the appearance of the same element in either a different epic poem or elsewhere in the same poem, and then show how the meaning of the element's use in Homer is deepened and enhanced by knowing the prior uses of the same element. The text in neoanalysis is essentially and inescapably allusive, divided between the poem in front of the reader and the absent poems against which it makes sense and makes its difference.

Since, for the most part, evidence for the content of poems in the Homeric tradition earlier than the *Iliad* and the *Odyssey* is difficult to come by, a major problem for neoanalysis is how to establish that a particular use of a repeated element is earlier than the Homeric use, or if it has instead been influenced by the Homeric poems.[71] The difficulty of establishing priority has led to the suspicion that the neoanalytic method is an inherently circular one, in which the scholar uses presuppositions about the Homeric evidence to construct the earlier poem, which can then be used to justify those presuppositions about Homeric evidence:

> A distressingly frequent defect in method, which first appears early in Kullmann's book, involves essentially the old Analytical fallacy, 'better is older', a doctrine which Kullmann clearly sees to be fallacious as it manifests itself in standard Analytical treatises, but which he apparently does not realize is also characteristic of the 'neoanalysis' which he so greatly admires. The neoanalysts will tell us, for instance, that the Homeric handling of some motif – say the rescue of Nestor by Diomedes – is artistically much inferior to the handling of the same motif somewhere else – say the rescue of Nestor by Antilochus in the *Aethiopis*. We are then asked to conclude, almost as a matter of course, that the better version is the older one, and the first thing we know we are presented with a 'source' for the *Iliad*, a 'Memnonis' or an 'Aethiopis'.[72]

These criticisms from Combellack's review of Wolfgang Kullmann's 1960 book, *Die Quellen der Ilias*, are directed against the project of neoanalysis in general, with no little validity. To propose lost poems as sources is always to risk a circularity of logic in which the object of inquiry is so constituted as to suit the expected result.[73] Combellack notes later that the question of which poem was the source and which the imitator is often resolved in neoanalysis using criteria that are not convincingly objective, thus putting the judgement of the priority of the poems into serious doubt. Indeed, Combellack would prefer that 'a sterner regard for the facts' prevail, and that the assertions about the priority of the poems, in various stages of existence, be rephrased as observations about the similarity of various themes, which would then be not saying very much at all.[74] What, then, is at stake in the neoanalytic position that holds onto the question of priority in the face of not unreasonable criticism? We will need to situate neoanalysis within its context, and in its relationship with the analytic method in particular.

The major division in modern Homeric scholarship prior to the twentieth century was between unitarian and analytic positions. The unitarian position argued for the unity of the Homeric poems as whole poems and as works of one creative mind, which often also implied their artistic quality and greatness. The analytic position sought evidence from all quarters to argue that the Homeric poems were patchworks of songs by different poets, edited together with more or less incompetence. By the turn of the twentieth century, the Homeric question had become a problem of interpretation. The critical method of late Homeric analysis, as represented by Wilamowitz's *Die Ilias und Homer*, is a way of confronting what appeared to be inconsistencies in the *Iliad* on the levels of logic, style, psychology and other such verisimilitudes.[75] Wilamowitz rejected older analytic approaches that sought to divide the poem into its component parts. Some of these approaches used technical criteria such as dialectal forms to divide the poems, which Wilamowitz rejected because it was a 'mechanization of research', and others followed Lachmann's interpretive attempt to see the poem as the stitching together of individual songs.[76] Instead, Wilamowitz proposes to account for inconsistencies by discerning layers of editing and addition worked upon a poem that was once a unity, which he called Homer's *Iliad*. Along with the other works of Homeric analysis which tried to locate a unity variously at the beginning, middle or end of the process that produced the existing text, Wilamowitz makes the assumption that perceived inconsistencies in the text are contradictions which should not be explained or interpreted synchronically, and therefore must be explained by invoking the carelessness of various editors during the history of the poem's coming into being.[77] Synchronic contradictions are resolved by distributing the contradicting terms through time.

There is a moment of forgetfulness in both the oral theoretical and analytic approaches. In oral theory, the themes and formulas which are repeated come 'out of a kind of universal pantry of oral tradition' and do not remember where and how they have been used before.[78] Sensitive to this characterization, oral theory has no resort other than to assert a timeless unity in which memory itself loses its meaning.[79] In the analytic approach, on the other hand, the specific verses which are variously inserted and displaced throughout the history of a text do retain a certain memory of where they used to be, which is how the analyst can claim to restore them to their original places and establish an original text. The moment of forgetting is ascribed instead to the editors and interpolators who are thus assumed to have overlooked the inconsistencies produced in the text through their blundering interventions. Turning back now to neoanalysis, it agrees with the analytic approach in understanding the repeated elements as differentiable between an original usage and a later usage, that is, they remember where they came from. Where neoanalysis differs from old analysis is in venturing to ask the question, what if those responsible for late interventions in the text knew what they were doing after all? What if the memory of a previous repetition was part of the poem, rather than only available to the outside perspective of the analytic scholar? These questions distinguish neoanalysis from both old analysis and the theory of orality.

While we are more interested in how the method of neoanalysis connects with our themes of the divided present and pure difference, let us consider one of the major lines of interpretation proposed by neoanalytic scholarship. Looking back at the foundational work of Ioannis Kakridis, Heinrich Pestalozzi and Wolfgang Schadewaldt, Kullmann reviews the earliest results of the neoanalytic method:

> The most important hypothesis of the neoanalysts is the so-called Memnonis hypothesis – or, better, the Achilleis hypothesis ... It postulates that the Iliadic description of the death of Patroclus, the vengeance Achilles exacts for it upon Hector, and the consequence that Achilles must also die are, with respect to their motifs, modelled on another tale, one that is known to us from the cyclic epic *Aithiopis*. In this epic is told how first Penthesileia, then the Ethiopian king Memnon came to help the Trojans ... At the end is told how Nestor's son Antilochus sacrificed himself in rescuing his father from a dangerous situation in battle and was killed at the hand of Memnon. Thereupon Achilles entered the battle and took vengeance for his friend Antilochus on Memnon, and thereby forfeited his own life. He falls to the arrow of Paris at the Scaean gates, just as his mother Thetis foretold the case, should Memnon die. The lament of Thetis and the Nereids and the Muses follows, then the funeral games in honour of Achilles.[80]

In Kullmann's version, then, neoanalytic scholarship proposes that scenes and plot points in the *Iliad* are modelled upon themes from earlier epic poetry. But let us note that this passage also offers important details in its rhetoric. The specific phrasing here, 'with respect to their motifs (*motivisch*), modelled on another tale (*Erzählung*), one that is known to us from the cyclic epic *Aithiopis*', is a retreat from the original positions held by Pestalozzi and Schadewaldt. For Kullmann, the *Iliad* draws upon earlier motifs, not earlier texts. Pestalozzi, in contrast, conceived the source of the Iliadic story not as merely an unfixed *Erzählung*, from which motifs were taken and which also resulted in the cyclic epic *Aithiopis*, but rather as a fixed text:

> The comparison with the corresponding motifs of the *Iliad* proves fully and unquestionably the priority and originality of the old *Achilleis*. And hence a clearly recognizable poem (*klar erkennbares Gedicht*) enters the picture as a model for the *Iliad*, both artistically and materially, in place of the 'pre-Homeric myth' that until now has been claimed or assumed.[81]

Schadewaldt, for his part, after acknowledging his previous belief in a common thematic source for the *Iliad* and the *Aithiopis*, recants and, citing the view of Pestalozzi, states that 'the *Aithiopis* is a pre-Homeric poem (*Gedicht*), model for the *Iliad*, and therefore a way to gain insight into how Homer wrought the *Iliad* and to recognize with clarity of vision the Homeric in Homer'.[82]

What is at stake in the difference between an unfixed tale and a fixed text? What interests us here is not which position is historically correct.[83] The significant distinction here is between different ways of conceiving the nature of the link between Homeric and pre-Homeric poems. For Kullmann, the category of the motif provides a way of conceiving an essential continuity in how the Homeric poems relate to what comes before them. The motif gains a certain consistency and identity in itself, so much so that Kullmann is able to define neoanalysis as 'research of the history of motifs'.[84] While it is undoubtedly true that Pestalozzi and Schadewaldt were themselves concerned with motifs and with proving the similarities between their use in Homeric and pre-Homeric contexts, the insistence on the existence of another text puts the emphasis on discontinuity rather than continuity, difference rather than identity. Schadewaldt states explicitly that it is not so much about seeing what is in common as 'what, within the same frame, is different'.[85] Insofar as every repetition of motifs involves similarities and differences, the choice between emphasizing difference or identity is an active decision, rather than the result of empirical inquiry. The decision is furthermore prior to interpretation; it provides the conditions for interpretation.

In making difference the fundamental basis of interpretation, the earlier scholars Pestalozzi and Schadewaldt can be distinguished, within the neoanalytic school itself, from its later representative Kullmann.[86] Early neoanalysis brings out the force of difference as an essential moment of reading. The neoanalytic interpretation of the description of Achilles as he grieves for Patroclus, 'And he lay stretched out in the dust, mighty in his might' (XVIII. 26), argues that it was originally used in the context not of the death of Patroclus in the *Iliad*, but of the death of Achilles in another text.[87] The Iliadic context of the death of Patroclus thereby gains in resonance in its evocation of Achilles' death, to which it narratively leads. Here, the verse which we read in the *Iliad* does not exist immediately in itself, nor does it, as traditional referentiality would propose, import the full totality of its traditional meaning. Rather, it takes a detour, a circular movement from Achilles grieving for Patroclus in the *Iliad*, to Achilles dead on the battlefield while fighting raged on around him in a lost *Aithiopis* or a hypothetical *Achilleis*, and back again.[88]

If the moment of the Homeric hero is split between the present of action and its *kleos* in future song, the moment of interpretation in neoanalysis is split between the existent Homeric text in front of us and an absent text of which it is supposed to be a repetition and an allusion. Other studies have amply investigated and debated the questions of whether there could have been other texts to which the Homeric poems could have alluded, or of the validity of the criteria by which neoanalysis judges what is and is not an allusion, or of the literary value of neoanalytic interpretations of such allusions.[89] What is at stake for us is how the method of neoanalysis itself repeats – not consciously, to be sure – the difference that divides the time of the *Iliad*.

Is the neoanalytic division of the moment of interpretation a local division or a generalized division? Recall our examples of local divisions in the *Iliad*: Hector and Agamemnon referring their present moment of action to a particular version of their *kleos* which they desire or fear, or Agamemnon and Patroclus comparing the different meanings of an event in the time when it happened and in a later time. The characteristic of a local division is, thus, that difference is extracted from the comparison of two pre-existing identities. This is clearly the case for the specific interpretations that neoanalysis has proposed. If the Achilles–Patroclus–Hector triad in the *Iliad* is modelled on the Achilles–Antilochus–Memnon triad of a hypothesized *Aethiopis*, then we clearly have two pre-existing identities from which neoanalysis extracts the difference, which it sees as the art of Homer. This is thus a case of local division. Indeed, what neoanalytic scholars have striven to do is to maintain the possibility of extracting difference from identities by arguing tirelessly for the plausibility and existence of the pre-Homeric text, which is necessary to act as the second *comparandum* next to the Homeric text. For this goal, neoanalysis braves the slings and arrows of critics like Combellack, the core of whose argument is precisely that the second *comparandum* is not clearly enough distinguishable from the first – the Homeric text – and thus the comparison which needs two pre-existing identities from which to draw an allusive difference collapses into a single pole. The criticism that an argument is circular is, at its core, that the circle collapses into a point, and no allusion remains because difference has vanished into identity.

What if we acknowledge the circularity of neoanalytic arguments, but also assert that the circle never collapses? It is along this line that we will be able reach an account of generalized division and pure difference within neoanalysis. This is not a possibility argued for by neoanalytic scholars, since they are invested in maintaining the conventional structure of comparison with its two pre-existing *comparanda*. It is instead a possibility released in the encounter of the image of time that we have found in the *Iliad* with an argument stated most explicitly by Ken Dowden. As well as helping us think the notion of pure difference, it also productively connects poetry and scholarship.

Dowden observes first that the *Iliad* is often 'uncanonical' from the perspective of the epic tradition, that is, it 'stands aside from the *Faktenkanon*, but continually echoes it'.[90] The fact that many incidents from the epic tradition, which are known from other sources, are left out of the Homeric poems has often been explained as the result of a Homeric sensibility that exercises a certain restraint towards the more fantastical and sensational elements of the tradition, such as, to give Dowden's examples, the sacrifice of Iphigeneia, the centaur Cheiron or the prophetic ability of Cassandra. Dowden interprets this neoanalytically as Homer making a particular point by leaving out the fantastical: 'If he meant his work to be so perceived, it could only be so perceived in contrast to the prevailing character of a tradition, which therefore included these motifs and *to which, by refusing reference, he made reference*.'[91] Dowden argues that 'Homeric silence does not necessarily mean that [a tradition] was unknown to him', and we can sometimes access those traditional episodes, not found in Homer, in other sources.[92] The key point is that if Homeric silence is an 'active' silence of omission rather than of ignorance, then we can read Homer's silence as a form of meaningful allusion.

What are the implications here for the structure of comparison? Where a conventional neoanalytic argument asks us to compare a Homeric passage with a pre-Homeric one, Dowden, in replacing Homeric passages with Homeric silence, is perilously close to taking away one of the *comparanda* – not the pre-Homeric text this time but the Homeric text. The boundaries of acceptable interpretations are now maintained only tenuously by the limits of what we *happen to know* to be absent from Homer, because we are aware of the *presence* of those same elements in other, non-Homeric sources. But the meaning-making power of Homeric silence, once invoked, cannot be contained within the boundaries of what we happen to know from other sources, but must rather expand to encompass the entirety of the Homeric poems. This is because Homeric silence about something, being the lack of a thing rather than the presence of a thing, can only be detected through its context. So, for instance, it is only because the *Iliad* makes Agamemnon call Calchas a 'seer of evil' (1. 106) without mentioning the sacrifice of Iphigeneia that we can say the *Iliad* is silent about the sacrifice of Iphigeneia, and it is only because we know of the sacrifice from elsewhere that we can identify the Iliadic silence in its context. But, given our incomplete knowledge of non-Homeric traditions, we cannot know what else the Homeric poems are silent about. To what unknown stories might the Homeric poems be making reference through their very silence, and what unheard allusions might the Homeric text be framing, as 'seer of evil' frames Iphigeneia, without our knowing? The situation with the *comparanda* is reversed, and indeed is endlessly reversible: comparing an absence in the Homeric text to a present motif elsewhere is in fact interchangeable with comparing existing elements of the Homeric text to unknown motifs elsewhere, because the silence that is compared in both cases is not a positive element but a structural effect. With Dowden's intervention, every part of the Homeric text has become part of a potentially significant silence, and thus every moment in reading the Homeric text is divided between the present text and an unknown absent text.[93] The situation parallels how, for Achilles, because he does not know how or when he will die, every moment is divided between what it means in the present of action and in the site of *kleos*, since every moment could potentially be significant as part of the framing for the moment of death. Death in this case acts as the unknown element that distributes the potential for significant silence throughout every moment.[94] Achilles and Dowden's neoanalysis are thus united here in producing a logic of *kleos* as the pure difference of a generalized division of time.

* * *

This chapter has tied together a number of topics and concepts across the Homeric poems and neoanalytic scholarship, and it would be useful to conclude with a clear overview of how the main ideas fit together with each other and within the broader claims of the book. The core of the argument relates *kleos* to an image of time, a relation which comprises two stages, two ways in which *kleos* breaks the present. In the first stage, the anticipation of future *kleos* divides particular, local moments into the meaning they take from the immediately available context and a meaning that takes place in another time or another site. Instances of this first, local division of the present include: Hector and Agamemnon at what they thought were critical points in their lives, thinking about how those points will appear from the perspective of future song; Agamemnon and Patroclus re-evaluating specific past events and dividing their meanings between how they had appeared then and how they now appear; and neoanalytic interpretations which divide the moment of reading between the present text and the absent text to which allusion is made.

The local division of particular moments gives way to a generalized division of every moment when *kleos*, the agent that divides or differentiates, is recognized as unknowable, and the site of *kleos* in the song to come is recognized as inaccessible. Because it is no longer possible to know *which* moments will turn out to be significant, *every* moment comes to be divided between what it seems to mean and what it may turn out to mean. We see the transition in the career of Achilles, as he comes to learn that he cannot control the meaning of his *kleos*. The generalized division itself is seen in Achilles' anticipation of his own definite, indefinite death; Helen's expectation that heroic misfortune will find meaning in future song; and Dowden's extension of the neoanalytic method so that silences can be read as meaningful.

The apparatus of *kleos* and the generalized division is connected to difference, and the distinction between local and generalized forms of division maps onto a distinction between conventional difference and pure difference. Conventional difference is drawn from the comparison of pre-existing identities, which map onto the two different meanings or states of affairs produced in the local division of particular moments. Pure difference arises when there is nothing to which a moment can be compared, but, because every moment is split in generalized division, difference still inheres. What props up the structure of comparison in this case is *kleos*, the unknown *comparandum* which holds open a space for pure difference. Hence we rejoin the thesis of the introduction, that *kleos* expresses difference, not identity. We also pick up the methodological gambit of the introduction in demonstrating that both Homeric poems and scholarship – in this case, neoanalysis – participate in the movement towards generalized division and pure difference.

In the following chapters, we will consider how Homeric scholarship, in particular oral theory, and the Homeric poems react to and refigure the concept of *kleos*-as-difference we have drawn out here, and what forms of time are produced therein.

3

The Dream of the Instant

The preceding chapter connected a series of concepts important for the Homeric poems and their scholarly reception: *kleos*, difference and time. We have seen how *kleos*, as the form in which meaning is bestowed in the Homeric poems, breaks the present into a 'now' of action and 'another time' of the meaning of that action. We have also seen that, because *kleos* is unknowable, every moment could come to take on a different meaning and every present loses its self-identity. This is what is expressed in the notion of a song to come, a heroic song which will give meaning to the actions and sufferings of the heroes, but one projected out of the heroes' present. The song is always to come and never accessible, which is why it can give expression to the unknowability of *kleos*. The unknowability of *kleos* that divides every moment also expresses pure difference, which divides the meaning available to the present of action from the meaning that action will come to take on in the other time. We have seen these propositions demonstrated in figures from the Homeric poems, as well as through the methods and presuppositions of neoanalytic scholarship. Scholarship and poetry are thus joined through the thesis that *kleos* expresses difference instead of identity.

Neoanalysis is but one of the protagonists of Homeric scholarship of the past hundred years, and it is to the other major force in Homeric studies that we will now turn, the theory of orality. We examined oral theory, in the first chapter, in the form of one of its developments, Foley's traditional referentiality, but we will consider here another influential expression in the work of Gregory Nagy. Hence the broad question which motivates our discussions in the present chapter: How does oral theory, in particular the work of Nagy, take up and express the division of the present occasioned by the logic of *kleos*?[1]

A tension immediately emerges in response to our question. We had argued previously that oral theory expresses a major image of the Homeric tradition dominated by the ideals of continuity and self-identity. Foley's traditional reference allows the recovery of meaning by connecting the present performance epiphanically to the resonances of its past, maintaining the self-identity of tradition through the continuity of performance. But Nagy, on the other hand, emphasizes change through time, and thus would seem to be the last to valorize self-identity. Indeed, Nagy also seems to reject the continuity of tradition, emphasizing instead the incompatibility between different layers of the oral poetic tradition: 'Consequently, the language of a body of oral poetry like the *Iliad* and the *Odyssey* does not and cannot belong to any one time, any one place: in a word, it *defies synchronic analysis*.'[2] Is Nagy then fundamentally different from the image of oral theory we had extrapolated from the work of Foley? In answering this question, what is at stake here is less a question of empirical continuities or discontinuities, but rather a choice between different conceptions of time. These different conceptions of time turn on the question: is a self-sufficient moment or instant possible? From the perspective of the division of the present as we worked out in the previous chapter, the answer would be 'no'. Since meaning is not contemporaneous with the moment of action, each instant is divided by an irreducible temporality. Meaning takes a certain amount of time = x, the time inhabited by pure difference, even when we cannot know what shape that difference will take. This is the structure imposed by the logic of *kleos*. What kind of structure underlies the evolutionary development of the Homeric tradition according to Nagy? As in the case of Foley and traditional referentiality, we will need to describe the context of Nagy's work within the history and reception of Parry and Lord's theory of orality.

I. The instant from Parry to Nagy

Nagy's work inherits the question of the origins of the Homeric poems, which has driven research in the field throughout its modern history.[3] Within the context of the second half of the twentieth century and the ascendancy of the theory of orality in anglophone Homeric scholarship, this question appears in the form of the need to reconcile the seemingly undeniable 'oral' poetics of the Homeric poems, taken as already substantially proven by Parry, with the also undeniable fact of their existence as fixed, written texts. How did the poems progress from their fluid, oral beginnings to become fixed in texts? Nagy's response to this question is based on two strongly held positions, one inherited and one innovative, the first addressing the synchronic aspect of the particular poet, the second addressing the diachronic aspect of a developing tradition. The first position is that of composition-in-performance, inherited from Parry and

Lord, the notion that the oral poet does not memorize a fixed text but rather composes the verses in the moment of performance.[4] The second position is that of evolution and fixation: although each individual poet composes in performances that can vary greatly from the performances of another poet, a specific configuration of social and cultural forces in the Greek-speaking world during the archaic period effected the gradual homogenization of the Homeric tradition, leading eventually to fixed texts of the *Iliad* and the *Odyssey*. Nagy identifies the cause of the gradual homogenization as Panhellenism, the increase in contact and commerce through the eighth to sixth centuries between certain classes of citizens from previously isolated city states. Nagy's evolutionary model thus offers an explanation for the existence of a more-or-less standard written text of the Homeric poems while staying true to the theory of orality's crucial distinction between oral and written poetics.

Let us enter the discussion at a specific point. Nagy's 1996 collection of papers, *Homeric Questions*, opens with an essay which functions as a manifesto of sorts. It should be noted that Nagy is invested in defending the positions of Parry and Lord as representative of oral theory as a whole. This means that Nagy's defence of oral theory against accumulated critiques often takes the rhetorical form of a 'return to Parry' and a 'return to Lord', pointing out the critics' deviations from Parry and Lord's intended meanings, even in places where Nagy seems to be making advances of his own. One footnote, however, seems sufficiently confident to concede some ground: 'All this is not to say that we cannot find gaps in Parry's argumentation. For an attempt at pinpointing such gaps, I cite the subtle arguments of Lynn-George 1988: 55–81. The issues raised by Lynn-George call for an *Auseinandersetzung*, the scope of which would surpass what is being attempted in this presentation.'[5]

The *Auseinandersetzung* called for here has thus far not been forthcoming, and Michael Lynn-George's subtle arguments remain unanswered. Lynn-George's work is especially relevant for us because it brings out clearly what I have argued is the nexus of ideals that governs oral theory: continuity, self-identity and instantaneous creativity. Unlike in the cases of oral theory's other critics, Nagy does not accuse Lynn-George of misunderstanding Parry and Lord. Lynn-George's arguments are thus still open questions and loose threads, and still relevant in considering Nagy's development of the theory of orality – despite protestations, Nagy's oral theory is not that of Parry and Lord. An examination of these arguments and how Nagy's work responds to the contradictions within Parry's oral theory – described for us by Lynn-George, though not explicitly taken up by Nagy – will help us understand oral theory's more recent developments. The air of general neglect which rests on Lynn-George's work renders a brief rehearsal of his points relevant and necessary.[6]

Lynn-George attacks Parry's theory of orality on three distinct but related fronts. He argues that Parry's conception of an oral poet is determined – through opposition, as a negative counter-image – by a Romantic conception of art and creativity; that the traditional language of orality is a misapplication of structural linguistic categories; and that the problems occasioned by these foundational misconceptions cause contradictions throughout Parry's system and its development. As we recapitulate Lynn-George's critiques, we will also note how they bear upon the two contrasting forms of time which organize the central confrontation of this chapter: the possibility of a self-sufficient and self-identical instant, versus an irreducible temporality marked by difference.

Parry's system relies on a successive series of distinctions: formula and essential idea, language and thought, oral and written. These distinctions form a coherent series in that each of them restate and reinforce, on different levels of analysis, 'a traditional form–content dichotomy which would distinguish rigorously between thought and language, where words are no more than the instrument for the expression of ideas which remain independent from language, divorced from it as anterior, exterior and superior to what should serve as their transparent vehicle'.[7] While the dichotomy between form and content in Parry's conception of language can seem to cursory examination to parallel the signifier–signified distinction familiar from Saussurean structural linguistics, it does not take into full account the consequences of Saussure's emphatic insistence on the differential nature of language as a system: 'Everything that has been said up to this point boils down to this: in language there are only differences. Even more important: a difference generally implies positive terms between which the difference is set up; but in language there are only differences *without positive terms*.'[8] In contrast to Saussure, positive terms abound in Parry; every essential idea that comes to be represented through language has its own positivity. The formulaic epithet in Parry therefore gains its meaning through being identical to itself, whereas meaning in structuralism derives from a word's difference from other words.[9]

In conceiving of language as the 'transparent vehicle' of a thought that is beyond language, Lynn-George argues, Parry's system runs into an initial contradiction. It asserts that Homeric language allows transparent access to the essential idea or thought, but it was the difficulty of interpreting formulaic language that motivated Parry's project in the first place. Parry's insistence on maintaining 'the direct and substantial nature of Homeric thought' is at odds with what he himself in fact recognized as a problem, the 'experience of so many epithets which do not clearly reveal the intention of the author'.[10] Lynn-George points out Parry's 'ambivalence' towards the concept of style as an indication of this contradiction: while maintaining, on the one hand, that style is the essential factor in determining whether a text is oral, Parry is also able, on the other hand, to dismiss as inessential everything in an expression which is 'purely for the sake of style'.[11] This contradiction within the concept of style – the way it is simultaneously essential and entirely superfluous – mirrors the contradiction about whether Homeric language is transparent or not, and can only be resolved through the invocation of a metalanguage. Homeric language only gains its transparency if there is an implicit set of metalinguistic rules linking the expression to its thought or idea. In the absence of this metalanguage, Homeric language becomes opaque. Thus, the difference between 'essential' and 'superfluous' accounts of style is the difference between 'before' and 'after' establishing the traditional metalanguage. Before we have the notion that a metalanguage connects every formulaic expression to a specific meaning, style is 'essential' because it is what drives us to the realization that such a metalanguage exists. After establishing that a metalanguage links sign and sense, the specifics of formulaic expressions become 'superfluous', since we now understand them perfectly. Just as in Foley's conception of a traditional reference, the implicit metalanguage of Parry's theory operates to erase the allegorical split of the sign and to produce a tradition composed of continuous, self-identical wholes.[12] Meaning in both Parry's and Foley's conceptions of oral poetry no longer depends on a process of interpretation which could bring differences, but rely on a set of pre-established correspondences between sign and sense.[13] The metalanguage thus removes time from interpretation and makes meaning instantaneous. While there may be an arbitrary period of empirical time taken for the audience to retrieve the correct associations – whether that be a fraction of a second for an archaic Greek listener to recall the traditional resonances of a phrase like 'the plan of Zeus', or the days or weeks for a modern scholar to track down and rebuild those same resonances from the corpus of surviving Greek myth – the interpretation takes no logical time once the necessary associations have been established. We see again how oral theory in Parry and Foley seek identity and the instantaneous, at the expense of difference and time.[14]

The basis for Parry's system are formulas which are so perfectly fitted to expressing the essential idea intended by the poet that the formula is directly reducible to this idea. But another contradiction arises here, since the purpose to which the formulaic system is put is in direct conflict with the poet's intention, since the oral poet is always without choice and 'obliged to use the words of others'.[15] The distinction between the words of others and the words of one's own is mapped by Parry onto the distinction between oral poetics and written poetics. Lynn-George argues that this opposition is determined by the Romantic notion of art in which the Romantic artist, as a creative individual in free command of his self-expression, is mapped onto Parry's conception of written poetics, while oral poetics represents its negative counter-image, a poet constrained by the traditional language which alienates him:

> The theory of orality was a major restatement of Romanticism. All Parry's presuppositions concerning the artist and the work of art were emphatically Romantic; orality was both constructed from, and determined by its opposition to, this concept of art. The historically earlier position of the artist, completely caught within the rigid confines of a common language before writing, allowed later liberation for the Romantic individual.[16]

Oral poetry is thus less an alternative to written literature than a product of its fantasy, the retrojection into the historical past of the bondage to the language of others that functions to recuperate the possibility of individual expression in the present. The freedom of the Romantic artist is underwritten by the unfreedom of the oral poet. Lynn-George marks the distance between Parry and Saussure: 'Saussure had already maintained that all language, spoken and written, "constitutes a system" as well as confirming that, "no matter what period we choose or how far back we go, language always appears as a heritage of the preceding period".'[17] Parry contradicts Saussure when he imagines that the poet, once released from oral tradition, can wield language freely as his own as a purely creative artist. Parry's Romanticism is not immediately obvious because it comes in the form of a rejection of Romanticism, but is nevertheless determined by it. Responding to Lord's remark that the 'method of language is like that of oral poetry, substitution in the framework of grammar', Lynn-George notes: 'The terms in the comment, however, need to be reversed: oral poetry participates in a system of language,' rather than language participating in the system of oral poetry.[18] Notice here that, in contrast to the emphasis on identity and the instantaneous in the rest of Parry's system, oral poetics incorporates the structuralist insight of the fundamental difference between the subject and the structure in which he is embedded. This inconsistency in conceiving the relationship between the poet and his language is what led to the contradictions we have seen before.

One further aspect of Lynn-George's critique remains to be considered for the purposes of introducing Nagy's responses and innovations. Lynn-George observes that Parry's conception of oral poetic language as a versifying system requires a certain 'incompatibility of signification and versification'.[19] A system of formulas linked to essential ideas through metalinguistic fiat would only be necessary if the words which might otherwise be best for expressing those ideas were unmetrical, that is, if the best words for signifying were not allowed due to the constraints of verse. What makes the incompatibility between the requirements of signification and versification actually operative as a concrete problem is the context of performance, in which the poet does not have enough time to fit the word to the idea:

> In his unlimited freedom the writer can move along an 'unrestricted range' of thought, language and time. The poet without writing, on the other hand, is caught completely 'in the stress of the moment', the pressure of time which at this primitive stage fetters him absolutely to the immediate present: he does not plan ahead or revise, he does not anticipate and has no memory of what has just passed; he does not ponder, has no room for reflection.[20]

Time hurries the individual poet along, but in doing so preserves the traditional formulaic system from change. It is too useful for both the poet who, in the instant of performance, has no time to compose, and the listener who, caught in the same instant, has no time to spend on interpreting the meaning of any untraditional element. Oral tradition is thus the antidote to time, encountering it always within each performance and always emerging victorious. The traditional language of the oral poet is, despite everything, a timeless construct, one that is preserved in 'the immediate presence of the spoken word'.[21]

The context of performance thus realizes the three determining notions of oral theory: the *self-identity* of the essential idea, expressed through an oral formula which is *continuous* through tradition, enabling the *instantaneous* moment of performance in which tradition – the natural sign, unsplit and immanently whole – is epiphanically presented by the poet and immediately received by the audience. Nagy's reconception of oral theory will shift oral theory in distinct ways with respect to the points of weakness pointed out by Lynn-George, in particular with respect to the question of the contradiction between what the poet wants to say and what the traditional language constrains him to say. But, as we will see, Nagy maintains throughout the ideal self-identity, continuity and timeless instantaneity of the oral tradition, although often in problematic and contested ways which testify to the innovativeness of his work.

* * *

Nagy's work radically revises the bases of oral theory. A common charge against Parry's conception of the formulaic system is that it exerted a compulsion on how a poet expresses the intended meaning. The oral poet is thus said to be always dogged by a mismatch between what he wants to say and the means he has of saying it metrically, or, as Lynn-George puts it, the language of traditional oral poetry requires an 'incompatibility of signification and versification'.[22] Nagy responds to all such objections by arguing that there is never such an incompatibility because the poet never *wants* to say anything that exceeds the traditional language. Nagy makes this audacious response plausible by boldly reconceiving the relationship between form and content, between what the poet can and what he wants to say. The synchronic problem of meaning and means is, in Nagy's work, projected into its diachronic dimension: the poet is not to be conceived at any given time as an individual who, while potentially free to conceive anything imaginable, is lamentably constrained by the relative poverty of traditional language, but instead is constrained by a past tradition that places constraints on what he can conceive in the first place. Nagy's operation here can thus be understood as another historicization, and solves the mismatch between signification and versification using a particular conception of time, but, as we will soon see, it is a conception of time as a timeless unity.

Citing the evidence of historical linguistics and comparative mythology, Nagy demonstrates the great antiquity of themes in archaic Greek poetry, which he argues are part of the common Indo-European inheritance of Greek culture.[23] The themes of archaic Greek poetry, Nagy argues, are so old as to precede the metres of Greek poetry, the dactylic hexameter in the case of epic.[24] Not only do themes precede metre, the metre of poetry is itself determined by the content of the themes and the formulas which express them, and not, as commonly conceived, the other way around.[25] Through this radical inversion of the relationship between theme and metre, content and form, Nagy is able to argue that the usual criticism of oral theory starts from false premises. Form never inhibits content because form is determined by content:

> To assume that whatever is being meant in Homeric poetry is determined by such formal considerations as formula or meter (as when experts say that the formula or meter made the poet say this or that) is to misunderstand the relationship of form and content in oral poetics. Diachronically, the content – let us call it *theme* – determines the form, even if the form affects the content synchronically.[26]

In the move from the synchronic to the diachronic dimension, the subject who is responsible for the making of oral poetry is no longer the individual poet, but rather the tradition to which individual poets are subordinate. Nagy forcefully expresses this subordination: 'To my mind there is no question, then, about the poet's freedom to say accurately what he means. What he means, however, is strictly regulated by tradition. The poet has no intention of saying anything untraditional.'[27] After Nagy's reconceptualization of the relationship between metre and content, there can be no question of 'incompatibility of signification and versification', no incompatibility of content and metre, because the metre itself is already determined by and fitted to the content, which has priority.[28]

Does this argument defuse Lynn-George's critique? It is undoubtedly persuasive, and the influence – and even precedence – of theme and formula over metre is tantalizingly attractive. It does not, however, entirely address Lynn-George's point, in which what is under attack is not – in its essence – the mismatch between intention and expression, but rather the very distinction between an intention prior and exterior to language and language as a vehicle for such an intention. This distinction is fully maintained by Nagy and can be seen in the way Nagy responds to criticisms of oral theory on the mismatch between intention and expression. In each case, Nagy summarizes in single sentences what he sees as mistaken conceptions of oral theory, each of which is then rebuffed in Nagy's own voice. What is important here is the similar form of all the mistakes Nagy stages for himself to correct: 'The formula made the poet say *it* that way. The meter made the poet say *it* that way. The poet had only one way of saying *it*. Homer had a new way of saying *it*.'[29] In each of these cases, Nagy maintains the distinction between the 'it' that the poet wants to say and the way in which he says 'it'. While Nagy does not remain on the level of the individual poet with his own artistic intention and his own use of language, the escape into the diachronic dimension of the problem does not alter oral theory's reliance on the form–content dichotomy governing language and its meaning. Instead, Nagy's response to the mismatch between form and content is to construct a prior harmony between them in the determination of metre by theme.[30]

With the shift from the level of the individual poet onto the level of tradition in assigning responsibility for the making of oral poetry, the artistic will to create songs that was always assumed for individual poets can no longer occupy its former position as the origin which orders and disposes content. Indeed, although Nagy takes pains to emphasize the long history of traditional themes and formulas, tradition itself is still, as Lynn-George observed of Parry's conception, a timeless construct. Objecting to the hypothetical statement, 'Homer had a new way of saying it', Nagy denies the possibility of escaping from tradition: 'Granted, to the extent that the performer controls or "owns" the performance in conjunction with the audience, the opportunity for innovation is there. Such innovation, however, takes place within the tradition, not beyond it.'[31] Parry's latent Romanticism, as pointed out by Lynn-George, reappears here in exactly the same configuration, in that both Parry and Nagy oppose the condition of the oral poet, bound within language-as-tradition, to the presupposed freedom of a free artist. Saussure and Lynn-George's rejoinder here, as before, would be that insofar as all speakers of a language must enter into the language of others, and insofar as 'language always appears as a heritage of the preceding period', what is being claimed for oral tradition here can be said of every work of every period.[32] It is still the Romantic aspiration of an absolutely free and original artist that sustains the implicit distinction within both Parry and Nagy's versions of oral theory.

Since the poet now has no intention except what is in the tradition, the position of the individual's artistic will as origin has been vacated. The categories of myth, cult and ritual step in to fill some of this vacancy. The answer to the question of what is expressed in an oral poem is no longer the will of an individual, but the needs of ritual. Nagy's defence of the metrical and formulaic aspects of oral poetics rests on the unity and continuity of the traditional themes from which the formal aspects derive, and the categories of myth, cult and ritual allow Nagy to ground the unity of the epic tradition on historically existing social and religious practices. The epic tradition is supposed to be unified and continuous because it derives from the cultic and ritual practices which made up the total social reality of Greek and pre-Greek societies as they historically existed: 'Myth, in societies where it exists as a living tradition, must not be confused with fiction, which is a matter of individual and personal creativity. Rather, myth represents a collective expression of society, an expression that society itself deems to be true and valid. From the standpoint of the given society that it articulates, myth *is* the primary reality.'[33] Later in the same work, Nagy would reject the approaches of those who sought the genesis of the Homeric poems and their assumption of an 'essence through origins', and yet, in grounding the essential unity of epic tradition upon myth and the unity that myth is assumed to inherit from its Indo-European provenance, the essence of the origin is reasserted.[34] Furthermore, in the emphasis on myth as the 'collective expression of society', one that is 'true and valid' and 'the primary reality', Nagy sets up the entire category of myth as the positive signified, of which epic is the signifier. Throughout the history of oral theory from Parry and Lord to Nagy and Foley, the unity of signifier and signified has always tended to expand. In Parry, that unity bound the formula to its essential meaning, while Nagy binds the epic register itself as a signifier writ large to the signified of social reality.

The grounding of epic on the security of a positive signified continues in the elaboration of cult and ritual. Following Walter Burkert, Nagy defines ritual: 'Ritual, in its outward aspect, is a programme of demonstrative acts to be performed in set sequence and often at a set place and time – sacred insofar as every omission or deviation arouses deep anxiety and calls forth sanctions. As communication and social imprinting, ritual establishes and secures the solidarity of the closed group.'[35] Further, cult is defined as 'a set of practices combining elements of ritual as well as myth'.[36] The links are thus complete, and a great chain binds metre and formula, on the side of poetry, through epic themes governed by the myth and ritual of hero cults, to the diachronic unity of Indo-European inheritance and the synchronic unity of the 'solidarity of the closed group' on the side of culture. Thus conceived, the presupposed unity of epic is coextensive with the presupposed closedness and uniformity of ancient societies, with all the political consequences such a conception implies. Epic poetry becomes an object of positive science. The positive facts of Indo-European inheritance can be established through historical linguistics and comparative mythology, and those of Greek society and religion through history, psychology and archaeology. Epic is therefore rationally explicable, its language transparent, at least to those who can see the links between each element of Nagy's chain. The language of epic thus becomes an image of Nagy's definition of *ainos*, 'a difficult code that bears a difficult but correct message for the qualified and a wrong message or messages for the unqualified'.[37]

It would not be saying much to merely repeat after Lynn-George and Saussure that 'there are only differences without positive terms'.[38] What is the nature of the Homeric poems in Nagy's system? An oral poem in this system is blocked from interpretation as a process, because all interpretation has been pregiven in the thematic unity of the chain that ties poetry to history and society. To pick one example among many, Nagy traces the unified theme of grief, *akhos-penthos*, pain, *algea*, and devastation, *loigos*, in order to interpret the name 'Achilles' by deriving it from *Akhi-lāwos, 'he who has the host of fighting men grieving'.[39] Interpretation is equated with derivation. The unity traced here is found in reconstructed etymologies and ritual necessities, extending throughout the poem in an 'automatic distribution', behind the poem's back. When Nagy claims a feature of epic as traditional, that tradition takes place on the level of myth or ritual and is inexplicable within the epic poem itself.

The tradition is capacious. Not only does it determine the meaning and diachronic unity of themes, as in the derivation of 'Achilles', it also governs formal features like the unity of the poem. It might at first seem that the formal unity of a particular poem or performance is one of the features that would be most resistant to assimilation into the tradition, given the fact that the degree of unity is a property of specific performances, but Nagy's system turns this formal feature into another kind of content:

> From the intensive studies of Parry and Lord on the nature of formulaic language, we expect to see in Homeric poetry the automatic distribution of set phraseology appropriate to set themes. Conversely, our knowledge of formulaic behavior tells us that we cannot expect any given composition within the tradition to require any alterations or modifications in the inherited phraseology of its hexameters for the purpose of accommodating the composition's own sense of its unity. If we do indeed discern the reality of an artistically unified *Iliad*, then we must also be ready to say that the unity of our *Iliad* is itself traditional.[40]

Deriving the full implications of his convictions, Nagy insists here that the formal unity of a poem cannot be judged on terms exterior to the tradition; it would not do to use, say, Aristotelian notions of logical unity to judge whether or not the *Iliad* forms a whole. Instead, if the *Iliad* is unified, it is because the tradition says it must be, on the same metalinguistic level that was previously invoked by Parry and Foley to justify interpretation. Conversely, even if we detect contradictions or inconsistencies within the *Iliad*, as the analysts were wont to do, those contradictions mean nothing and leave no meaningful trace since the tradition had already spoken the unity of the poem.[41] Nagy thus parallels Parry in establishing a metalanguage of epic poetry. This time, that metalanguage is based on the diachronic unity of themes, themselves based on myth and ritual. Only the metalanguage provides the understanding that makes transparent what would otherwise remain obscure, and the possibilities of hermeneutics are severely constrained. The knowledge Nagy gains from his analysis is thus an unconscious knowledge, known *of* the poem that is not known *by* the poem. Like Foley's traditional referentiality, Nagy's reconception – a recreation or refounding – of oral theory recovers the possibility of interpretation freed from Parry's strictures, but, again, that recovery has come at a high price. In contrast to the neoanalytic moment of interpretation that is always divided between a present text and an absent one, oral theory retrieves everything – themes, contents, potential contradictions, formal unity itself – into the instantaneous moment of a predetermined harmony.

We see again that oral theory maintains the instantaneity of meaning. Once we have established what meaning is traditionally given – whether that be through what comes 'instantly and easily' to the mind of Parry, or through tracing a traditionally resonant word with Foley, or by following up the meanings of Achilles' name in myth and ritual – no further time is taken for interpretation, and tradition brooks no change of meaning. This stands in strong contrast with neoanalytic reading, in which the meaning of a present text is always open to revision by a potential allusion, and with the processes of meaning in the Homeric poems themselves, in which the meaning of a present action is always subject to change because we do not have access to the future song of *kleos*. As noted at the beginning of this chapter, this contrast is predicated on different answers to the question of whether a self-sufficient moment is possible, or if there is an irreducible temporality dividing each moment from itself. Oral theory so far falls on one side of this choice, while neoanalysis and the Homeric poems fall on the other. The question facing us now is the status of diachrony in Nagy: how can we maintain that Nagy neglects the time of meaning, when he so strongly advocates for the importance of diachronic change through the oral tradition? We will need to examine more precisely the functions of synchrony and diachrony in Nagy's system, with a brief detour through Auerbach's famous essay on Odysseus' scar. What we will see is that 'diachrony' for Nagy – in contrast to 'history' – is not a temporal category of change, but a reaffirmation of synchrony.

II. History and diachrony

The distinction between synchrony and diachrony is fundamental to Nagy's work, where synchrony describes a snapshot of a cultural-linguistic system with all its relations at a particular instant in time, and diachrony describes how the system and its elements change through time: 'Fieldwork in the study of oral poetry as it is performed requires a synchronic perspective, for purposes of describing the actual system perpetuated by the tradition. When it comes to delving into the principles of organization underlying the tradition, that is, the reality of cultural continuity, the diachronic perspective is also needed.'[42] The synchronic–diachronic dichotomy maps directly onto the claim for the objective status of research into oral tradition: 'Whereas a given tradition may be perceived in absolute terms within a given society, it can be analysed in relative terms by the outside observer using empirical criteria: what may seem ancient and immutable to members of a given society can in fact be contemporary and ever-changing from the standpoint of empiricist observation.'[43] Hence 'fieldwork' corresponds with the gathering of synchronic data from the subjective viewpoints of those within a tradition, and diachronic inquiry with the objective, scholarly study of someone who stands outside the tradition and makes empirical observations. These dichotomies map further onto Parry's distinction between the oral poet, unable to transcend the pregiven boundaries of his tradition, and the writer, moving freely in the frictionless medium of his language. These distinctions allow both Parry and Nagy to distribute knowledge and ideology within their metalinguistic systems. Thus, knowledge lies on the side of the external, objective observer of the tradition in its diachronic aspect, while the internal, subjective participant of the tradition only has access to its timeless, synchronic aspect, which is a form of ideology.[44]

We can note briefly one obvious objection to these distinctions and the distribution they perform, although I will not pursue this line of argument. To what extent is the objective scholar free to stand outside tradition, when, as Lynn-George argues, that tradition encompasses not only oral poetry but language itself? Lynn-George remarks, about Parry's reports of observation and fieldwork in action, that 'the "observer" constructs more and more his own account of what the author "thinks"'.[45] There is a distinct sense that researchers performing the objective task of fieldwork are not immune from putting their interpretations of the logic of oral poetics into the mouths of their subjects. Lynn-George quotes from Parry: 'The finished singer will boast that he knows . . .'; 'When asked how . . . he will say briefly . . .'; 'But if one is able to point out . . . he will then say . . .'; 'Questioned further, he will explain that . . .'; 'What he means, *though never having reasoned about his art he cannot say*, is that . . .'[46] Oral theory deploys these objective observations in support of a specific interpretation of oral poetics that valorizes a timeless conception of tradition, which, as we have seen, manifests as the instantaneous moment of composition-in-performance that has no time to do anything except unchangingly reproduce traditional language. If we expand this moment to include also the reproduction of traditional *themes* in addition to traditional *language*, we can see that Parry's timeless tradition is also the synchronic field held by Nagy as one pole of the synchrony–diachrony pair in his system. It is in support of this image of oral poetics that the objective observer blurs the boundaries between himself and the oral poet, in order to supply the thoughts that the oral poet must have meant, 'though never having reasoned about his art he cannot say'. Lynn-George again quotes Parry, who eventually 'no longer writes in terms of "recovery", "reconstitution" or "reconstruction"', but instead picks out 'the instant when the thought of the poet expressed itself in song' as 'that moment which criticism must seek to *create*'.[47]

Leaving aside the line of argument in the previous paragraph, I would like to further examine the temporality of synchrony and diachrony in Nagy's work. A useful point of reference here is Auerbach's conception of Homeric time. Although the connection is not explicit, Lynn-George's analysis of the creative moment in oral theory parallels his critique of Auerbach's well-known essay on Homeric narrative.[48] Lynn-George connects Auerbach's conception of Homeric narrative's need for 'full illumination' with Auerbach's need to see Homeric narrative as dominated by the present. Commenting on the foot-washing scene in *Od.* xix in which the narrative is interrupted by a long digression on the provenance of Odysseus' scar, Auerbach argues that Homeric narrative expresses a need for everything to be fully illuminated: 'Here is the scar, which comes up in the course of the narrative; and Homer's feeling simply will not permit him to see it appear out of the darkness of an unilluminated past; it must be set in full light, and with it a portion of the hero's boyhood.'[49] What are the stakes of this division into light and darkness, in which the Homeric narrative must be preserved in the light of its illumination? Lynn-George argues that the metaphor of light and darkness is explained by Auerbach's conception of time in Homeric narrative. The light which illuminates every part of Homeric narrative in Auerbach's conception is the light of the present in the moment of narration: 'What he narrates is for the time being the only present, and fills both the stage and the reader's mind completely.'[50] It is in order to protect the unity of the present that Auerbach's Homer cannot leave the scar unexplained and unilluminated. He anticipates the audience's question about the provenance of the scar, because otherwise curiosity about Odysseus' past would split the moment of performance between what the poet is narrating and what the audience wonders about. This cannot be allowed to happen, and so Auerbach's Homer, by telling the story of the scar at the earliest possible moment, removes in advance the lacuna that would have been caused by the lack of an explanation for Odysseus' scar.[51] The violence of the temporal jump between the foot washing and Odysseus' youth matters nothing for Auerbach's Homer, as long as no questions arise to cause the dehiscence of the present. This is a subtler point than it may first appear. What is avoided is not the past, but instead the kind of double vision that breaks the *narrative* present into awareness of both past and present.

The story of Odysseus' scar avoids this double vision by *making present* the past of the story, hence the present *of narration*, irrespective of whether it narrates the *chronological* past or present, remains singular and unified. Just as the theory of orality preserves the instantaneous moment of performance through the use of a metalanguage that assigns formulas immediately to the essential ideas they are supposed to express, suppressing all hermeneutic doubt, Auerbach's Homer, too, presents a perfectly illuminated present, in the form of a frame through which all narration smoothly passes.

In Auerbach's quest to recover the stability of a present moment even from such a stark temporal transition as in the story of Odysseus' scar, Lynn-George identifies the desire which Nietzsche describes as man's envy of unhistorical experience:

> Then the man says 'I remember' and envies the animal, who at once forgets and for whom every moment really dies, sinks back into night and fog and is extinguished for ever. Thus the animal lives *unhistorically*: for it is contained in the present, like a number without any awkward fraction left over; it does not know how to dissimulate, it conceals nothing and at every instant appears wholly as what it is ... Man, on the other hand, braces himself against the great and ever greater pressure of what is past.[52]

The Homeric poems certainly are responses to the problem of the past that presses upon the present. What Parry, Auerbach and Foley offer are ways of reading the Homeric poems which respond to this problem in a manner parallel to Nietzsche's animal, living unhistorically – that is, without the split that divides the subject in the present with the awareness of another time, or the Freudian notion of the unconscious as 'another scene', *eine anderer Schauplatz*. Oral theory's covering over of this split is made all the more palpable for us since we have already worked through the logic of neoanalysis in the previous chapter, which precisely makes the split appear. But while Parry, Auerbach and Foley can be seen to valorize a timeless present, how is it possible to say the same of Nagy, whose system places such a great emphasis on evolution and diachronic change? We turn back now to Nagy in order to see how synchrony and diachrony work in action.

Two points underpin Nagy's conception of synchrony and diachrony. The first is an explicit, absolute separation between synchrony and diachrony, and the second is a mostly implicit dependence of diachrony on synchrony. Throughout his work, Nagy insists on the incommensurability of the synchronic and diachronic levels of analysis. 'Consequently, the language of a body of oral poetry like the *Iliad* and the *Odyssey* does not and cannot belong to any one time, any one place: in a word, it *defies synchronic analysis*.[53] The diachronic here always exceeds the synchronic, and the attempt to make sense of an oral poem synchronically is always doomed to failure:

> What I resist is simply the insistence of some scholars on the notion that an original composer of an original composition in oral tradition can be recovered *as a synchronic reality*. The parallels of historical linguistics imposes itself. Within the conceptual framework of this discipline, we can claim to be reconstructing an earlier phase of a language on the basis of cognate forms, but we cannot ever say that we have recovered an original phase. The different details that we reconstruct cannot be reassembled into one synchronic reality, one glorious instance of real speech as really spoken in one time and one place.[54]

The argument here is that, because the different elements of what will have become our *Iliad* and *Odyssey* – these elements may be linguistic, thematic or plot-related – have each their own processes of development with their own external pressures, the poem that they compose at any given moment in time cannot be understood as a unity that overrides the individual developments of the individual elements. Hence there is no synchronic time at which every part of the poem makes sense, which is why there never was 'one synchronic reality'. This stipulation connects with what we have seen earlier, Nagy's assertion that formal unity is not a property of any instance of performance but of the tradition: because the elements are independent, any coherence between them must exist only through a kind of traditional fiat. Nagy thus removes the possibility of interpretation from the particular poem or performance, conceived as merely synchronic, and asserts that only the diachronic level offers the possibility of interpretation, which has in the process become the study of derivation.

A comparison can be made with what Freud called 'secondary elaboration' in the making of dreams. Dreams for Freud, like the Homeric poems for Nagy, are also made up from disparate elements with independent origins, displaced and condensed in order to become expressed. Secondary elaboration is what happens after these elements have been amalgamated, and the dreamer tries to make some narrative sense of it all. The process of secondary elaboration is thus analogous to the act of the audience or receiver of a Homeric poem, trying to rationalize an amalgamation of elements which do not 'originally' belong together. The distinction between Freud and Nagy emerges at this point. Where for Nagy, the lack of an original unity blocks interpretation since there was no 'glorious instance of real speech as really spoken at one time and one place' to interpret, for Freud, on the other hand, secondary elaboration is fully part of the dream work and can itself be interpreted.[55] In terms of the stakes of this chapter and the question of whether a self-sufficient instant is possible, for Nagy, meaning requires a synchronic instance of speech – that is, a self-sufficient instant – and the lack of such an instance blocks interpretation. For Freud, as well as for neoanalysis and the other figures of the splitting of the present we have examined, the lack of a fully present and independent synchronic reality is a part of meaning-making itself.

The absolute separation between the synchronic and the diachronic is imposed as part of an unspoken comparison to written texts; the latter is assumed to have one author and one synchronic origin, free from the burden of the past of language. But, more pertinently, it is necessary to see that behind Nagy's separation of synchrony and diachrony and the valorization of the diachronic perspective over the synchronic, there lies a hidden yet essential subordination of diachrony itself to a more fundamental notion of synchrony. This hidden subordination of diachrony to a more fundamental synchrony undercuts the explicit valorization of diachrony over synchrony, but is also what supports that explicit valorization. In what way is diachrony subordinate to a more fundamental synchrony?

For Nagy, diachrony is only ever the description of changes in synchronic systems. This is explicitly stated in a key footnote: 'I am using the terms *diachronic* and *synchronic* ... not as synonyms for *historical* and *current* respectively. It is a mistake to equate *diachronic* with *historical*, as is often done. Diachrony refers to the potential for evolution *in a structure*. History is not restricted to phenomena that are structurally predictable.'[56] What is at stake in distinguishing diachrony from history is precisely the need for a second, more fundamental level of synchrony. Synchrony is what can be apprehended in one logical instant, taken in with a single glance.[57] The stipulation that the instant of synchrony is a 'logical' instant here distinguishes it from an empirical instant in the sense that, while it may take time in the synchronic study of a language for a student to learn, say, verbal forms before moving onto nominal forms, the verbal forms studied earlier do not change while the nominal forms are studied – the same synchronic level occupies the same logical instant, no matter how long practically it takes to enumerate the various elements of that level. What distinguishes history from diachrony in the passage quoted is that, because diachrony is restricted to 'phenomena that are structurally predictable', it relies on the logic of synchrony, while history is not restricted in this way. In order to know which *historical* events to select in forming a *diachronic* sequence, we must already have a *synchronic* structure to guide us, because diachrony selects among historical changes only those which will prove to make sense within a synchronic structure, while everything else in history is discarded.[58] A map of diachronic changes through a period of time is closed because all those changes must fit within a synchronic structure, thereby producing a second level of synchrony as we apprehend the whole map in a single instant. In contrast, history, within Nagy's distinction, is not mappable, or can only be an open map, because there is no predetermined structure. Finally, to restate this point on one more level: every diachronic change gains its full meaning the moment it happens, while historical events are open to revaluation and reinterpretation because there is no pre-established structure in which to understand them. Hence we refind in Nagy's theoretical distinction between diachrony and history the contrast between a present that is self-sufficient and self-identical, and one that is divided by time and difference – the fault line running through and connecting our analyses of poetry and scholarship.

Let us flesh out the theoretical discussion with the actual context of Nagy's discussion of the Homeric tradition. Nagy posits five stages in his evolutionary model of the fixation of the Homeric tradition, from pure oral tradition in the early second millennium, through a 'definitive period' of performance starting in the Athens of the Peisistratidai, to an age of relatively standardized texts inaugurated by Aristarchus' edition.[59] The conceptually decisive period, however, spans only the distance between pure orality and the performances of the time of the Peisistratids, because it is through this timespan that the Homeric tradition loses 'the immediacy of the performer–audience interaction expected in the context of ongoing recomposition in performance' and becomes instead performances that are only 'aiming at a verbatim repetition – not at an act of recomposition'.[60] Although Nagy maintains that writing was not empirically required for 'textual fixation', this distance is in effect, conceptually, that between living orality and the dead fixity of writing.[61] What happened to shift Greek culture from one form of performance to the other? The centrepiece of Nagy's answer to the question of how the Homeric and other archaic Greek oral traditions traversed the gap is an account of Panhellenism.

Panhellenism is the 'surge of intercommunication among the cities from the eighth century onward'.[62] Whereas previously an oral poet performed in the intimacy of a single city state and its religious and mythical traditions, problems arise with the advent of Panhellenic festivals and their audiences from diverse city states, each endowed with its own local traditions. A unified, synthetic tradition is therefore necessary in order to be valid in Panhellenic contexts.[63] The synthetic tradition entails a claim to absolute truth so as to be able to assert its validity ahead of any local traditions it may contradict. As the synthetic tradition embraces the influence of and asserts its authority over more and more local traditions on its way to becoming truly Panhellenic, it also becomes more fixed, resulting eventually in the ideal of verbatim repetition.

It is in this crucial transitional stage that we will see a conflict in Nagy's work between a commitment to Parry and the more profound potential of his own system, which opens up new directions for oral theory and could have brought it into conversation with neoanalysis through the division of time which we have been pursuing. Those new directions were however foreclosed because the conflict was resolved – as an unsatisfactory compromise – in the concept of diachrony that we have just described. We will therefore first explore the problematic transition in the status of the performer brought about by Panhellenism, then describe the potential of a new direction for oral theory, and finally see its foreclosure in the diachronic compromise.

Nagy asks us to conceptualize the transition brought about by Panhellenism as one between two kinds of poetic performers and two kinds of performance. On the one hand, there is the older, pure idea of the oral poet as *aoidos*, 'singer'. The *aoidos* represents the pre-Panhellenic period in which the performer belonged to his local community. The performance of the *aoidos* is thus considered to be the harmonious expression of the values and mythological and ritual needs of an enclosed society.[64] On the other hand, there is the figure of the Panhellenic poet, *rhapsōidos*, 'rhapsode'. The rhapsode performs not only for his own community, but travels to other places, with different values and mythological traditions. Thus, where the *aoidos* is enclosed in harmony and has the function of embodying the return of the same, the rhapsode must contend with the differences which arise within the Panhellenic context between one locality and another.[65]

There are subtle interplays of sameness and difference in the figures of the *aoidos* and the rhapsode. On the one hand, there is a straightforward formula for the difference between the two: 'Whereas the oral poet recomposes as he performs, the rhapsode simply performs' – that is, ideally 'verbatim'.[66] But on the other hand, Nagy warns that it is 'simplistic and even misleading to contrast, as many have done, the "creative" *aoidós* with the "reduplicating" *rhapsōidós*'.[67] The *aoidos* performs songs that may change in accordance with the changing values of the community to which he belongs, but those changes – in song and in values – are never acknowledged within the performance community, since the authority of traditional poetry rests on their remaining the same.[68] The rhapsode, on the other hand, is charged with making sure that his song is in fact, objectively, the same each time, but this sameness is alive with the implicit differences to be encountered in different localities which it subsumes. How is it possible to reconcile the sameness of the rhapsode's song with what local audiences would have been used to? The answer, which Nagy does not state explicitly, is that the Panhellenic rhapsode no longer logically or notionally performs for local audiences, whatever may be the case empirically. If a rhapsode is performing in, say, Athens, the local audience may be Athenians with Athenian expectations, but the rhapsode does not perform for them. Instead, the rhapsode performs for a projected Panhellenic audience that remains the same everywhere, because it is also absent from everywhere. The function of Panhellenic song is not to express the values of an existing Panhellenic audience – that audience does not exist, since there are only ever local audiences – but it is instead to call such an audience into being through its own performance.[69] There is therefore no parallel between the *aoidos*–audience relationship and the rhapsode–audience one: the local audience determines the performance of the *aoidos*, while the rhapsodic Panhellenic performance determines its Panhellenic audience.

It is at this point, through the figure of the Panhellenic rhapsode, that we can produce a series of connections to the division of the present by difference. Just as, in a neoanalytic reading, the present text is haunted by its potential allusions to an absent text, and just as, for a Helen or an Achilles, the present meaning of an action is accompanied by its potential revaluation in a song to come, the rhapsode also produces a song that is aimed not at the audience before him, but at a Panhellenic audience that will come into being as the audience of Panhellenic song. The audience members, too, are transformed from those which listened to the *aoidos*. Let us imagine an audience member who is plucked from an *aoidos*-performance – in which all is in harmony with his expectations and with the values of his community – and placed instead in a rhapsodic performance: we can well imagine that he might be offended by any part of the rhapsodic performance which differed from expectation. But a habitual audience member of rhapsodic performance would instead recognize that any unfulfilled expectations he might have are not signs of the rhapsode's deficiency in harmonizing with his local community, but rather signs of the audience member's own deficiency in comparison with an ideal Panhellenic audience.[70] Nagy's figure of the Panhellenic rhapsode, taken to conclusions beyond those Nagy himself had reached, implies breaking out from the harmonious self-identity of an oral tradition that confirms and reconfirms itself, and into an open-ended creation of a song and an audience to come.

The transition from *aoidos* to rhapsode is accompanied, in Nagy's work, by a change in the meaning of mimesis, or what he calls the 'destabilization of the conceptual world of mimesis'.[71] In outline, this destabilization is a change from a 'dramatic' sense of mimesis as *re-enactment* of myth in ritual, to a reduced notion of mimesis as mere *copying*.[72] The logic of the older, 'dramatic' form of mimesis entails the idea that performance is taken to *really be* what it claims to be:

> The singer of Homeric poetry begins the song by praying to his Muse: 'sing!' ... What he then tells his audience is supposed to be exactly what he hears from the Muse or Muses, goddesses of memory, who are conceived as the infallible custodians of the *ipsissima verba* emanating from the Heroic Age. The words of Homer are supposed to be the recordings of the Muses ... what Homer *narrates* is exactly what the Muses *saw*, and what Homer *quotes* in his narration is exactly what the Muses *heard* ... When a Homeric hero is quoted speaking dactylic hexameters, it is to be understood that heroes 'spoke' in dactylic hexameters, not that they are being *represented* as speaking that way ... My argument is that the rhapsode is re-enacting Homer by performing Homer, that he *is* Homer so long as the mimesis stays in effect, so long as the performance lasts.[73]

The possibility of epiphanically remanifesting, in a present performance, the original 'Homer' depends on making the original 'absolute', or, in other words, divine: 'So long as the represented "that" remains absolute – that is, absolutized by the myth – the representing "this" remains a re-enacting "this".'[74] When, in the Panhellenic transition, mimesis changed from re-enactment to mere imitation, this change was accompanied by a change in the status of the absolute origin: 'Once you start imitating something that is no longer absolute, however, you can no longer re-enact the absolute: then you can only make a copy, and your model may be also just a copy.'[75] Although Nagy does not make this explicit, there is a change in the image of time between these two conceptions of mimesis: the mimesis of an absolute origin entails the image of a divine, circular time, the time of the festival which returns year after year, of the sacrifice ritual which brings back the first sacrifice. But when the ritual origin returns no longer, when the gods are absent, then time can no longer double back, and we can only make copies, always separated from its model by the straight line of time.

Nagy describes rhapsodes as performers who 'persist in appropriating to themselves the persona of the composer' using the idea of the 'recomposed performer', that is, the rhapsode 'becomes recomposed into Homer every time he performs Homer'.[76] But, at the same time, the rhapsode who is recomposed into Homer must aim not at recomposition but at verbatim repetition. The figure of the rhapsode is thus caught between two kinds of performance, two forms of performer–audience relationship, and two different images of time. The combination of such contradictory features within a single figure reflects Nagy's conflicting commitments. On the one hand, the whole thrust of Nagy's originality in the Panhellenic argument brings the poet out of the harmony and self-identity of Parry's conception of oral performance, along the straight line of time and difference. But on the other hand, in the assertion of a literal identity between the performance and what it represents and between the performer and Homer, we see Nagy's argument still constrained by Parry's doctrine, becoming an example of what Howard Bloch calls 'the fantasy of a semiotic utopia, in which word and referent meld'.[77] We might ask: at which level is this fantasy is to be found? If the fantasy is ascribed to the rhapsode, it becomes difficult to reconcile this insistence on the literal truth of poetry, the *ipsissima verba*, with the fact that the need for this very rhapsode arises in response to the pressures of Panhellenism, in which the rhapsode is confronted precisely with the choice between different versions of what is true: 'What was held to be true by the inhabitants of one place may well have been false to those of another. What is true and false will keep shifting as the poet travels from place to place.'[78] If, instead, the fantasy is taken to be part of the inherited conceit of traditional poetry, the difference between the singer and the rhapsode becomes difficult to account for, since the purely traditional singer evidently felt free to recompose, a privilege denied to the rhapsode, who is at least partially freed from his tradition through the contact with other traditions that defines his position. If, finally, the fantasy is ascribed to the audience, one begins to wonder whether it is a response of the ancient audience or if it is rather the modern oral theorist who is under its spell, in the fascination of 'the immediate presence of the spoken word'.[79]

Throughout the evolutionary model of the fixation of the Homeric text, the notion of a Panhellenism that takes the poet out of the closed circle of performance and places him before the potential, absent audience of all the Hellenes is locked in conflict with oral theory's insistence on holding onto a vision of plenitude in which all is present, unified and accounted for by tradition. This is the conflict, in essence, between a diachrony which serves the sameness and continuity of a tradition that preserves itself as self-identical, and the unpredictable, unstructured differences which occur within a history not predestined to fit into a 'structurally predictable' synchrony.[80] The conflict manifests concretely around the question of how each conception handles differences between traditions. The Panhellenic poet, the figure which leads to the gradual fixation of the oral tradition and the eventual production of written texts, owes his existence to an awareness of the differences between local traditions and the need to reconcile them. The poet of oral tradition, on the other hand, is strictly barred from the recognition of differences because every performance is supposed to be the *ipsissima verba* of the tradition. On the one hand, Nagy would like to preserve the oral theoretical ideals of continuous self-identity in the instant of performance, the oral poet of the pure present as conceived by Parry and Auerbach; this figure is preserved in Nagy's system as the *aoidos* and the *aoidos*-like features of the rhapsode. On the other hand, Nagy cannot escape his own recognition that epic necessarily exceeds the synchronic dimension, that oral tradition 'defies synchronic analysis' and hence cannot be contained within any pure present of performance.[81]

The compromise solution to this problem lies in Nagy's concept of the diachronic. The diachronic is that which produces a tradition that is allowed to change through time and hence exceeds every present of performance, but remains analysable as a unified system because the changes have been preselected to make sense within a synchronic structure – that is, remains beholden to a fundamental synchrony. Nagy states this dependence explicitly: 'A synthetic and critical tradition purports to represent a prototype of variant traditions, and *the diachrony of its evolution thus becomes its own synchrony*. Homeric synchrony, to take the clearest example, operates on the diachronically oldest recoverable aspects of its own tradition.'[82] The selection of thematic aspects from multiple traditions during the process of evolution is parallel to the historical linguist's method of deducing the prototypical form of a word or other linguistic element by comparing cognate words in related languages. The synthetic, Panhellenistic tradition produced through the evolutionary model is conceived as a mirror image of the oral theorist's own method of historical linguistics and comparative mythology. This comparison is telling because historical linguistics, at the level we are considering here, takes words as the positive objects of its study, without any pretension of interpreting the documents in which it finds those words. Similarly, Nagy's method treats themes as the positive objects of its study, and renounces interpretation of poems, which is consistent with the fundamental distinction in Nagy's programme between the objects of knowledge available from outside the tradition and the ideological illusions of the merely subjective perspective.

Despite the warnings that 'the different details that we reconstruct cannot be reassembled into one synchronic reality', the evolutionary model produces its own 'Homeric synchrony'.[83] The diachrony of evolution is actually the synchrony of the synthetic tradition, which demonstrates the extent to which diachrony in Nagy's conception is subordinate to a fundamental synchrony. Moreover, that synchrony is, as we have seen, always self-consistent and unified; the evolutionary model has no response to differences except their elimination as senseless contradiction. This is seen whenever two local traditions conflict on a particular point: one of them always prevails, and the other is eliminated from the synthetic tradition. Like Auerbach's elimination of double vision from the narrative present, the evolutionary model eliminates the double vision of conflicting versions. Nagy seems to explore the possibility of conflicting versions in describing the rhapsode as 'he who sews together [*rhaptō*] the song(s) [*aoidē*]', in which 'the many and the various become the single and the uniform – and yet there is supposedly no loss in the multiplicity and variety of the constituent parts', but the possibility is immediately recuperated within the unity of the tradition in a footnote that assimilates the category of paradox itself as 'a working convention within the tradition'.[84] The extent of this system's engagement with the existence of differences is to afford them a preassigned place within tradition. Difference and multiplicity are neutralized as merely conventional, and history is homogenized as diachrony.

The evolutionary model well deserves its name, in the sense that the mechanism which chooses between conflicting versions contending for the Panhellenic synthetic tradition operates by a logic of life and death. 'The synthetic tradition, in order to survive, must prevail over the countless variant traditions from which it was constituted.'[85] Only one of the competing traditions can prevail and survive in the Panhellenic synthesis – this logic reflects the oral theoretical requirement that the synchronic level of each performance be self-consistent and unified, which means that each version of traditional myth can only be either true or false. Just as in biological evolution, death takes the vanquished, which are then lost in subterranean oblivion until, as fossils and relics, they present themselves to the objective, inquiring eye of the oral theorist as palaeontologist:

> There may be at any given time a multitude of latest performances by a multitude of performers in a multitude of places. Still, each latest performance is a crisis for what has been said in all previous performances, and the cumulative trends of latest performances determine what ultimately survives and what is lost ... In any case each latest performance helps determine what is highlighted and what is shaded over, with the ever-present possibility that the shading will lapse, with the passage of time, into total darkness.[86]

The possibility of memory is foreclosed – to remember a different performance would break the spell of the present, which is disallowed by Nagy as it is by Parry and Auerbach. The lost leave no echo, but go gentle into the darkness of that good night.

What, then, actually produces the Homeric poems in the form in which they exist? This does not happen 'by invoking the genius of a poet who stands out from among the rest'.[87] Nagy answers with reference to the material found in the epic cycle, often assumed to contain older traditions from which the Homeric poems take their themes: '[T]he Panhellenization of the Homeric tradition entailed a differentiation from older layers of Panhellenic epic tradition, and that these older layers were gradually sloughed off in the process of Homeric streamlining. Such an explanation would account for not only the artistic superiority of the *Iliad* and the *Odyssey* but also the thematic archaism of the Cycle.'[88] The abstract framework of the evolutionary model, operating on a diachrony dependent on the unity of the synchronic, has nothing to say about the actual production of the Homeric poems. That is left, in a sweeping gesture, to processes not under the control of the diachronic and not selected by it. Disavowed for being 'not restricted to phenomena that are structurally predictable' and marginalized under the abstractions of 'sloughing off' and 'streamlining', it is history itself, *il miglior fabbro*, that returns in Nagy's evolutionary model to account for the artistically superior *Iliad* and *Odyssey*.[89]

Nagy does not deny that the *Iliad* and the *Odyssey* seem fundamentally different from the poetry of the oral conception of tradition. 'Yet such pan-Hellenic poetry, ascribed to the ultimate poets, is itself no longer oral poetry in the strict sense: it is being performed by rhapsodes ... Moreover, oral poetry, at least in the form represented by the medium itself, has not survived.'[90] But recognizing that the Homeric poems differ from the ideals of oral theory does not displace the desire to recover oral theory in the descriptions of singers in the Homeric poems. Nagy insists that how 'an actual epic' was composed is still recoverable in the representation of the singer Phemios in the *Odyssey*, despite warning, elsewhere, that 'self-references in Archaic Greek poetry may be diachronically valid without being synchronically "true".'[91] The Homeric poems are thus no longer actual epics. An air of irreality hangs over them, just as the rhapsode sings in the irreality of an absent audience. An oral poetics that insists on real performance within a real society on themes from myths that form a 'primary reality' serves only to mark its own distance from the Homeric poems.

Bloch writes, on theories of orality: 'It is not merely a question of determining with certainty the dogged question of origins, whether oral, written, or somewhere between the two, but of allowing a critical supposition concerning orality to dominate what it is we look for in a literary text.'[92] In the field of

Homeric scholarship, on the question of empirical origins, it can easily be conceded that no writing was involved for much if not all of the prehistory of the Homeric text. It is the critical supposition concerning orality that is in question, one which tends to insist on a strict division between orality and writing in an age before the existence of writing – and therefore also before the existence of orality, unless orality is itself made to have a positive, self-definitional and self-sufficient value, self-engendered and self-engendering. The figure of the Panhellenic audience, and even the opposition between orality and writing itself, serve less as objects of empirical research, and more as the objective correlates supporting presuppositions about the goals and means of reading. The theory of orality from Parry to Nagy remains the dream of a plenitude without history, a communal fantasy without end.

III. Difference and multiformity

Thus far in this chapter, we have seen how oral theory is strongly motivated by the image of a self-sufficient instant in which all is given. This instant manifests as the moment of composition-in-performance, and is supported by the apparatus of traditional language and traditional referentiality which maintain the self-sufficiency of the moment by short-circuiting the time of meaning and interpretation, making both instantaneous. We have also seen that, while Nagy's innovative account of Panhellenism provides an escape from the enclosed self-sufficiency of the instant by opening performance up to difference, his commitment to Parry's oral theoretical model leads, at least explicitly, to a form of diachrony that still serves synchrony and the instantaneous moment. In what remains of this chapter, I would like to use these results to expand on a comparison with the division of the present and thus build on the discussion of previous chapter, in particular concerning the ways in which Nagy and neoanalysis treat difference.

Difference is treated differently in Nagy's evolutionary model and in neoanalysis. A recurring concept in Nagy's work is that of the foil, which is an abstract concept of difference: 'What is true and false will keep shifting as the poet travels from place to place, and he may even resort to using alternative traditions as a foil for the one that he is re-creating for his audience;'[93] 'Such excessive *phthonos* on the part of Iros is directly comparable to *phthonos* in its function as a traditional negative foil of praise poetry within praise poetry;'[94] 'Throughout the poem, she is treated as a negative point of contrast – a veritable foil – to the other girl.'⁹⁵ That which is different, for Nagy, has the function of being a foil, an abstract negative image; it works to affirm the unity of the good and true tradition, which shines out all the more brightly against the darkness of the bad and the false.

A contrasting view of how a traditional poem can relate to different, absent traditions is offered by Karl Reinhardt: 'But in the *Iliad* the story of Patroclus does not stand as a story next to other stories: it draws into itself all the others in the form of presentiment or memory.'⁹⁶ Not as a story beside other stories (*als Geschichte neben anderen Geschichten*) – not as the true relates to the false, relegating the latter to obscurity or resurrecting it as a foil only to reaffirm its own truth – but as a presentiment or memory (*Ahnung oder Erinnerung*). The vacillation between presentiment and memory – the former referring to a future, the latter to a past – shows that it is not a simple matter of travel along a straight line from the past, through the present and into the future. The neoanalytic 'Achilleis hypothesis' demonstrates this: the Patroclus–Hector story in the *Iliad* is hypothesized to repeat the story of Antilochus, Memnon and Achilles in a possible *Aithiopis* or *Achilleis*. The existence of both the Patroclus–Hector story and the Antilochus–Memnon story would be contradictory if we try to fit both in the same 'timeline' or 'universe',⁹⁷ since Achilles would have to be simultaneously doomed to early death both for killing Hector as well as for killing Memnon. But instead of demanding that one version prevail over the other, Reinhardt offers the possibility of presentiment as the inkling of a future that could never come, and memory as the memory of what never happened. Against the experience of unity and self-identity in the instantaneous present of performance in oral theory, neoanalysis installs difference at the heart of the experience of Homeric poetry.

The contrast between the foil and presentiment or memory captures part of what is at stake, but another step is necessary. After all, Nagy, along with the editors of the Homer Multitext Project, Casey Dué and Mary Ebbott, do place great importance on interpreting the different versions of oral poems.⁹⁸ Dué's recent work, for instance, explores questions like what differences in meaning and theme might have emerged in a version of the *Iliad* which gave greater prominence to the presence of Penthesileia as both lover and enemy to Achilles.⁹⁹ This interpretative aspect of the oralist multitext project begins to look like neoanalysis, although the resemblance goes unacknowledged due to the continuing differences in how the prehistory of the Homeric poems is conceived in the two camps. But the position I would like to develop from the multitext project and oral theory's approach to difference can be approached most directly with reference to a development already seen in the context of neoanalysis. In the previous chapter, we distinguished between local and generalized divisions of the present, a contrast expressed in various Iliadic figures on the level of poetry, and in neoanalysis as the difference between neoanalytic readings founded on actual comparisons, on the one hand, and Dowden's reading of Homeric silence, on the other. We had said that an actual comparison – say, of the use of the verse 'And he lay stretched out in the dust, mighty in his might' (XVIII. 26) in the context of the death of Patroclus compared to Achilles' death – expressed a local division of the present in which difference depended on and was drawn from the comparison of pre-established identities, whereas Dowden's suggestion about Homeric silence, in which every part of the poem could potentially be silent about something that we do not know, expressed the generalized division of the present because every moment of the poem is split between present meaning and an unknown potential allusion. A pure difference makes its force felt, prior to any possible comparison between actual identities.

A parallel analysis holds for the creation of a multitext of all known variations of an oral tradition. In the creation of a multitext, what is expressed is the desire to place all known versions before the eyes of the viewer in a single glance. It is the desire for the self-sufficient instant, replayed on another level. In its interpretations of different versions of how a poem might have been performed – does Penthesileia appear or not? – there is reflected the local level of comparisons between actual versions. But beyond this, there is the generalized question of how a poem thematized multiformity, or the possibility of different versions *as such*. Were the Homeric poems able to come face to face with the fact of multiformity, even as each performance is necessarily bound to tell a single version? How must meaning and interpretation work for something like a 'presentiment or memory' of absent pasts and impossible futures to be possible? With these questions, we are able to connect the concerns of the multitext with our interests in time and *kleos*, because *kleos*, along with the structure of the song to come and the generalized splitting of the present it implies, is the form in which multiformity – reconceived as the possibility of difference – comes to be thematized in the Homeric poems. Where oral theory – so much like neoanalytic and analytic scholarship before it – sought evidence of multiformity in the contradictory details of the Homeric poems and of visual depictions of the myths,[100] the possibility of multiformity was prefigured in the song that Helen projected for a future audience.

4

Sutures

We have seen so far how the logic of *kleos* and the image of time it entails have been able to connect figures and preoccupations from Homeric poetry and scholarship. However, these connections have for the most part remained purely formal, in the sense that we have focused primarily on the form of meaning-making in these discourses: Patroclus' retroactive assignation of meaning to the expedition of the Danaans, for instance, implies a *formal* division between the meaning available in the present and one that was still to come, but the contents of what those meanings are have only been incidental. This focus on form – temporal and differential – follows from the nature of the concepts themselves, since the essential feature of the logic of *kleos* is that, in dividing every present moment, a pure difference is inserted and overturns the stability and self-identity of any particular content.

While an insistence on formal purity helped us connect discourses and figures which initially seemed distant from each other, reducing their thematic and narrative richness to illustrations of formal principles makes for sterile readings of the Homeric poems. The task of this chapter is to move beyond mere formalism by demonstrating some of the ways in which the formalism of *kleos* interacts with and enriches the thematics of the Homeric poems. The itinerary will begin by examining the ways in which Homeric heroes sometimes substitute a positive meaning content for the space or the gap of pure difference; then, we will see a substitutability between pure difference and objects or objecthood; finally, I will offer an interpretation of an odd detour in book vi of the *Iliad* in which Hector, seeking his wife Andromache, initially fails to find her at home – why does Hector come upon his empty house?

Before embarking on this itinerary, let me reframe the logic of *kleos* to bring to the fore those aspects important for the upcoming discussion. The basic proposition is that *kleos*, because it is unknowable and inaccessible, divides every present moment in terms of meaning. It indicates an interruption in the possibility of meaning-making because the present meaning of our actions is not the final meaning they can take on, which is projected into an inaccessible future song – another meaning can always come to overturn what we think or intend in the now. The hero does not know his *kleos*, but the hero sometimes *knows* that he does not know, and therefore must work with this awareness, just as someone working through an equation with an unknown variable is obliged to carry the unknown quantity through every subsequent step. But the persistence of the unknown does not prevent the hero from living and making judgements and meanings. In making those judgements, it is possible, of course, to simply forget the gap imposed by *kleos* and thus to neglect the unknown variable. It is in fact difficult to find clear examples of this in the *Iliad*, but Parry's demand for meanings that come 'instantly and easily come to mind' may be the purest expression of the effacement of the gap – we have seen how Foley and Nagy complicate and historicize this position – which is why it produces such a clear and useful comparison for bringing out the contrasting position in the Homeric poems.[1] The figures which we will be examining here, however, do not simply efface the gap in meaning, but preserve it even as it is enfolded into or expressed as meaning. This is part of the reason for the concept, suture, that stands as the title of this chapter; a suture closes a gap, but leaves the seams visible.[2] We will therefore be looking for both the division and difference entailed by the logic of *kleos*, and the figures which foreclose them.

I. Suture in speech

The first form of suture we will examine is found on the level of the heroes' motivation. What are the ways in which a hero can draw motivation from the division of the present imposed by *kleos*? This question is deliberately phrased: what we are after here are not the ways in which heroes are motivated by *kleos* – wanting fame – but instead ways in which there is a short circuit between the unknowability of *kleos* and a particular decision or motivation. An apparent contradiction arises: if, as we have outlined, the logic of *kleos* is a *formal* feature of meaning-making – it imposes upon every present meaning the shadow of a pure difference anticipating a meaning to come – then how is it possible for this empty formal structure to produce a positive *content* and guide a hero to one decision or another? It cannot, except through sutures or short circuits which are to various extents 'illegitimate' or 'improper', fusing the level of form with that of content and borrowing the force of the former under the mask of the latter.

Let us examine three instances of this kind of suture, which will include two figures we have seen before in Achilles' speech to Lykaon and Helen's anticipation of future song, as well as a new passage involving Hector's attitude towards divination. Before starting, let me set up the framework in which these three figures will appear, and also explain the order of presentation. The three figures form an *ordered* series – they are ordered by *how* 'improper' their sutures are. A suture is *more* improper when it short-circuits the formal gap of *kleos* with a *more specific* content, such as a particular decision to be made in the narrative. This will be represented by Achilles' speech to Lykaon. Helen's anticipation of future song lies on the other end of the scale because, as we will argue, it is barely connected to any particular content. In the middle is Hector's attitude towards divination, which connects the temporality of *kleos* with a principle of action. For clarity of presentation, I will first discuss Hector's speech, the middle figure of the series, before moving onto Achilles, and finish with Helen.

This middle figure, then, is found in book XII in Hector's reply to Polydamas, who has interpreted a bird sign and, on the basis of which, counsels Hector to pull back from the Achaean ships. I am particularly interested in the following verse in Hector's rejection of Polydamas' advice: 'One bird sign is best: to fight in defence of the fatherland.'[3] What appears as a simple statement of patriotism that seems closed in upon itself actually expresses a form of openness in suturing a generalized division of time. Let us first examine the speech of Polydamas which prompted Hector's response. The Trojans, successful in the field, are driving the Achaeans before them. The fighting reaches the Achaean wall, and a portent appears. Polydamas interprets it as an unfavourable one for the Trojans:

> Let us not go on and fight the Danaans by their ships. I think it will end as the portent was accomplished, if the bird sign that came to the Trojans as we were trying to cross was a true one, an eagle, flying high and holding to the left of the people and carrying in its talons a gigantic snake, blood-coloured, alive, but let it drop suddenly before winning his own home, and could not finish carrying it back to give to his children. So we, even though in our great strength we break in the gates and the wall of the Achaians, and the Achaians give way before us, we shall not take the same ways back from the ships in good order; since we shall leave many Trojans behind us, whom the Achaians will cut down with the bronze as they fight for themselves by their vessels. So an interpreter of the gods would answer, one who knew in his mind the truth of portents, and whom the people believed in.[4]

Polydamas' advice relies on a conception of time that seeks to erase the gap imposed by *kleos* and to restore an undivided present. The logic of the argument begins with the present intentions of the Trojans, which is to break through the Achaean wall. This act of breaking through the wall initially carries a triumphant meaning, but that meaning will change as the Trojans pay for the breakthrough with high casualties. Fortunately for Polydamas, a bird sign has appeared in the present that tells the Trojans what their present act of breaking through will mean in the future, and therefore, Polydamas counsels, Hector and the Trojans can avoid the disastrous change in meaning by changing their present act. In this sense, the bird sign as a premonition of the chronological future allows for the erasure of the difference in meaning of the present act, thereby ensuring that the intended act does not misfire, and that the present remain undivided.

From the perspective of the logic of *kleos*, this is an attempt to circumvent its inaccessibility: to be sure, if the Trojans fall back, they may avoid the casualties they would have taken, but the meaning of that retreat would itself be subject to change. Divination does not escape from the retroactive nature of meaning, and does not provide a secure ground for action.[5] In this context, let us read Hector's reply:

> But you: you tell me to put my trust in birds, who spread wide their wings. I care nothing for these, I think nothing of them, nor whether they go by on our right against dawn and sunrise or go by to the left against the glooming mist. No, let us put our trust in the counsel of great Zeus, who is lord over all mortal men and all the immortals. One bird sign is best: to fight in defence of the fatherland.[6]

Hector's reply can of course be read as characterizing his arrogance and fatalism, and as an example of how rejecting prophecy leads to disaster.[7] More interesting is how Hector, in refusing Polydamas' advice, expresses a different form of temporality. Hector does not only refuse Polydamas' advice, but forcefully rejects the interpretation of bird signs as such. But why does Hector seem so hostile towards the interpretation of bird signs here, or, better, what is it that has come to be expressed as hostility towards this form of interpretation?

On the level of content, it is of course possible to say that Hector is simply displeased by an unfavourable omen against his wishes. Formally, however, the last quoted verse shows that something else is also at stake. When Hector declares that 'to fight in defence of the fatherland' is the 'one bird sign' that is best, 'bird sign' – literally, 'bird' [*oiōnos*] – clearly no longer refers to actual birds or omens, but has instead become a label for what we might call a principle of action. The principle of action that Hector rejects, as we have shown in the logic of Polydamas' advice, relies on a conception of time that tries to use the foreknowledge of the future provided by omens to avoid the division of the present. This rejected principle situates itself in the chronological future revealed by the omen and applies it to the present, as if the meaning of the present action were decided and located in that future moment, a moment made accessible by divination, and not in the inaccessible site of a song to come. In rejecting the interpretation of bird signs, Hector thrusts all of this aside and puts in its place the principle of 'fighting in defence of the fatherland'. But what form of time is implied in this principle? In contrast to divination's manipulation of chronological futures, 'to fight in defence of the fatherland' is clearly a principle of the present – no knowledge of the future is required to apply this principle in any particular present circumstance. But calling it a principle of the present only leads to another question: what *kind* of present? Is it a self-identical and self-sufficient present, in which case we would see Hector as a self-deluded fool, blindly confident in his own judgement and thereby leading his people to disaster? Or is it instead a divided present, in which what Hector asserts against the calculations of divination is not the certainty of self-belief, but rather the awareness that the potential for meaning to change in the logic of *kleos* persists beyond all calculation?[8]

There is no way to make the choice between these alternatives definitively. We might say that Hector himself does not know, or, perhaps better, that Hector can only express the latter in the form of the former. What we can observe, however, is that a short circuit operates here, in which the radical unknowability and openness of *kleos* channels its centrifugal force against the chronological calculations of divination, joining with Hector's own inclinations to produce, as an overdetermined condensation, the formulation, 'one bird sign is best: to fight in defence of the fatherland'.

In this figure, we see a suturing of the logic of *kleos*. It short-circuits the form–content gap in connecting the formal proposition that final meaning is inaccessible with a guiding principle for specific action, to fight for the fatherland. The patriotic principle gains in conviction and persuasiveness by borrowing the force of the divided present – which runs throughout the poem – to overturn Polydamas' divinatory calculation that seeks to forestall potential changes in meaning. Hector's words are thus improper insofar as a short circuit is operating, but not as improper as it could be. The next figure to be examined is more improper because it connects form not to a principle, but to a specific decision.

This figure, which we have examined before, is found in Achilles' encounter with Lykaon. Captured by Achilles, Lykaon asks for his mercy, but Achilles is in no mood to keep him alive to be exchanged for ransom and slaughters him. How does Achilles reason about his decision? His reasoning is given in a brief speech that begins by recalling Achilles' loss of Patroclus and his need to exact vengeance:

> Poor fool, no longer speak to me of ransom, nor argue it. In the time before Patroklos came to the day of his destiny then it was the way of my heart's choice to be sparing of the Trojans, and many I took alive and disposed of them. Now there is not one who can escape death, if the gods send him against my hands in front of Ilion, not one of all the Trojans and beyond others the children of Priam.[9]

This first half of Achilles' reasoning explains his decision to kill instead of ransom Lykaon perfectly well in terms of the hatred Hector incurred for his family and all the Trojans by killing Patroclus. But Achilles does not leave things here. He proceeds to generalize the fact of death to all mortals: 'So, friend, you die also. Why all this clamour about it? Patroklos also is dead, who was better by far than you are. Do you not see what a man I am, how huge, how splendid and born of a great father, and the mother who bore me immortal? Yet even I have also my death and my strong destiny.'[10] All mortals are equal in their mortality: the stark consciousness of mortality is a prominent theme of the *Iliad*, as the standard interpretations affirm.[11] But a question remains: why does this reflection occur here? What draws together the theme of Achilles' revenge upon the Trojans and the common mortality of man? The connecting statements – 'So, friend, you die also. Why all this clamour about it? Patroklos also is dead, who was better by far than you are' – cannot be taken at face value: even if all men must die, nothing in that fact entails that they should do so without clamour. Moreover, the common mortality of man does not motivate Achilles' slaughter of the Trojans, still less the particular slaughter of this particular Trojan. A short circuit has occurred here between generality and particularity, between the formal structure of mortality and the specific content of death.

Mortality here is formal because it is the form of meaning for a mortal life. The fact of mortality gives form to a life, but no content: nothing is given about *how* death comes. We saw previously the emphatically definite indefiniteness of Achilles' understanding of his own death: 'There shall be a dawn or an afternoon or a noontime when some man in the fighting will take the life from me also either with a spearcast or an arrow flown from the bowstring.'[12] What is definite is the *form* of a life: it will end in death. What is indefinite is its content, or when and how it will happen. Achilles' speech is drawn to this figure, vividly combining absolute formal certainty with an ostentatious indefiniteness with regard to content, highlighting the short circuit that allows the force of formal generality to enter the specific decision to kill Lykaon. Recall the connection made previously between the way that the indefiniteness of death has the potential to reorder and reinterpret the meaning of all events in a life, and the logic of *kleos*, which is the generalized form of the retroactivity of meaning and the splitting of the present: death, with its attendant circumstances, is only one expression of how present meanings are subject to retroactive revision. Achilles has therefore conflated death as the avatar of contingency with the specific decision of inflicting death on Lykaon. This is the short circuit or instance of suture, improperly linking the openness of pure difference to a particular content.

In moving from Hector's to Achilles' speech, we went in the direction of more impropriety. For the last figure, we move in the opposite direction from Hector's principle. We can afford to be relatively brief here, as the third figure is Helen's words to Hector already discussed in chapter two (VI. 358): 'Zeus set a vile destiny upon us so that hereafter we shall be made into things of song for the men of the future.' The relevant analysis remains the same as before. Faced with the lack of coherent meaning for the suffering of the present, Helen projects that absent meaning into future song. Instead of a lack of meaning in the present, we have a plenitude of meaning, but deposited in the inaccessible site of a song to come. A short circuit operates in this case in what we might call the positivization of lack; the failure of meaning-making is turned into the promise of meaning, or, the *form* of ignorance is turned into a *content* of knowledge. What we can add to the earlier analysis is in placing this figure into series with the previous two figures. In suturing the form of meaning to its content, where Achilles produced a particular *decision* to kill and Hector a generalized *principle* of patriotism, Helen produces only the promise of meaning's possibility, the barest stain of content upon the purity of form.[13]

In this series of three figures, we have seen three of the ways in which the heroes are able to enfold the openness of *kleos* into the present of action. These forms of the suturing operation operate on the level of the heroes' individual motivation and self-understanding. In the next section, we will see how the suture works on the level of Homeric poetics, and in particular in the function and meaning of objects and objecthood; by this latter, I have in mind instances in which features of objects are attributed to characters. Helen provides a convenient segue. While we have just seen how Helen projects meaning into a future song, she also reflects the events of epic in yet another way in weaving 'a great web, a red folding robe, and working into it the numerous struggles of Trojans, breakers of horses, and bronze-armoured Achaians, struggles that they endured for her sake at the hands of the war god'.[14] Some form of metapoetic substitutability between the verbal narrative of song and the visual depiction of textiles is often noted, and this handiwork of Helen's, with its depiction of epic struggles, makes the connection in a particularly salient way.[15] If we consider the invitation to compare song and weaving in the context of our present interests, a question arises: what is the relation between weaving and the inaccessibility which we have been emphasizing in the figure of the song to come? What does the status of the robe – as an object substituting for a story – mean for the interruption that characterizes meaning-making under the logic of *kleos*?

II. Objecthood and meaning

This section elaborates a thesis that can be succinctly stated: Homeric poetics expresses the failure of meaning through objecthood. Two notes, one about each of the two terms of this thesis, are necessary to connect previous discussions to what follows. First, on the failure of meaning: given that the unknowability of *kleos* divides every now between a present meaning and a meaning to come, there is a moment in between the two meanings in which the earlier meaning fails. This failure of meaning may be actually realized – as in the cases of Agamemnon realizing the consequences of the truce for Menelaus or Patroclus retroactively reassigning the meaning of the Achaeans' expedition – or it may remain a pure possibility; the latter corresponds to the pure difference that inheres in generalized division. Hence the failure of meaning is part of the logic of *kleos*. The second note is on objecthood: objecthood for the context of this discussion contrasts with the order of language and sense; where the latter is filled with meanings and significations, the former expresses muteness and the refusal of signification.

My treatment of objects picks up, obliquely, on recent trends in scholarship inspired by versions of New Materialism and object-oriented ontologies, the complexity and importance of which require an elaboration of what I see as the philosophical stakes and the orientation of my argument in relation to them. The first thing to note is that it is difficult to generalize about this scholarship – I will briefly discuss work by Alex Purves, Lilah Grace Canevaro and Jonas Grethlein – despite their often being in reference to each other. This is in no small part because their philosophical inspirations are themselves not easily generalizable; substantial differences separate names often cited together like Jane Bennett, Graham Harman, Levi Bryant or Brian Massumi.[16] A second difficulty with characterizing the connections between Homeric scholarship and object-oriented ontologies is that the former tends to be focused on literary topics which are relatively distant from the philosophical and political commitments of the latter. Scholars have recognized considerable challenges in attempting to connect objects which appear in the Homeric poems – literary representations – to the philosophical turn towards real-world objects.[17]

The fact that Homeric objects appear in a poem and are therefore constructions of human intentionality and agency points to a central question for all these works, that of the distinction between the human and non-human. To apply a New Materialist perspective to the Homeric poems has therefore taken the form of highlighting the ways in which non-human objects resist or are at least independent of human intention and meaning. Let me discuss some representative applications along these lines, before situating my own approach. Purves offers an example of resistance to the traditional tendency to read objects 'as signs, as fixed symbols waiting patiently for their significance to be unlocked at key moments in the plot'.[18] Instead, Purves's reading of Ajax in his armour at XVI. 102–11 allows us to see these objects as acting with an agency of their own: 'It is, I want to suggest, the interconnectedness of these materials – missiles, helmet, shield, breath, and sweat – that count. Together, they join forces with Ajax' body to tell the story of what is happening at this particular moment in the poem.'[19] In this account, Purves experiments by following Bennett closely in attributing agency to objects.[20] In contrast, Grethlein is more ambivalent about the possibility of objective agency. He points out, for one, that previous cited examples of Homeric objects that seem to have agency or intention – such as spears 'full of desire to sate themselves with skin' (λιλαιόμενα χροὸς ἆσαι, XI. 574) – are likely examples of metaphor rather than ontological claims.[21] For another, he recognizes that even objects like Odysseus' bed, which do play a role as an agent in advancing the plot of the *Odyssey*, only do so 'in conjunction with a story'.[22] Canevaro, finally, also declines to grant independent agency to Homeric objects, pursuing instead a tiered approach in which human subjects as 'primary agents' delegate agency to objects as 'secondary agents'.[23] This is because her work pursues a productive tension between New Materialism and the broad tradition of feminist and gender theories, for which ontologies based on the subject–object division are still important for their social and political dimensions.[24]

In relation to these debates regarding the borders between the human and the non-human about *whether* or *to what extent* objects can have agency and intentionality independently from human subjectivity, I would like to instead show the way in which objects and objecthood in the *Iliad* appear at the edges of a limited subjectivity.[25] Between the full independence of objects from the regime of human meaning or intention and their complete subjugation to that regime – existing as mere symbols – there exist other possibilities. Canevaro works with one such possibility, that Homeric objects have agency only secondarily, dependent on a human 'primary agent' or 'originator'.[26] I am suggesting another, that the resistance of objects to human agency appears when human meanings fail, hence my thesis: Homeric poetics expresses the failure of meaning through objecthood.[27] This will be demonstrated by reading for the connection between expressions of the mute incomprehensibility of objects and failures of meaning-making. The failure of meaning-making connects with our broader preoccupations because the divided nature of Iliadic time embeds this failure into every provisional meaning.

If we were to pick up from the segue at the end of the last section, the correspondence between Helen's weaving and her projection of a song to come, the thesis would not find strong support based on this instance alone. This is because no part of the description of Helen's weaving brings to the fore its muteness or resistance to signification, which we have claimed to be the key features of objecthood in this context.[28] Let us turn instead to a series of connections between Achilles and objecthood, not just in the objects associated with him but including also what he says and how he is described. A key instance is found in a figurative object from Achilles' speech, when he finds out that Patroclus is dead: 'Now, since I am not going back to the beloved land of my fathers, since I was no light of safety to Patroklos, nor to my other companions, who in their numbers went down before glorious Hektor, but sit here beside my ships, a useless burden on the good land.'[29] In this striking image, Achilles experiences himself as a burden (*akhthos*), a word which foregrounds the feeling of weight and heaviness.[30] The 'good land', *arourēs*, indicates cultivated, productive, arable land. The metaphorical object that forms Achilles' experience of himself at this juncture, then, is contrasted with the living earth as its negation, stripped of all properties except its weight as a burden, a negation made all the more emphatic by the description *etōsion*, 'vain' or 'useless'.[31] Why does Achilles experience himself as a burden on the land? What is meant by this strange object that is characterized by the weight of its negativity? We can approach these questions by considering where it appears in the context of Achilles' career.

The burden on the land emerges at a moment of the failure of meaning. Previously, we saw Achilles' trajectory through the *Iliad* in terms of a formal change in how he understands the relationship between his *kleos* and his acts. Before the death of Patroclus, Achilles acts as if he could manipulate the meaning of his *kleos* from outside history, where 'history' is understood as the series of events that are included in *kleos*, as opposed to events which are not. The death of Patroclus teaches Achilles that he is fully within history, which, moreover, exceeds the conscious manipulation of any of its participants by always containing the potential to change the meaning of their acts and choices. Here, we retain this analysis but shift the emphasis from the formal change to the moment at which it occurs. Achilles' realization that *kleos* escapes his conscious manipulation entails a failure of meaning. When he is told of the death of Patroclus, Achilles recognizes that his previous choices and the set of values which led him to make them no longer make sense. It is at this moment of the failure of meaning – more precisely, the failure of Achilles' meaning-making structure – that Achilles experiences himself as a burden on the land, a weight about which nothing is known except its unspeaking, unsignifying negativity.

Until the death of Patroclus, Achilles had been making decisions based on a calculus of honour, fame and recompense. As previously noted, honour and fame – *timē* and *kleos* – are conflated at this stage, and Achilles thinks that his *kleos* depends on his *timē*. While the stakes of Achilles' quarrel with Agamemnon are defined in terms of the insult done to his honour, *timē*, what gives the anger of Achilles its particular intensity is Achilles' relation to *kleos*. Achilles' relation to *kleos* sets him apart from other heroes: he thinks he knows what his *kleos* will be, and is told by his mother Thetis that he has the option to choose between a long and undistinguished life or a short life with *kleos aphthiton*, 'imperishable fame'. Despite the seeming openness of this choice, Achilles at the same time always seems to have already made the choice, or, more precisely, seems to already have had the choice made for him. He is always said by Thetis to be short-lived, as if the other choice of long life without glory was never an option: 'Ah me, my child. Your birth was bitterness. Why did I raise you? If only you could sit by your ships untroubled, not weeping, since indeed your lifetime is to be short, of no length. Now it has befallen that your life must be brief and bitter beyond all men's.'[32]

Achilles seems to have always already chosen a short life in return for an imperishable *kleos*, and it is this relation of recompense that lends a specific intensity to Achilles' relation to *timē*.[33] Jean-Pierre Vernant notes: 'Dedicated from the outset – one might say by nature – to a beautiful death, he goes through life as if he were already suffused with the aura of the posthumous glory that was always his goal.'[34] Achilles takes every insult to his *timē* as a threat to the brilliance of his *kleos*, bought at so high a price: 'As a heroic character, Achilles exists to himself only in the mirror of the song that reflects his own image.'[35] If there is a conflation in Vernant's account here between the concepts of *timē* and *kleos*, this only reflects the short circuit between those two levels in Achilles' own thinking. Until the death of Patroclus, Achilles' choices are made in this context, in which his *timē* is a paramount yet controllable element of the imperishable *kleos* which is the recompense for the brilliant brevity of his life.

To this Achilles, the death of Patroclus arrives as a blow from an unexpected quarter. Even though he warns Patroclus about the dangers of the gods, especially

Apollo, if he should attack the city without Achilles, Achilles' concern for Patroclus is suffused with concern for his own *timē* within the *timē–kleos-*recompense conjunction: 'When you have driven them from the ships, come back ... you must not set your mind on fighting the Trojans, whose delight is in battle, without me. So you will diminish my honour [ἀτιμότερον δέ με θήσεις].'[36] When Achilles is told of the death of Patroclus, a consequence of his own choices stretching back to his prayer for the temporary victory of the Trojans, he realizes that the terms of the *timē–kleos*-recompense conjunction are no longer – and never were – an adequate context for conceptualizing what is meaningful for his life. Deprived of the conceptual framework in which his previous decisions and wishes made sense, Achilles' past choices cease to be recognizable to himself. It is at this point – where signification and the symbolic conceptual order fail – that Achilles experiences himself as a mute, inexplicable weight, a useless burden on the land.

I am thus advancing a reading of the burden on the land as a figure of the failure of signification at a precise point of Achilles' career through the poem, the point at which he becomes incomprehensible or unreadable to himself. Achilles' tendency towards unreadability – his position outside existing systems of symbolic signification – is corroborated by the number of other descriptions of Achilles in which he seems inaccessible to sense and meaning.[37] Let us first note a few examples of this figure, before turning to establishing a link between Achilles as a site of the failure of signification and an interpretation of his shield.

First, then, Achilles is figured as incomprehensible and outside the social order by other heroes. Ajax during the embassy calls Achilles 'hard', with an 'implacable heart' outside the social systems of exchange.[38] Patroclus himself calls Achilles 'pitiless: the rider Peleus was never your father nor Thetis was your mother, but it was the grey sea that bore you and the towering rocks'.[39] Achilles is not unique in this respect, since other heroes are also figured as having incomprehensibly hard or 'iron' hearts.[40] But Achilles' unreadability is more strongly and uniquely marked in the persistent descriptions of a brightness or brilliance associated with the hero himself and his arms, in particular after the death of Patroclus. Where earlier associations between Achilles and hardness can be attributed to the circumstances – typically, he is characterized this way by a speaker who has failed to obtain something from him – a striking series of images after the death of Patroclus can be more productively linked through a connection between the failure of meaning and those aspects of objecthood which resist interpretation. In the realm of the visual, this is often marked by a brightness that overwhelms direct perception.[41] For instance, when Priam watches as Achilles sweeps across the field of battle, the poem describes him: 'In full shining, like that star which comes on in the autumn and whose conspicuous brightness far outshines the stars that are numbered in the night's darkening, the star they give the name of Orion's Dog, which is brightest among the stars, and yet is wrought as a sign of evil.'[42] In one of the poem's most striking images, Achilles stands up, unarmed, in the midst of the fighting and shouts out terrifyingly in rage and grief, and a brilliant flame, *selas*, is made to shine out from his head, like a bright fire shooting high, visible across the seas (XVIII. 203–29).[43] In this last image, the specifically unreadable and non-signifying nature of the association between Achilles and brightness is reflected in the conjunction of the visual aspect of brightness with the aural aspect of Achilles' cry. Just as the sight of Achilles is bright with *selas*, his voice, *phōnē*, is compared to the wordless blare 'screamed out by a trumpet'.[44] Where we expect the human voice to bear meaning, we have only a pure, non-signifying scream.

Let us draw out a series of consequences from the preceding discussion to advance the discussion of the broader concerns of this chapter. First, the object-like characteristics associated with Achilles – the muteness of the burden on the land, unreadable brightness and the non-signifying sound of a scream – gain their meaning as part of a contrast between meaning or interpretation and an objecthood resistant to meaning. To this extent, the discussions here pick up on the gesture that Purves makes in seeking to read objects beyond their human significations: 'Homeric objects are allowed, indeed often required, to carry histories with them (this is especially true in the case of armor and shields), but when read only in terms of plot they end up in danger of being understood as closed and inert.'[45] Second – and here, my goals diverge from those pursued by New Materialist readings – the resistance to meaning expressed through these figures of objecthood should be connected to the *narrative* career of Achilles, in that the association between Achilles and objecthood comes most sharply into focus after the death of Patroclus. This is the most direct point of contrast between our discussions and Purves's, since we are connecting the function of objects with precisely the human concerns of plot from which Purves wishes to free them. But these positions are not in direct opposition, since – and this is the third of the propositions I wish to demonstrate – we do not connect objecthood with any positive meaning in the human concerns of the plot, but instead with the failure of meaning. Achilles' objecthood is associated with the narrative moment in which he loses his initial meaning-making apparatus, the set of coordinates formed through the *timē–kleos*–recompense conjunction.[46] Fourth and finally, the failure of meaning associated with Achilles' objecthood is intimately connected with the logic of *kleos*; it is this logic – the projection of meaning to the site of a future song and the concomitant inherence of difference and the generalized division of the present – that Achilles learns as he recognizes the failure of his attempt to control the meaning of his *kleos*.[47] In this way, then, we can see how, in their mute materiality, objects and objecthood express pure difference, suturing it in a precarious identity.

The point can be sharpened by considering the moment when Achilles faces the very brightness, *selas*, with which he is often identified. This occurs when his mother Thetis brings him the set of arms freshly crafted by Hephaestus: 'Trembling took hold of all the Myrmidons. None had the courage to look straight at it. They were afraid of it. Only Achilleus looked, and as he looked the anger came harder upon him and his eyes glittered terribly under his lids, like sunflare [*selas*].'[48] Stephen Scully, in an article on 'reading the shield of Achilles', notes the affinities between Achilles himself and his shield, in particular the way that both are associated with brightness, *selas*.[49] Scully argues that, towards the end of the *Iliad*, Achilles adopts a 'divine synoptic perspective' which is 'inhuman' and 'breaks the sense of the special status of the human'.[50] Scully proposes that the shield, in framing the human world within a cosmic perspective, shares this inhuman divine perspective, and that the convergence of perspectives between the shield and Achilles explains why Achilles alone is able to read the shield and indeed delight in it, while other mortals tremble and do not dare to look at it.

Scully's reading therefore shares certain similarities with ours, as well as important differences. It is similar insofar as Scully, too, posits a change in Achilles' 'perspective', or his meaning-making apparatus; for both readings, Achilles loses the value system comprised of the conjunction *timē–kleos–*recompense, which he had used to give meaning to his actions and choices. What distinguishes the two readings is in what happens afterwards, in the kind of change triggered by the initial loss. It would be natural to expect that the loss of one value system would lead to its replacement by another, and indeed this is Scully's reading when he ascribes to Achilles, after the death of Patroclus, a 'divine synoptic perspective', that is, a divine perspective in which mortal concerns are no longer significant. Where Scully's position involves a change in content from human to divine, our discussion, in contrast, focuses on a suturing function that short-circuits content and form. It is not that Achilles begins by judging the events which happen in the narrative in a human manner and ends by giving them meaning within the inhuman perspective of the divine, but instead, more radically, the way in which Achilles understands the formal relation between narrative content and the meaning of narrative changes.

What is the nature of this change? Objects and objecthood play an important role in mediating and expressing the change in Achilles. For Scully, Achilles' affinity with objects and with the shield in particular derives from the harmony between their points of view upon the human world. The reason why Achilles is able to look upon the shield while other mortals cannot is because, after the death of Patroclus, he shares the divine perspective expressed by what Scully understands as the detached, synoptic view upon the human experience depicted on the shield. For us, however, Achilles' affinity with brightness and the shield is based not on their convergence in the mutual comprehensibility of their divine perspectives, but rather in their common incomprehension, or negation, of human understanding. Achilles does not understand – no more than the terrified Myrmidons – the divine perspective of the shield, but his affinity with the shield is precisely based on this incomprehension.[51] Parallel to his assumption of unknowable death in his speech to Lykaon, as Achilles looks upon the shield, he sees and commits himself to the failure or the beyond of meaning. Or, to draw another connection, Achilles' encounter with the shield parallels Helen's projection of meaning into a future song; where Helen's positivization of lack turned it into a promise, Achilles finds it in the inhuman brightness of an object.

III. Vignette and simile

Through the examination of the figures of objecthood connected with Achilles – the burden on the land, the brightness of the shield, the wordless scream of the trumpet – we have worked out a nexus of concepts connecting objects, the failure of meaning and the logic of *kleos*. Objecthood as such can express the cut in meaning imposed by the unknowability of *kleos*. As a corollary, let us build on this thesis by examining two more categories which extend the *kleos*-structure. Both are prominent features of episodes of the deaths of minor warriors: first, the vignettes of their lives, and second, the similes which accompany their deaths. For both, we will demonstrate how they each express a break in meaning-making and moreover are related to each other through this property.

The death of a minor warrior is frequently accompanied by a vignette of their lives. The death of Skamandrios exhibits the typical form of these vignettes:

> Menelaos son of Atreus killed with the sharp spear Strophios' son, a man of wisdom in the chase, Skamandrios, the fine huntsman of beasts. Artemis herself had taught him to strike down every wild thing that grows in the mountain forest. Yet Artemis of the showering arrows could not now help him, no, nor the long spearcasts in which he had been pre-eminent, but Menelaos the spear-famed, son of Atreus, stabbed him, as he fled away before him, in the back with a spear thrust between the shoulders and driven through to the chest beyond it. He dropped forward on his face and his armour clattered upon him.[52]

The first thing to note about this passage is the way it provides another exemplification of the retroactive nature of meaning that we first saw in Agamemnon's realization of the meaning of his oath and Patroclus' belated recognition of the meaning of the Danaan expedition. At the moment of death, the dying man's life gains its meaning, and everything in that life comes to be retroactively reconfigured in relation to death. The moment of death provides a form of finality that, as in the cases of Agamemnon and Patroclus, allows the temporary and improper occupation of the perspective of the song to come.[53] The poem makes explicit this new relation to death, which Benjamin formulates succinctly:

> 'A man who dies at the age of thirty-five', said Moritz Heimann once, 'is at every point of his life a man who dies at the age of thirty-five'. Nothing is more dubious than this sentence – but for the sole reason that the tense is wrong. A man – so says the truth that was meant here – who died at thirty-five will appear to *remembrance* at every point in his life as a man who dies at the age of thirty-five.[54]

Our desire or pretension to know what an event or a life really and finally means is what is at stake in Benjamin's emphasis of 'to *remembrance*'. In the case of Skamandrios, it is the hunt at which he excelled which takes on a new meaning that is now seen to have always already been the meaning of the hunt in the life of Skamandrios, as that which would not be enough to save him from Menelaus. In the case of others, it is the nurture of parents which will not be repaid, or wealth which will no longer avail, or a new wife whose embrace will never be known. It is often remarked by those arguing for the possibility of invention for the traditional poet that the biographical vignettes of the heroes who are summoned as grist for the mill of battle are not traditional but rather invented for this purpose. We can agree with this if we also specify that this purpose is precisely so the divided time of *kleos* can appear even within the description of battle, which might at first seem to be most concerned with presenting a vivid, undivided present of narration.[55]

The vignette, as a form, expresses the retroactivity of meaning. Furthermore, it is important to note that the retroactivity of meaning does not exchange one meaning content for another, in the way Scully understands Achilles to have exchanged a human meaning for an inhuman, divine one. Instead, what is staged is the negation or overthrow of meaning. The meaning of the hunt in Skamandrios' life and of his dedication to Artemis turns out to be that which 'could *not* now help him'. What impresses itself in particular about the meanings imposed on the lives of the minor warriors at their deaths is not only the finality of death but also the incompleteness of life. The Trojan war cuts across the lives of these warriors and what they anticipated doing in those lives. A humanist reading will interpret this aspect of the *Iliad* as a comment on the evils of war, which would be borne out by those passages which dwell on the interruption that war has brought to the tranquillity of peace, such as those marked by the phrase, 'before the coming of the sons of the Achaians'.[56] But the theme of the tragic interruption of peaceful lives caused by war is only a materialization, only one form of manifestation of the structuring principle of the Homeric tradition that is the interruption of all settled meanings and expectations. The overturning of Achilles' expectations through the course of the *Iliad* cannot be parsed in an anti-war interpretation, but nevertheless demonstrates the interruption of Achilles' expectations, the putting back into motion of a framework of meaning that Achilles had thought settled.

How do the discussions so far relate to a second prominent feature of the minor warriors and their deaths, the similes which often accompany them? The link between similes and the biographical vignettes just examined is the way in which they both reach, from within one narrative and the meaning-making apparatus it entails, towards the possibility of other stories, and thus expressing the pure difference that inheres within any meaning. The vignettes make this difference appear through the confrontation of biographical narratives that cut across each other, and we might recall here Grethlein's discussion of the contingency that cuts between experience and expectation; for the biographical vignettes, the contingency always appears as the death in battle that breaks apart the link between the minor warrior's experience – of hunting, for instance, or parental nurture, or marriage – and the expectation that experience carried but which will not be fulfilled.[57] Where the vignettes present different versions or re-visions of a single life, the similes are freer in the form in which they make difference appear.

One characteristic way in which this happens is for the Homeric simile to elaborate a little more than necessary, to seem to go on just a little too long.[58] The usual expectation for a simile is for it to present the terms involved – the tenor and vehicle – in such a way that the relations between the two are made clear. But Homeric similes often have a way of lingering in the world of the vehicle, as if the time of the narrative were briefly forgotten and the poem dwells in a different time, if only for just one extra verse. To take a well-known example, when Menelaus is wounded by the arrow, the flow of blood is compared to purple dye: 'As when some Maionian woman or Karian colours ivory with purple, to make it a cheekpiece for horses; it lies away in an inner room, and many a rider longs to have it, but it is laid up to be a king's treasure, two things, to be the beauty of the horse, the pride of the horseman.'[59] The second half of the simile on the fate of the dyed cheekpiece corresponds to nothing in the scene it is supposed to be describing, and escapes into the time of its own narrative. The dyer and the ivory are summoned to illuminate one moment in the narrative, as the blood spreads over Menelaus' skin, but the ivory cheekpiece persists beyond that moment, into an indefinitely extended time of waiting among the king's treasure. A simile that ends when it 'should' – that is, when it has accounted for all the terms being compared between the world of the simile and the main narrative – is easily retrieved into the narrative time that it serves. But similes that are too long, as they often are in the *Iliad*, tend towards escaping this assimilation.

We find another object that bears a contrasting temporality in a simile when Ajax fells the Trojan Simoeisios:

> He dropped then to the ground in the dust, like some black poplar, which in the land, low-lying about a great marsh, grows, smooth trimmed yet with branches growing at the uttermost tree-top: one whom a man, a maker of chariots, fells with the shining iron, to bend it into a wheel for a fine-wrought chariot, and the tree lies hardening by the banks of a river.[60]

While the rest of the simile can be read as a description of the warrior and his fall, the final verse, 'and the tree lies hardening by the banks of the river', extends the time of the simile beyond the time of the narrative, where nothing can correspond to the long duration of the drying trunk beside the running river. Specific correspondences haunt the hardening trunk and the warrior Simoeisios, since, just before the simile, Simoeisios is said to have been named after the river Simoeis because his mother bore him on the river's banks.[61] The potential correspondence between Simoeisios born by the Simoeis and the tree hardening on the riverbanks emphasizes all the more starkly the non-identity of narrative time and the duration of the drying tree.

Vignette and simile thus converge in the case of this minor warrior. In addition to the simile just examined, a brief vignette accompanies the death of Simoeisios, relating the origin of his name: 'Simoeisios, whom once his mother descending from Ida bore beside the banks of Simoeis when she had followed her father and mother to tend the sheepflocks. Therefore they called him Simoeisios; but he could not render again the care of his dear parents; he was short-lived.'[62] The context of parental nurture that accounts for and gives meaning to his name is broken by his death at the hands of Ajax; the name 'Simoeisios' itself remains as a relic of the former meaning-making apparatus. Here, a humanist reading would perhaps highlight the senselessness of the violence that indiscriminately cuts across the fragility of human meaning – the force that makes men into objects, as Simone Weil once wrote – and I retain and presuppose this reading.[63] But the *Iliad* goes beyond the loss of meaning, and we can see how if we keep in mind the operation of suture that turns a formal and inescapable break in meaning-making into a palpable representation. Through the set of correspondences and associations already identified between Simoeisios and the tree, an affinity is established between not just the way they both lie in their stillness, but the excess and the lingering of the simile imparts to the death of Simoeisios some of the meaning and purpose it finds in the tree, felled in order to build a 'fine-wrought [*perikallei*] chariot'. We cannot import the contents of the meaning from the simile to the narrative context; there is obviously no connection between the death of Simoeisios and chariot-making. What is translated across this gap is not the purpose but only a formal purposiveness, the hope that a senseless death now might be redeemed, that is, might turn out to have a purpose or meaning at the site of *kleos*, in the song to come.[64] The link is not through an identity or harmony in content, but through formal difference. Where we have so often pointed out the destructiveness of the logic of *kleos* in terms of its overturning of meaning, the disjunctive connection between vignette and simile in the death of Simoeisios reminds us that *kleos* also has a redemptive side, which is precisely what was expected when Helen projects the meaning of present suffering into a future song.

Before moving onto the final section of this chapter, let us take stock of the argument so far with a brief summary. The overarching notion that joins all the threads here is the form of meaning – the insistent potential for it to change through a time divided by *kleos* – and the chapter is organized as a series of explorations of the different ways in which that formal structure comes to be thematically expressed in various kinds of content. In section one, we saw how the inaccessibility of *kleos* is sutured to specific decisions, principles and attitudes of heroes. Section two took one moment of the process through which meaning changes, the failure of an earlier meaning, and argued that this moment could be represented through objecthood. Within a regime in which the inaccessibility of *kleos* hangs over the understanding of every moment and event, narrative meaning can only be contingent and 'stochastic', and, in this section, we have seen how its precarious nature is staged in the contrasting and contradictory proliferation of what might be called micro-narratives of vignettes and similes.[65]

The way in which difference is extracted from contrasts between proliferating micro-narratives leads to the topic of the next section. In vignettes and similes, the micro-narratives are short and fleeting – hence 'micro' – and produce local contrasts. But there is also a persistent and overarching narrative which is always available for producing difference, and which is privileged as definitive: the final version of *kleos* in the song to come. The final song will put every event in its place, and it has an effect on meaning-making for the heroes even though it is inaccessible to them – this is again a suturing operation in which the formal element of a song to come comes to be represented in the content. In the next section, then, we will read for the way that the division between a precarious present meaning and the definitiveness of *kleos* comes to be expressed thematically in the encounter of Hector and Andromache.

IV. The doom of Troy

Two problems from the meeting of Hector and Andromache in book VI motivate the discussion in this section, one more obvious than the other. The more obvious problem is an apparent contradiction in Hector's vision of the outcome of the Trojan war and its consequences. On the one hand, Hector foresees the defeat and destruction of his city: 'For I know this thing well in my heart, and my mind knows it: there will come a day when sacred Ilion shall perish, and Priam, and the people of Priam of the strong ash spear.'[66] But on the other hand, Hector also prays in apparent contradiction to this gloomy forecast that his son might thrive and make his mother proud – his mother, who in the earlier passage Hector foresees enslaved in an Achaean household:

> Zeus, and you other immortals, grant that this boy, who is my son, may be as I am, pre-eminent among the Trojans, great in strength, as am I, and rule strongly over Ilion; and some day let them say of him: 'He is better by far than his father',

as he comes in from the fighting; and let him kill his enemy and bring home the blooded spoils, and delight the heart of his mother.⁶⁷

While it is of course possible to explain the conflict psychologically – say, Hector's gloomy mood was dispelled by the sight of his son – we will be asking what it can tell us formally. I will argue that the thematic and psychological logic of the scene express an underlying temporal and formal split in how fate is implicitly understood, a split which is expressed thematically as a contrast between the public aspect of the hero and the personal or intimate aspect.⁶⁸ Put simply, the intimate and the personal takes its meaning from a contrast with the finality of *kleos*.

The other problem is less obvious, and may not seem like a problem or even especially odd. I am referring to the fact that Hector almost misses his meeting with Andromache. Recall that, after his visit to the household of Helen and Paris, Hector heads to his own home as the final stop in his brief return to the city. But Andromache is not at home: '[F]or she, with the child, and followed by one fair-robed attendant, had taken her place on the tower in lamentation, and tearful.'⁶⁹ Andromache, as Hector finds out from the housekeeper, 'heard that the Trojans were losing, and great grew the strength of the Achaians. Therefore she has gone in speed to the wall, like a woman gone mad.'⁷⁰ The description of Andromache here, 'like a woman gone mad [*mainomenēi eikuia*]', will be echoed by the description of her as 'like a raving woman [*mainadi isē*]' (XXII. 460) in the context of the eventual death of Hector. Hector has therefore, in book VI, arrived at a reflection of the place of his own death. Hector's presence while living at the house marked by the absence of his death mirrors his absence while dead from that same house in book XXII, marked this time by the false assumption that he was still alive.⁷¹ A strange untimeliness hangs over Andromache's relation to Hector's death: she misses it both times by being too early to mourn him in book VI, and too late in finding out in book XXII.⁷² Hector's presence in the empty house, in book VI, thus constitutes a detour that is strangely without consequence for the course of the narrative while being replete with untimely ironies. Some kind of accounting for this seems necessary, beyond the – merely formal – labelling of its irony.

I will offer an accounting – a not-quite-solution to these not-quite-problems – that ties the two issues together. The contradiction in the fates of Troy presupposed by Hector will be parsed as a thematic expression of a formal distinction. The formal distinction is that between a provisional meaning, still liable to change, and the final meaning projected into future song. This formal distinction comes to be expressed thematically between, first, what is assumed to be fated and to form the public exploits of *klea andrōn*, and second, in the interstices, the level of the personal and intimate. The intimate personal narratives, in my account, retrieve a present meaning from the insistent potential of its failure and overturning, and operate a suturing of difference in a precarious identity. The same distinction informs Hector's detour and his almost missed encounter with Andromache in ways to be seen.

Let us first note that – this will seem a digression – beyond the specific dramatic stagings we have seen in the vignettes and similes, the difference between contexts of meaning – along with the potential for the loss or change of meaning as contexts are lost or replaced – can appear at the level of concepts itself, unattached to the narrative of particular heroes or minor warriors. A succinct example is found in the recurrent notion of divine and mortal names, such as the name of a hill near Ilium: 'This men call the Hill of the Thicket, but the immortal gods have named it the burial mound [*sēma*] of dancing Myrina.'[73] The meaning content of this phenomenon has not been satisfactorily explained, but the significance is in its gesture, in the difference itself established between the human and divine contexts. This particular example of a divine name is especially pertinent for us, because it demonstrates that difference in contexts of meaning can be connected to forms of time. Grethlein begins to go in the direction in which we are aiming when he observes that the burial mound, *sēma*, expresses the loss of memory:

> For men, the marker of Myrine has turned into merely landscape; artefact has become nature. Only the gods, who are endowed with a better memory, are aware of its original significance. The underlying semiotic process is implied in the Greek word σῆμα, which can signify both 'sign' and 'tomb'. For humans, the 'sign' of Myrine's 'tomb' has lost its original significance and has gained a new one.[74]

We can build on Grethlein's hint of the gods' 'better memory'. The name 'Hill of the Thicket', which Grethlein notes is 'merely landscape', draws its meaning from the present; its significance is what can be seen in the here and now. 'The burial mound of dancing Myrina', on the other hand, is the sign of another time, a lost memory. What kind of difference does this gesture towards a divine meaning context stage? The logic of pure difference returns here: we are not given any adequate information about Myrina and thus cannot produce an actual meaning content with which to contrast the human name 'Hill of the Thicket'. All we can say is that a contrasting meaning exists – marked by the vanishingly enigmatic epithet 'dancing' or 'leaping' – and thus what is staged is a virtual or pure difference.

Divine names like 'burial mound of dancing Myrina' are puzzling and inexplicable because being inexplicable is precisely the point.⁷⁵ This is the same logic which follows from the unknowability of *kleos* and the inaccessibility of the song to come into which that *kleos* is projected. Thus, from the perspective of the structure of difference which we have been elaborating, it is insufficient to equate epic with the narration of the glory of heroes, *klea andrōn*, at least in the case of the Homeric poems and in particular the *Iliad*.⁷⁶ The *Iliad* is at once more and less than the *klea andrōn*, because *kleos* is not the poem, but is projected from within the poem into the site of a song to come. The *klea andrōn* fulfil the same role as the divine name, holding open a comparison despite never being present or known, with the goal of making difference appear in or as that opening. We have seen that the present in the *Iliad* is always divided; the *klea andrōn* is what it is divided *from*.

The stipulation that *kleos* be unknowable is a formal structural requirement: it can divide *every* present only if it is a formal element without content. However – and here, we return to Hector in book VI – the function of suture is precisely to turn form into content. How does this work in the context of the problems we posed at the beginning of this section? What Hector stages in the contradictory visions of the fate of Troy is the materialization of a properly contentless *kleos* as a present meaning content; he sutures content to a formal element. Hector puts, in the place of contentless *kleos*, the fatal prediction that 'there will come a day when sacred Ilion shall perish' (VI. 448). The vision of the city's doom shares with *kleos* the property of being the final meaning that overturns the provisional meanings produced along the way. The 'proper' logic of *kleos* says: no matter what an event seems to mean in the present, that meaning is not secure because the final meaning is inscribed in the song to come. In comparison, Hector's 'improper' logic has placed a specific content in place of the unknowability of *kleos*: no matter what we do, the city will fall. Both *kleos* and the city's doom are thus alienated from the hero in the present; the city's doom is alienating not only because of its content – this is the thematic explanation – but also because it borrows this property from the pure difference of *kleos*, the formal element whose position it occupies.

The fact that the city's doom is alienating because of its formal position is not clearly demonstrated here at VI. 448, because the formal explanation overlaps with the thematic one: it is entirely to be expected that Troy's defender should be put off by the thought of Troy's destruction. The difference between the formal and thematic levels is more clearly demonstrated in the verbally identical repetition in the speech of Agamemnon (IV. 163–5). We expect Agamemnon, as the enemy of the Trojans, to be entirely in harmony with the prophecy of the city's doom, but, most strikingly, the city's doom is presented as *contrary* to Agamemnon's wishes. The context is all-important; this speech occurs as Agamemnon looks over the injured Menelaus, who, he thinks, has been fatally wounded:

> For I know this thing well in my heart, and my mind knows it. There will come a day when sacred Ilion shall perish, and Priam, and the people of Priam of the strong ash spear, and Zeus son of Kronos who sits on high, the sky-dwelling, himself shall shake the gloom of his aegis over all of them in anger for this deception. All this shall not go unaccomplished. But I shall suffer a terrible grief for you, Menelaos, if you die and fill out the destiny of your lifetime.[77]

The doom of Troy, which in terms of thematic content should be close to Agamemnon's heart, is presented instead as an external and inevitable event, in contrast to what Agamemnon really cares about, which is the death of his brother. Hence we see that the doom of Troy occupies the position of the *other* meaning, one with a permanence and inevitability against which the ephemerality of a present meaning is contrasted and, through the contrast, gains its force.[78]

Hector's contradictory visions of the fate of the city thus stage or give content to a formal distinction. The level of *kleos* is staged as the fated doom of Troy, against which his present hopes for his son stand out all the more brightly. This formal distinction, when staged, comes to be represented by a thematic distinction: in this case, the contrast between the public, heroic aspect of the warrior and the private intimacy of the family. But we should not lose sight of the formal bases of the thematic contents, not least because thematic contents can be contradictory while preserving the formal bases. Let us consider the status, for instance, of Hector's prayer for his son. Thematically, it is an expression of hope, but what does it express formally? We can answer this question by noting that the prayer is contrasted with the doom of Troy, and then ask what else is contrasted with that doom. Parallel to Agamemnon's speech over Menelaus, the public and heroic aspect of the fall of Troy is set against an intimate and personal concern: 'But it is not so much the pain to come of the Trojans that troubles me, not even of Priam the king nor Hekabe, not the thought of my brothers who in their numbers and valour shall drop in the dust under the hands of men who hate them, as troubles me the thought of you.'[79] Hector then proceeds to paint an image of Andromache enslaved. We can observe here, first, the contrast of the public and the personal, and second, more interestingly, the thematic contrast between the image of Andromache enslaved and the prayer for his son. The joyful vision of the prayer strikes a strong thematic contrast with the enslavement of Andromache on the level of content, but the two line up on the same side of the formal contrast with the doom of Troy.

What, then, do the thematically contrasting images of Andromache's enslavement and the thriving of Astyanax have *in common*, which allows them both to stand out against the doom of Troy? It is a commonality on the level of form, more specifically, the form of time involved in each case. The doom of Troy, being the 'improper' materialization of *kleos*, expresses the final image fixed at the end of time – all our strivings will, in the end, amount to the realization of the fall of the city. In contrast, both Hector's vision of the enslavement of Andromache and his prayer for Astyanax express the openness of possibilities within time. In the prayer for Astyanax, what Hector expresses is that *even though* and *in contrast to* the closed finality of the city's already fixed doom, there is, in the present, the space for hope, an openness onto possibilities already foreclosed at the level of *klea andrōn* – showing again that the *Iliad* is not reducible to *klea andrōn*. But in the case of the prayer, the thematic content of hope is still not well distinguished from the formal property of openness. The vision of Andromache's enslavement, on the other hand, allows us to disentangle the two. On the level of content, the enslavement of Andromache – along with the death of Hector himself and everything else it entails – is the closure of possibilities and the loss of hope. But why then does Hector describe this awful vision? We do not feel that Hector is being cruel. Instead, what is important here is the formal level: Hector contrasts the closed finality of the meaning of Troy's doom at the end of time with the provisional, intra-temporal act of imagining a possible future itself. What Hector says to Andromache is that the meaning that matters is not the final doom of the city, but his own, precariously imagined meaning that exists within the present.

Two notes will clarify the argument here. First, we should disentangle the associations between *kleos*, fate and the properties of fixity and openness. The immediately preceding discussion of fate as 'final' and 'fixed' ought to have provoked some anxiety, given that we have associated fate with *kleos*, and *kleos*, according to previous analyses, ought to be open. The openness of *kleos*, let us recall, is precisely what made possible the generalized division of the present: *kleos* is open because it is unknowable, which means that because we do not know *which* moments will turn out to have been significant, *every* moment becomes divided between its present and an unknown future revision.[80] The question therefore arises: why is *kleos* open but the doom of Troy, which occupies the place of *kleos*, closed? The answer lies precisely in the suturing operation that enabled a specific content, the doom of Troy, to occupy the place of *kleos*. The aim and point of the suture *is* the substitution of a thematic content for a formal element. Hence, where *kleos* is projected as final, in the song to come, and as open – the result of its unknowability – the doom of Troy has inherited the finality of *kleos* but, of necessity, cannot inherit its openness, since it has to have a known content in order to exist. This is precisely why suture is 'improper', a short circuit rather than 'normal' operation. As a result and at the same time, the openness of *kleos* becomes displaced – to those images which contrast with the doom of Troy: Andromache's enslavement and the prayer for Astyanax.

For the second note, to briefly take a point of orientation from further afield, this openness can be compared with what Peter Szondi, writing about Walter Benjamin's *Berlin Childhood*, calls 'hope in the past':

> [T]he future is precisely what Benjamin seeks in the past. Almost every place that his memory wishes to rediscover bears 'the features of what is to come', as he puts it at one point in *A Berlin Childhood* ... Benjamin listens for the first notes of a future which has meanwhile become the past. Unlike Proust, Benjamin does not want to free himself from temporality; he does not wish to see things in their ahistorical essence. He strives instead for historical experience and knowledge. Nevertheless, he is sent back into the past, a past, however, which is open, not completed, and which promises the future. Benjamin's tense is not the perfect, but the future perfect in the fullness of its paradox: being future and past at the same time.[81]

Before making the comparison, it is necessary to note an adjustment that needs to be made: with the suturing operation that attaches a known content such as the doom of Troy to the place of *kleos*, fixedness in the Homeric poems appears in the future from the perspective of the heroes, and the contrasting openness appears in the heroic present. In the context of Benjamin's *Berlin Childhood*, however, the point of fixedness is in the writer's present, while openness appears in his past. What this means is that the temporal labels are shifted between the two contexts, so that, for Benjamin, openness is sought in the past in contrast to the fixity of the present – 'Benjamin listens for the first notes of a future which has meanwhile become the past' – while, in the Homeric suture, openness is sought in the heroic present in the despite of the fixity of the future. With this shift, we can see that both Benjamin and Hector oppose the knowledge – in Hector's case, assumed knowledge – of an already fixed outcome to the open possibilities that still existed before what is fixed had become fixed.

But what is the point of this operation? If openness is sought in the past or the present, what is being sought *in* that openness? The response to these questions can be worked out more explicitly in the case of Benjamin than in the Homeric context, because we are much better informed about Benjamin's historical situation. Here is Szondi again discussing what Benjamin sought in an open past, this time in the context of technology:

> Benjamin's conception of technology is utopian rather than critical. What he criticizes is the betrayal of utopia that was committed in realizing the idea of technology. Accordingly, he directs his attention not to the possibilities latent in technology – which today are largely destructive – but to the time when technology first represented a possibility, when its true idea still lay on the horizon of the future ... The way to the origin is, to be sure, a way backwards, but backwards into a future, which, although it has gone by in the meantime and its idea has been perverted, still holds more promise than the current image of the future.[82]

The backward glance is in fact oriented forwards, into the future. It seeks in the foreclosed possibilities of an open past the resources for rewriting what appears irrevocably fixed in the present; this is 'hope in the past'. In the Homeric context, it is the rewriting, rereading, or re-vision produced in the vignettes. Once again, we must distinguish the formal and thematic levels. On the thematic level, the death of Skamandrios the hunter is a closure of the possibilities of his life. But on the formal level, it expresses the openness of *kleos* in the overturning of the already established meanings. What is at stake for the Homeric poem that it stages, through such a variety of different figures, this openness in opposition to fixity?[83] A definitive response is perhaps impossible, for historical reasons, and because the demand for definitiveness is precisely what is overturned.[84]

Let us return to Hector and Andromache. In their meeting, a formal opposition between fixity and openness underlies a thematic opposition between the public heroic sphere and the personal. Personal and intimate meanings take place in the shadow of the fixed destination of the city's doom. Both Hector and Andromache carve out the space for intimacy through repurposing epic and heroic language and themes. Does this allow us to provide some form of account for the second of the problems that introduced this section, the oddly inconsequential yet potently resonant detour in Hector's journey that sees him fail to find Andromache at home? I suggest that what the detour emphasizes is precisely the boundary of the public or heroic and the personal, and that it is a *coup de théâtre* in which we are set up to expect a failure of meaning but find instead an affirmation of meaning in all its precarity.

The detour initially sets us up to expect, once again, the overriding of intimate and personal stories: the house in which Hector and Andromache miss each other is resonant with correspondences between the living Hector missing Andromache because she feared his death, and Andromache drawing a bath for the dead Hector, thinking he was still alive. With these resonances, it seems that what is being staged is a scene in which the fixed destiny of the *klea andrōn* would again foreclose the possibility of intimate, personal meanings – 'again', because we have so often seen the overturning of personal meaning, as in the vignettes of the lives of minor warriors, in which precarious meaning is swept away, leaving only the echoes of what might have been but never coming to pass.

And indeed, by the end of the detour, Hector leaves his house, as if to return to the battle without seeing Andromache: 'Hektor hastened from his home backward by the way he had come through the well-laid streets. So as he had come to the gates on his way through the great city, the Skaian gates, whereby he would [*emelle*] issue into the plain …'[85] If we put aside our knowledge that Hector and Andromache will in fact meet, there is nothing in the passage to indicate that the meeting will happen. The key word is the one that I have given in Greek here, *emelle*, 'he was going to, he was about to'. The imperfect form of *mellō* frequently indicates precisely the boundary that separates the fixity of what is fated from all the other possibilities that could have taken place, but which will turn out to have been foreclosed.[86] Hector, then, is on the cusp of leaving the city, re-entering the public and heroic world of death and battle from the ambiguous, resonant space of his empty house. It is at this point, at the fateful Skaean gates where he would face Achilles, that Andromache meets Hector: 'So / as he had come to the gates on his way through the great city, / the Skaian gates, whereby he would [*emelle*] issue into the plain, there / at last his own generous wife came running to meet him, Andromache …'[87] Against my usual practice, I have indicated Lattimore's verse breaks for a couple of observations. First, he preserves the prominent verse-initial position of 'the Skaian gates'. Second, he adds, with no basis in the Greek, the emphatic and again verse-initial 'at last' to bring out the appearance of Andromache at this particular point, as if against expectation. The translator, at least, feels the significance of the moment and wishes to underline it, and I would argue that his instincts are justified and reflect the overturning of our expectations.[88] Instead of the expected sharpening of a resonant but missed encounter, the meeting of Hector and Andromache is restored to us, only a little delayed after the failed detour to the empty house. The detour is thus essential: it is only through the empty detour that the encounter can be perceived as restored, since otherwise it would never have been missed.

The meeting of Hector and Andromache takes place, therefore, on two boundaries: that between the interior spaces of the city and the plains of battle and the *klea andrōn* outside, and that between the city's certain doom and the intimate meanings wrested in its despite. The thematic contrasts produced in the encounter – between men and women, war and peace, patriotism and family – are undergirded by the structured forms of time that opposes openness to fixity. We have seen how this opposition is derived, via the suturing of a thematic content to the logic of *kleos*, from a temporal structure that informs so many other facets of the poem and, beyond that, of its scholarship. All the forms of suture we have discussed in this chapter thus perform, in one capacity or another, what Hector and Andromache perform in their encounter on the wall, the redemption of meaning from and through the time of its overturning.

5

Three Syntheses of Time

This final chapter serves two connected purposes. The first is a consequence of the way the discussions in the previous chapters have been carried out. These previous discussions have been anchored in the themes and preoccupations of the Homeric poems and their scholarship, and have as a consequence been structured by the pre-existing landscape of those themes. On the one hand, this way of following existing contours has the virtue of showing the roots of our interests within the Homeric poems and the scholarly discourse. For instance, in the first chapter, which the previous sentence describes particularly aptly, we allowed the problem of difference and interruption to emerge from a mapping of Foley's work on continuity and identity; the opposing terms confronted each other in the interpretation of the *sēma*. On the other hand, constrained by the form of organization of existing discourses, we have not been able to present the novel concepts and figures – *kleos* as difference, song to come, generalized division, suture – introduced throughout this procedure in the structure which makes as clear as possible their own development and justification. One of the goals of this chapter, then, is to remedy this by putting these concepts and figures back into circulation and reconstituting them as moments of an ordered series in which they maintain more clearly their positions and relations.

The form used to structure our discussions in this chapter is Deleuze's philosophy of time, and tracing the connections between Deleuze and the Homeric themes we have been preoccupied with is the second goal of this chapter. Deleuze and other explicit theoretical considerations – in particular, those related to structuralism – have so far led a subterranean existence in the notes of earlier discussions; this was again to allow the Homeric discourses to take centre stage, but in this chapter I will address them directly. In particular, the aspect of Deleuze's work to be added to the existing configuration of poetry and scholarship is the account of three syntheses of time, found for the most part in *Difference and Repetition*, influenced as well by the later conceptions of the two-volume work on *Cinema*.[1] In the three syntheses, Deleuze presents three interrelated forms of time, each centred on the present, the past and the future, respectively, although these are not the present, past and future of a chronological conception of time and will have to be further specified. Particularly important for our purposes is the fact that the three syntheses are not discrete and disconnected, but are mutually related and motivated, each providing the impulse for transitioning to another. What Deleuze's syntheses bring to our discussion is therefore not a static framework into which to fit Homeric concepts, but a dynamic one that connects different moments and establishes articulations between and within them. We will see how these movements between different forms of time are expressed in the Homeric poems and scholarship.

In reordering and rearticulating the concepts and figures we have previously derived, this chapter serves the function of a conclusion, although we will not only be retreading the same ground in a new order. We will begin by describing Deleuze's first synthesis, that of a present that never passes, and show how a variety of approaches in Homeric scholarship from Auerbach and Parry to Norman Austin exemplify the time of this living present. The possibility for a poet's intention to exceed what is possible to say in traditional language introduces a break in the living present, and leads to the second synthesis of a pure past. The pure past is a form of time that retrieves all events into an absolute memory, and is represented in the Homeric context by Nagy's conception of tradition and by various interpretations of the 'plan of Zeus', *Dios boulē*. The unifying force of the plan of Zeus, as the authority that gives sense to all possible events, mirrors the function of *kleos*, which is also a site in which all events gain their meanings. Does the availability of the concepts of the plan of Zeus and of *kleos* then imply that the meanings of all events in the *Iliad* are fixed and secure? We will see that the *Iliad* undermines such fixity by staging resistance to the plan of Zeus, offering alternatives to the canonical plot, and presenting the paradoxical nature of *kleos* in a series of figures from the poet to the muse and the sirens. The refusal of fixity expresses Deleuze's third synthesis, in which time comes to be 'out of joint'.

I. The living present

Deleuze develops a theory of time as a series of three syntheses which constitute the transcendental conditions for ordinary understandings of time.[2] The first of the syntheses is focused on the present, but it is not defined, as it would be in a chronological conception of time, as the moment of the now which passes indifferently along a linear timeline from the past to the future, the latter two conceived as a former present or a present to come. Instead, the present of the first synthesis is specifically understood under the labels 'habit' or 'living present'. In contrast to an instantaneous 'now', the living present or present of habit includes the immediate past in the form of retention and the immediate future as expectation or anticipation. Deleuze refers to Hume's example of the repetition of a sequence AB, AB, AB ... Through the repetition of the sequence AB, we come to expect B when we perceive A. We 'contract' the series of repetitions in order to produce the present of the first synthesis:

> A succession of instants does not constitute time any more than it causes it to disappear; it indicates only its constantly aborted moment of birth. Time is constituted only in the originary synthesis which operates on the repetition of instants. This synthesis contracts the successive independent instants into one another, thereby constituting the lived, or living, present.[3]

The instants which are contracted are not, of course, limited to abstract sequences like AB, but includes everything that affects an organism or thing – the first synthesis does not presuppose a human subject, but is a passive synthesis independent of any active consciousness: 'What we call wheat is a contraction of the earth and humidity, and this contraction is both a contemplation and the auto-satisfaction of that contemplation.'[4] In this first synthesis, prior to the constitution of subjectivity, each part of an organism performs its own contractions: 'At the organic level, each organ has its present or its own duration, so that the differences here are not only from one species to another: several presents, durations or relative *speeds* coexist in the same organism.'[5]

How does the living present of habit interact with what we have previously said about the present in the Homeric context? Let us take up again the discussion of Parry's conception of traditional oral poetry from chapter three, and add to it further observations from Lynn-George on the primacy of the present in Auerbach and Austin. Deleuze's first synthesis of habit will allow us to relate these different conceptions of the present.

To begin with Parry's system, we had concluded that what was established there was an instantaneity of meaning. Because traditional language was conceived as a 'transparent vehicle' for meaning, with traditional phraseology directly connected to a thought existing prior to and outside of language, meaning in Parry's conception of oral tradition was instantaneous and unseparated by any logical time.⁶ On this basis, we were also able to connect Parry's system with that of Foley; both conceptions of oral tradition entailed the instantaneity of meaning and only differed as to how we, as modern audiences, might be able to gain access to that meaning.⁷ The oral tradition therefore constitutes one single moment of instantaneous meaning even as it spans centuries of historical time. This is the first form of the present for which we need to provide an account.

The other forms of the present to be addressed here are the present of Auerbach and that of Austin. We will refer to Lynn-George's account of them, in which he argues that both Auerbach and Austin valorize the present at the expense of time. If there is a deficiency in Lynn-George's account, it is that he may have been overly hasty in identifying the two, though we will be able to build upon and supplement his arguments to finally support his basic thesis that Auerbach and Austin reflect the same conception of the present. Taking first Auerbach's essay on Odysseus' scar, we have already briefly discussed the way in which Homeric narration is there conceived as an unruffled present. It is a specifically *narrative* or *formal* present – a present of the *act or form of narration* – because it overrides any temporal disjunction in the *content* of narration. The episode that Auerbach places centre stage – the jump from Odysseus' foot washing into the past of the boar hunt, and further, into the past of his grandfather Autolycus' naming of the newborn Odysseus (xix. 386–466) – is chosen precisely because of the violence of the temporal dislocations in narrated content which, for Auerbach at least, the strength of the present of narrative form is able to absorb and cover over. No matter the *what* and the *when* of the content, the narration remains in whichever present happens to be the subject of the tale. When we discussed this previously in chapter three, we emphasized that Auerbach's insistence on the narrative present is in fact a denial of any possible split in the present that might be occasioned by the simultaneous awareness of a memory of the past or an anticipation of the future. Lynn-George writes:

> Here the transitory and destructive dimension of time is total. Every present is extinguished anew by an oblivion which obliterates entirely, the former scene forgotten at once in the foregrounding of that which follows: 'The broadly narrated ... story of the hunt, with all its elegance and self-sufficiency, ... seeks to win the reader over wholly to itself as long as he is hearing it, to make him forget what had just taken place during the foot-washing.'⁸

In the case of Austin, the text under discussion is his essay on digressions in the *Iliad*.⁹ While Austin's essay explicitly criticizes Auerbach, Lynn-George argues that both of them, in fact, drive towards the same goal of 'the celebration of a pure present'.[10] Like Auerbach on Odysseus' scar, Austin's is an argument that seeks the nature of Homeric narration, this time via an analysis of digressions. Austin reacts against interpretations which see the digressions as disconnected from the narrative contexts in which they occur, even when the lack of connection is seen as a positive aspect of oral poetry:

> Once condemned by the Analysts as irrelevant insertions added by later poets to satisfy personal whims or demands for local tradition, the digressions have become the hallmark of the oral style, the example *par excellence* of the poet's *amor pleni*. But this modern view has not so much acquitted Homer of the charge of irrelevance or incongruity as it has accepted irrelevancy as a characteristic of the oral style and thereby made of it something close to a virtue.[11]

In contrast to readings in which digressions are irrelevant to their narrative contexts, Austin argues that they derive from and perform meaningful work within them:

> The digressions, whether drawn from distant myths or family history or from the beginning of the Trojan War, *are securely anchored to the present by their pragmatic intent*. They reflect a pervasive need to justify an action in the present by an appeal to a past precedent. They go, however, far beyond simple justification of a present course of action. They are cogent examples of that mode of thinking which, as van Groningen has remarked, uses the past occurrence not merely as an edifying example but as the positive proof of a present possibility.[12]

For Austin, the digressions are a form of 'dramatic amplification' tied to the present of narration. Even as the digression tells stories of the distant past, they have a present existence and express the possibilities of the present: '[The Iliadic digression] brings time to a complete standstill and locks our attention unremittingly on the celebration of the present moment.'[13]

The question before us concerns the different forms of the present represented in Parry, Auerbach and Austin: given the differences in the terms and the structures of the three versions of the present, is it legitimate to group them together at all? Or, put more positively, is it possible to see Parry, Auerbach and Austin as expressing different aspects of the same present? Lynn-George describes the contrast between the latter two conceptions:

> The fixity of Austin's schema refuses the departure to another world and another time which is a fundamental and recurring feature of the epic narrative. In the unremitting focus locked on the here and now he eliminates the force of the

duration and the distance in a divergence which moves apart from, while remaining a part of, the present: something different and distant in the present while at the same time separate from it. If Austin tends to abolish the movement apart, Auerbach attempts to render it absolute, such that any connection is snapped, isolating an autonomous and self-sufficient world without relation. For both, the moment is never multiple or heterogeneous but remains monolithic.[14]

Lynn-George's conclusion that the moment in both Auerbach and Austin is monolithically unified contrasts clearly with our earlier demonstration of the generalized splitting of the moment, but the fact remains that, by Lynn-George's own analysis, Auerbach and Austin offer structurally different versions of the present. In what sense can these monolithic *moments* be considered *presents*?

Let us fill out and augment Lynn-George's argument: Auerbach and Austin, as well as Parry, can be connected through the living present of habit in Deleuze's first synthesis. We will see that Austin and Parry present two aspects of the living present, while the connection with Auerbach will emerge more clearly in the transition from the first synthesis to the second. First, Parry's conceptualization of oral traditional language describes precisely the contraction of instants in the synthesis of the living present. Parry contracts formulas as repeated identical instants as, in Deleuze's example, Hume contracts repeated occurrences of AB. The product of this contractile synthesis is the oral poetic tradition itself, which is a living present. The existence of the oral tradition as a living present explains the instantaneity of meaning which we have repeatedly noted: in Parry as in Foley, a meaning is directly connected with its linguistic expression without the loss of time because the whole system of oral poetry has already been conceived as a present. The unity and self-sufficiency of the living present is preserved in Nagy's conception as the subjective side of his contrast between the subjectivity of what the tradition knows about itself and the objectivity of an external observer. For Nagy, the tradition remains 'ancient and immutable' from within its own subjective perspective, even though it may be 'contemporary and ever-changing' for an external observer.[15] The tradition, as conceived here, does not appear to itself to be changing because any elements which have changed – for an external observer – do not remain and nor do any memories of them remain: they are no longer included in the sequence of instants which are contracted, and therefore fall out of the living present that is synthesized. Any element which does remain remains *as eternal*, where 'eternal' does not mean 'for all time' but rather 'as part of a present that does not pass', since the living present knows no past or future that it has not already contracted within its own present.

We can clarify this last point by way of reintroducing Austin into the discussion. It is of course the case that, chronologically, a sequence AB, AB, AB must include instances which occur earlier and instances which occur later, that is, some instances in the relative chronological past and others in the relative chronological future. But the contractile function of the first synthesis makes these relative chronological pasts and futures into part of the living present, as retention and expectation. The living present thus includes what would be called, from a chronological perspective, pasts and futures, but only insofar as they relate to and take their meaning as part of the living present itself. This aspect of the living present is expressed in Austin as the notion that Iliadic digressions are 'are securely anchored to the present by their pragmatic intent'.[16] What Austin takes pains to show is that, despite the fact that digressions may narrate events which occurred far in the chronological past, they remain relevant and active as 'positive proof of a present possibility'.[17] In other words, the chronologically past events of the digressions are retained as part of the living present, for the living present.[18]

Let us now bring Auerbach into the same conception of the living present. The immutability of the tradition's subjective perspective depends upon a choice or a selection of which elements to include in the sequence of instants to be contracted. Auerbach's conception of Homeric narration is one that asks readers or audiences to be extremely selective in what they contract. If for Auerbach, as Lynn-George observes, 'every present is extinguished anew by an oblivion which obliterates entirely, the former scene forgotten at once in the foregrounding of that which follows', this is by no means inevitable but rather the result of a choice.[19] The scene of the foot washing is obliterated by the subsequent story of the scar only because Auerbach's Homer is one that asks us not to include the former in the sequence of instants that we contract. Or, to put the issue in a way that is fairer to Auerbach's argument, what is at stake in his choice of the episode of Odysseus' scar is not an arbitrary request that we do not contract the foot washing with the story of the scar notion, but rather that we *cannot* contract them due to the abrupt nature of the transition and the great distance of time between them. Indeed, even in Deleuze's example from Hume, the sequence AB, AB, AB is contracted precisely because there is something repeated in them, an identity or a similarity among the elements. Auerbach, then, is arguing that there is insufficient similarity or relation between the two scenes, connected by the mere mention of the scar that, for him, should not have been enough to motivate such a long digression.[20] What is important for us in this argument is not whether or not Auerbach is justified in asserting that no connection is possible – we might very well assent to his sense of the violence of the break. Instead, what is significant is the fact that, for Auerbach, there is no connection possible outside of the contraction of the living present. This is the force of Lynn-George's observation that, in Auerbach as in Austin, 'the moment is never multiple or heterogeneous but remains monolithic'.[21] Neither conceives of a time that is not a homogeneous living present.

In connecting oral theory, Auerbach and Austin, Deleuze's first synthesis allows us not only to see them as expressions of a particular conception of the living present, but also to perceive their limitations and thereby help us transition to other conceptions of time. Why is it necessary to think time beyond the living present? Let us first follow Deleuze's argument and then turn to the Homeric context. The limitation of the first synthesis arises when we try to understand the passing of time. Since the contents of what the living present contracts is finite, the living present also changes or passes: one living present now, another in another moment. While we can say that the living present passes and one living present succeeds another, we cannot understand this change *from within* the living present, because the present passes only 'to the benefit of *another* present' and 'does not account for its own passing':[22]

> It is therefore necessary to explain the passing of time. The reason for the change is not in the present, which aspires only to continue. We never get to the past, still less to the future, so long as we make the present continue: what we call past and future (retention and anticipation) is only incorporated within a larger present that excludes any difference in kind.[23]

To be sure, the living present, as a duration, includes a past and a future, but only as the past and future of the present. We can recognize here the exact parallel of the internal half of Nagy's division between the internal and external perspectives on tradition: from within the tradition, all is eternal and a perpetual present, even when the tradition tells of the past.

Is there anything, within the Homeric context, that breaks out of the living present? Let us reconsider the status of traditional language in oral theory. Is traditional language one of the elements contracted into a perpetual present? Oral theory would like to answer that it is: the meaning of a traditional linguistic element ought to be immediately clear and the traditional resonances of a formulaic phrase must be directly present, without passing through the past of a remembered prior text or previous usages.[24] A challenge to this position arises from the possibility that traditional language might restrict what a poet could say.[25] What would it mean for the synthesis of the living present if there could be a difference between the poet's present intention and the possibilities afforded by traditional language? Traditional language would no longer appear as one of the present elements to be contracted. Instead of the harmonious presentation of traditional meanings, the oral poem would be divided by the gap between what the traditional language of the poet says and what the poet means.

We can reframe this gap in terms of Austin's embodiment of the living present. Austin wished to see apparently digressive elements as instead having an intimate connection to the present narrative context, thus becoming part of that present. For instance, his example of the description of the boar's tusk helmet in book x:

> The helmet is not merely a curiosity fossilized in the poet's repertoire. Its circuitous line of descent is significant. Autolykos had gained it by devious means … The desperate situation here calls not for heroic gestures but for nocturnal skulduggery. The boar's tusk helmet in its history and its appearance thus reflects the urgency of the crisis and the character of its wearer, who can adapt himself to non-heroic behavior when heroic strategies prove futile.[26]

In presenting the meaning of the helmet for Odysseus' situation, Austin argues for a continuity between the past of the helmet and the now of the narrative. The past of the helmet is therefore revealed to be only a relative past, in the sense of a past that could be contracted into the living present and become part of the present. If, on the other hand, the helmet *were* 'a curiosity fossilized in the poet's repertoire', then it would not be contractible into the living present and would thus leave a gap mirroring the one that would arise between the poet's intention and the resources of his traditional language.

Nagy's solution to this problem closes the gap between language and intention, but at a price. As we saw in chapter three, Nagy eliminates the possibility of any discrepancy between the poet's intention and traditional language: 'To my mind there is no question, then, about the poet's freedom to say accurately what he means. What he means, however, is strictly regulated by tradition. The poet has no intention of saying anything untraditional.'[27] We have already discussed the results of this argument, that it re-establishes the self-identity of the tradition and removes difference. Nothing new can come into existence within the tradition because even the new is already traditional: 'Granted, to the extent that the performer controls or "owns" the performance in conjunction with the audience, the opportunity for innovation is there. Such innovation, however, takes place within the tradition, not beyond it.'[28] This is not an empirical observation about innovations that did happen, but rather a transcendental argument in which every innovation is always already recuperated into tradition, every difference turned into the realization of pre-existing possibility.

With this radical position, Nagy has indeed saved the homogeneity of traditional poetry, but the present has been lost. Every potential – even the potential for the new – has now been retrojected into the past. Nor is this the relative past of retention in the living present, but rather an absolute past that maintains the same relation to every possible present.[29] The way in which everything that seems to be new is instead reanalysed as always already existing should remind us of the way Agamemnon reinterprets his oath as always having meant death instead of peace.[30] With these figures, we have left the first synthesis and realize the need for another form of time.

II. The pure past

To account for the passing or succession of the present, something more fundamental than the living present of the first synthesis must be thought: '[T]*here must be another time in which the first synthesis of time can occur.*'[31] This other time within which the first synthesis of the living present can happen is the product of a second synthesis, that of an absolute or pure past or, as Deleuze also calls it, a transcendental memory. The sequence of the first two syntheses thus runs from present to past, and from habit to memory. How can the present pass and become past? 'So long as we conceive time as a passing of instants, then we are condemned to an eternal present in which no instant is different from any other. At the very least, the phenomenon of passing requires that one instant be distinguished from another so that one might know that a present has passed.'[32] The passing of the present thus requires a time that is different from the relative past of retention within the living present.

It is crucial to emphasize that the pure past is not produced by the passing of the present, since the present cannot pass without the past:

> No present would ever pass were it not past 'at the same time' as it is present; no past would ever be constituted unless it were first constituted 'at the same time' as the present. This is the first paradox: the contemporaneity of the past with the present that it *was*. It gives us the reason for the passing of the present. Every present passes, in favour of a new present, because the past is contemporaneous with itself as present.[33]

The pure past is a condition for and not a result of the passing of the present, in the sense that the living present cannot cease being present since the contraction of a sequence of instants into the present is all it can do. We can contrast the requirements of a pure past with Austin's interpretation of Homeric narrative. Austin's Homer produces a living present and not a pure past because, no matter how distant the past stories told in digressions happen to be, they are still considered part of the present context in which they are told – they are contracted into the living present of narration. Auerbach, too, maintains the unity of the living present, but from the other direction, by disallowing the relation between present and past events and making the currently narrated time the only time. Homeric narration thus appears as a frame which does not change even as its contents change, continually designating those contents as present. The present in Austin and Auerbach is perpetual because it cannot pass. In order for the present to pass, there must already be a past against which the present can be seen to pass. There is no such past available in the conceptions of Austin and Auerbach. It is this past that is called pure, because it 'never *was* present, since it was not formed "after"'.[34]

The notion of the pure past strikes us as paradoxical, since it goes against all of our usual intuitions about the past being the state of something that used to be present, a former present. And yet it is what is at work in Nagy's stipulation that everything that occurs in traditional poetry is already traditional. With Nagy, we can see that the past in which the tradition of traditional poetry is supposed to be located cannot exist as any actual moment in the past: to the extent that traditional poetry is traditional, no matter how far back in history we situate ourselves, the tradition which recuperates all innovation would still appear in the past. Hence, the tradition is found in no actual or empirical past, but in a pure past that has never been present.

We might ask here whether the notion of a pure past is in fact part of the Homeric tradition, or if it is rather an aspect imported through our modernity. After all, the notion that tradition is never contemporary seems suspiciously similar to Saussure's proposition that 'language always appears as a heritage of the preceding period'.[35] Setting aside for now the problematic of deciding which notions are ancient and which are modern in the process of reception – see the brief discussion on 'deep classics' in the introduction – we can demonstrate that the pure past is an essential aspect of the Homeric poems. We have already touched upon this at the end of the previous section, in connection with Nagy, in noting the parallel with Agamemnon's understanding that his oath always already meant death for Menelaus. But as we have already analysed this figure in detail in chapter two, let us move onto another aspect of Homeric narration, its self-representation.[36]

The fact that Homeric narration represents its own activity of narration is obvious, not only in the explicit intrusions of the voice of the poet such as the invocations of the muse, but also in the depictions of poetic performances that we find in an Achilles or a Demodocus.[37] There are, in addition, more subtle reminders of the narratedness of narration in, for instance, the occasional apostrophe of a hero addressed in the second person, or, even more fundamentally, the implications of a description like *nēpios* for the difference in knowledge between the heroes and the poet.[38] We need not linger on the specific interpretation of these passages, but instead consider the question of what the fact of self-representation as such means for Homeric temporality. What is the connection between self-representation and the pure past? One of the arguments Deleuze uses in demonstrating the necessity of a pure past for the passing of the present is based on an analysis of the representation of a former present in memory.[39] Deleuze asks: what are the conditions for a past moment to be recalled in the present?

> Now the former present cannot be represented in the present one without the present one itself being represented in that representation. *It is of the essence of representation not only to represent something but to represent its own representativity.* The present and former presents are not, therefore, like two successive instants on the line of time; rather, the present one necessarily contains an extra dimension in which it represents the former and also represents itself. The present present is treated not as the future object of a memory but as that which reflects itself at the same time as it forms the memory of the former present.[40]

The present cannot represent a past moment or former present without also representing its own present representational activity, otherwise it would not be possible to tell which representation is the past, *represented* one, and which is the present, *representing* one. As a result, the present present and the former present in this activity of representation have fundamentally different structures. The former, represented present appears only once as represented, while the present, representing present appears twice: once in its activity of representing the former present, and a second time as represented in this activity. But if the present present must be *represented* as representing, what is doing this latter *representing*? There would be an infinite regress – every act of representation is represented, which must itself be represented, and so on – unless we posit an absolutely prior site of memory that can contain all the presents:

> As a result, the active synthesis of memory may be regarded as the principle of representation under this double aspect: reproduction of the former present *and*

reflection of the present present ... The whole problem is: with respect to what? It is with respect to the pure element of the past, understood as the past in general, as an *a priori* past, that a given former present is reproducible and the present present is able to reflect itself. Far from being derived from the present or from representation, the past is presupposed by every representation.[41]

The present is thus necessarily split in representation – necessarily, because representation itself cannot occur without presupposing the pure past that accompanies every present. Hence an initial answer to the question of whether the pure past is an aspect of Homeric poetics: yes, because the Homeric poems' self-representation as representing already presupposes the pure past.

This first demonstration of the pure past as part of the activity of representation is highly formal and abstract, even as this activity is often conspicuous in Homer. Let us therefore make the Homeric version of the pure past more concrete through further connections with the central concept of *kleos*. There has been much discussion of *kleos* that closely approaches a reading of *kleos*-as-pure-past, but it has taken place in the form of various interpretations of 'the will of Zeus'. As we saw in earlier chapters, *kleos* is that which accompanies and splits every present in the Homeric poems. We do not need to repeat those discussions, but will instead, first, indicate that *kleos* finds its place here as the expression within the Homeric poems of the pure past within the broader structure of a Deleuzian philosophy of time, and second, examine how interpretations of 'the will of Zeus' can be read as different approaches to the pure-past function of *kleos*. While *kleos* is in the past relative to the poet, it is in the future relative to the heroes, but this discrepancy does not worry us in calling it the expression of the pure past because the pure past is not a chronological past, but an a priori past.[42] We already have most of the demonstration needed for the logic of an a priori past in the discussion of Nagy's conception of tradition earlier. There, we observed that tradition expresses a pure past insofar as it always appears as further in the past than any arbitrary chronological moment. We only need to add that, despite being purely past in this way, it also applies forward, into any arbitrary chronological future, not so much in the sense that the logic of tradition will always exist in the future, but that the whole function of this concept of tradition is to take the innovation or novelty which may arise in any future time and resituate it within the past of tradition. This logic also applies to that *kleos* which is in the relative future of the heroes: no new or unforeseen event escapes the fate of always already belonging to *kleos*.[43]

When *kleos* is conceived in this way as a fixed fate, destiny or plan that orders mythological narrative, it converges with the plan or will of Zeus, the *Dios boulē* of the *Iliad*'s proem. The plan of Zeus is worth considering here because it allows us to see how the notion of the pure past interacts with the activity of interpretation. In particular, we will see how two different ways of interpreting the plan of Zeus respond to the pure past, by emphasizing its formal aspect or by suturing it.

Two levels of analysis are discernible in the question of the plan of Zeus, roughly divisible in terms of content and form. The first is the level of fictional content. This level assumes that the poem is a representation of events and beliefs which have an independent existence in themselves, even if it is in the form of myth or only in the poet's imagination. Hence, interpretations of the plan of Zeus at this level attempt to reason out what is being referred to by the phrase *Dios boulē*. James Redfield, reviewing previous discussions, counts five different interpretations, from the generalized notion that all is the will of Zeus, to interpretations which identify the plan of Zeus with the quarrel of Achilles and Agamemnon, the plot to glorify Achilles through the near-destruction of the Achaeans, the plan mentioned in the *Cypria* that Zeus wished to reduce the earth's burden of men through war, or the fulfilment of a prophecy of Troy's destruction.[44] The second level expands the scope of the question beyond the fictional referents of the poem, and makes the plan of Zeus a poetic principle and the *ratio* of the Homeric world. When scholarship takes up the plan of Zeus on this second, metapoetic level, it becomes an expression of that with respect to which every event which has happened or could happen takes on its meaning. The plan of Zeus, in these interpretations, take on the function of ordering past events and pre-ordering – ordering in advance – future events, and thus comes to occupy the position of Nagy's concept of tradition and of the Homeric concept of *kleos*. All three concepts express the pure past, and, by examining the properties the plan of Zeus takes on, we can see some of the functions of the pure past in the Homeric context.

Let us begin with William Allan's interpretation, which is particularly useful for our discussion because it explicitly makes *Dios boulē* perform a structuring and ordering role within an oral theoretical understanding of Homeric performance:

> We should therefore avoid talk of 'intertextuality', and a fortiori 'quotation', since the *Dios boulē* evokes a totality of stories characterized by Zeus's dominance, but does so without referring to specific texts. It is a traditional narrative element that … not only offers a distinctive explanation of human history, but also helps the bard generate, and situate, his performance within the wider stream of epic song.[45]

For Allan, *Dios boulē* represents the entire tradition of oral poetry and links various oral traditions through a common internal logic based on the dominance of Zeus. Like the concept of *kleos* as previously discussed, the plan of Zeus is an expression that manifests, within the content, the formal condition that governs it; Allan calls it a 'traditional narrative element' in the quoted passage. Allan also justifies our grouping of the plan of Zeus with Nagy's tradition and Homeric *kleos* by stating explicitly the property that unites them: '[T]he widest possible definition of the *Dios boulē* is best, because all events are seen to be part of that plan.'[46]

What comes to the fore here is how the logic of the *Dios boulē* affects the interpretation of the *Iliad* and every traditional mythological poem. For Allan, *Dios boulē* expresses faith in an ordered and rational unfolding of history: 'Although the *Dios boulē* covers a range of actions, they all relate to Zeus's power, both among mortals and his fellow gods. In short, the *Dios boulē* is nothing less than the rational articulation of history from the perspective of Zeus (as mediated by the epic narrator).'[47] This reading enables Allan to link the internal logic of *Dios boulē* to the scene of epic performance, and situate epic performance as part of the cosmic plan of Zeus: 'But as well as ensuring accuracy and truth, the poet's access to the will of Zeus, bolstered by his privileged relationship to the Muse(s), means that he can relate his song to the fundamental plan of the cosmos.'[48] Poet, tradition and the *Dios boulē* form a total system in which all is ordered, all is rational, and all is accessible to an eusynoptic vision of the whole in which the will of Zeus acts within history in the manner of the 'cunning of reason': 'The importance and usefulness of the *Dios boulē*, both as a narrative strategy and as a theological concept, is largely a product of the divine society itself, in which gods have their favourites and their schemes, yet their competing wills are shown to result in an order which is identified with the will of Zeus.'[49]

The oral theoretical issue that animates Allan's discussion and determines its interpretation of *Dios boulē* is the old chestnut of intertextuality and allusion. Because oral theory rejects the model of fixed texts or versions that appear at specific moments, any model of intertextuality in which the appearance of a particular phrase or concept in one poem can be understood as an allusion to the appearance of that phrase in another poem is inadmissible. In this context, Allan considers the repetition of the phrase 'and the will of Zeus was being accomplished [*Dios d' eteleieto boulē*]' in the *Iliad* and the *Cypria*. How can oral theory posit a relation between the two appearances without making one instance later than and thus alluding to the other? The solution is to make *Dios boulē* a concept of pure anteriority, pure past, which retrieves all actual instances into itself and thus relates them without making one earlier than the other. Hence, the plan of Zeus refers to no actual event but rather a formal principle. Insofar as both poems are in the Homeric tradition, both the *Iliad* and the *Cypria* presuppose the hegemonic power of Zeus, and this presupposition is what is expressed through the phrase *Dios boulē*. The influence of Nagy's distinction between external and internal can again be felt here. As a formal, metapoetic device, the *Dios boulē* stamps these poems with the mark of the Homeric tradition, which can be read as such by an external observer. As an ideological element, seen from within the tradition, the *Dios boulē* expresses the hegemony of Zeus. Through the intertextual logic of *Dios boulē*, we trace another path along which oral theory has solved the problems caused by Parry's initial presuppositions, charting its own way from the living present of Deleuze's first synthesis to the pure past of the second synthesis.

Sheila Murnaghan presents a different version of the link between the will of Zeus and the plot of mythological narrative. Rather than a rationalizing principle or an internal logic shared between different branches of the oral tradition, Murnaghan sees a single *Dios boulē* that subsumes all archaic epic. This entails not merely identifying the ambiguous *Dios boulē* of the *Iliad* with the plan to unburden the earth from the *Cypria*, but extends to positing a master narrative in the control of Zeus:

> Furthermore, as the scholium to *Iliad* 1 makes clear, the whole Trojan War should be understood as only one episode in Zeus's plan, which takes in the Theban War as well. And even this larger cosmic story encompassing both legendary wars, the story of Zeus's response to the earth's oppression by human beings, is itself only one episode in an even larger plot, in which Zeus is always and everywhere engaged in archaic mythology, and which finally transcends all specific narratives: the plot of mortality.[50]

The plots of archaic poetic traditions are here gathered into a master plot, merging the two meanings of plot as story and plot as conspiracy. Zeus is conceived as actively plotting death for man: 'Zeus constantly reasserts his nature and his power by assuring the existence for others of what he definitively lacks, repeatedly securing the mortality of mortals.'[51] Compared to Allan, Murnaghan's conception collapses the two levels of content and form. For Murnaghan, the will of Zeus is no longer the cunning of reason operating behind the back of epic history, but rather a manifest form of planning directing that history.

By positing death and the mortality of mortals as the goal of the plan of Zeus, Murnaghan makes the epic tradition a closed system. Zeus comes to be a malevolent deity behind all things; the structure of heroic society itself becomes only the context for the generation of conflict and war, and even the deferral of death becomes only the means for the prolonging of death in the future.[52] The entire mythological career of Achilles is read under the sign of the hegemony of Zeus. Even before his birth, Achilles was implicated in Zeus' plans for domination: due to a prophecy that the son of Thetis will be greater than his father, Zeus gave Thetis to marry a mortal instead of wedding her himself. The subsequent wrath of Achilles and its consequences in the *Iliad* are read as the means through which Zeus increases the death toll of a war which would have been less deadly had it concluded too quickly:

> Zeus's success involves seeing Achilles, the man who would have been his son, die; in this way, he protects himself against the challenge of a son who could be his rival and so maintains his immortality ... Both [Peleus and Priam] suffer through the actions of Achilles himself in his role not as the instigator but as the agent of Zeus's plan.[53]

Murnaghan's operation is thus one of suture, in the sense of the previous chapter. The pure past, as a consequence of the fact that it has gained specific actual content, loses its potential for ordering all possible events. By making Zeus the omnipotent and omniscient figure behind mythological history, those events in which Zeus is not in control or is actively deceived fall out of that history. As Ann Bergren points out, the *boulē* of Zeus does not in fact hold sway over all of the *Iliad*, since there is also the *boulē* of Hera which leads to Zeus' deception, a *Dios apatē* in contrast to the *Dios boulē*.[54] The pure past cannot properly be bound to any fixed content, and Murnaghan's interpretation is therefore a suturing, although, in defence of her argument, this suturing operation is one that was already being performed in the *Iliad* itself, as in Hector and Agamemnon's use of the doom of Troy or in Helen's use of the song to come; both, as we saw, were sutures that gave a specific content to *kleos*.

We have thus seen how Allan and Murnaghan resolve the paradoxical nature of pure past by, respectively, assigning it a formal function in oral theoretical terms or suturing it to an actual content. Each of these responses defines a relationship between events in epic and the meanings they take on as part of the *Dios boulē*, however we understand that concept. Now, we have already encountered a Homeric version of the relation between events and their meanings, in the form of the division of the present and the logic of *kleos*. What, then, is the relationship between the interpretations of Allan and Murnaghan, based on a pure past that encompasses all that happens, and the logic of *kleos* which divides every time? More pointedly, is *kleos* knowable either as a rational principle of history or as an actual plot? Our previous discussions have already answered this question – *kleos* is unknowable and is projected into an inaccessible song to come – but those previous discussions were, so to speak, empirical, since they derived from readings of the concept as presented in the Homeric poems. The goal here, in contrast, is to separate out the stages of what had been presented all at once, and to give each stage its place in a structure informed by Deleuze's philosophy of time. The unknowability of *kleos* is a piece of the puzzle that we already have; now the question is how to put it in the right place. Because *kleos* is unlike the interpretations of the *Dios boulē* based on the pure past, it exceeds the second synthesis and provides the impetus that pushes us to a third form of time, one focused on the future.

By way of transition, let us consider the encounter with the sirens in the *Odyssey*. The encounter with the sirens is a transitional moment because it both presents and takes away the figure of a knowable and fixed *kleos*. The sirens sing: 'For we know all the toils of the Argives and Trojans in wide Troy through the gods' despite.'[55] What is it that attracts Odysseus and tantalizes the audience in the sirens' song? The two attractions are commonly distinguished. Odysseus, it is said, is drawn by the warlike, epic nature of the promised song and how he himself is represented in it, while the audience is fascinated by a song that is promised but provocatively absent.[56] What the sirens seem to offer is a version of what the Iliadic muse offers, the *kleos* of the heroes. Odysseus seems to be attracted by his own story, a vision of his life and achievements given its proper meaning within the glorious martial context of the *Iliad*, as Pietro Pucci observes.[57] We recognize here the structural function of *kleos* as the site or context which gives meaning to all events: the function of the pure past.[58] What the song of the sirens promise, then, would occupy the same functional position as the plan of Zeus in Murnaghan's reading. To be able to know and understand the meaning of the deeds and sufferings of the heroic age is what Helen expects from the song to come, and it is what attracts Odysseus in the song of the sirens. But does Odysseus hear the song?[59] Do the sirens in fact know and sing of everything as they promised? The answers to these questions can only be speculative, but they also do not matter for our discussion, since what is significant is that the poem never gives us the definitive version of *kleos* as promised.[60] The *Odyssey* holds out the possibility of a song that tells all and takes it away again; this double gesture is not merely playful but connected to essential questions of *kleos* and the possibility of giving all events a final meaningful place. We can thus see that the two distinct forms of attraction that draws Odysseus and the audience to the song of the sirens are in fact two different moments of the same logic of *kleos*: *kleos* is first promised and then withheld, because it can only be given as withheld. In contrast to readings which would make of *kleos* a definite, knowable content, *kleos* and the pure past it expresses can only properly serve a structural function.[61] With the assertion of the unknowability of *kleos*, we are already on the verge of the third synthesis.

III. Time out of joint

Deleuze's third synthesis turns from the present of the first synthesis and the past of the second to orient towards the future. Our discussions in this section will not draw out its full philosophical consequences, which connect with many of Deleuze's interests outside the scope of what is at stake here, but will instead use motifs from the third synthesis to bring a series of Homeric problems into focus. This section will continue the question of the fixity and knowability of *kleos*, and will demonstrate that *kleos*, which previously appeared as pure past, is marked by an openness that reorients it towards the future. The particular motif from the third synthesis that ties together the argument of this section is Deleuze's borrowing from Hamlet, that 'time is out of joint'. Using this nodal idea, we will pull together the overturning of a fixed *kleos*, the Aristotelian understanding of plot and meaning and the place of the epic poet.

Beginning, then, by picking up the threads from the previous section: the way the siren song holds out and takes away the possibility of knowing *kleos* definitively as fixed repeats, at a different level, Achilles' career through the *Iliad*, in which his seemingly secure understanding of how his own *kleos* will play out is narratively overturned. The overturning of any fixity of meaning in the *Iliad* occurs even in small gestures of speech and narration. The repeated tag *ei pot' eōn ge*, 'if it/he ever was', marks a dissociation or dehiscence of the present from the past, as when Helen reminisces about her past relation with the Achaean heroes during the Teichoscopia (III. 180).[62] Lynn-George observes in the context of this phrase that 'the distance of this past, even in its return, elicits a sense of the possibility of its never having taken place'.[63] Even as the past is recalled and reconstituted in the present, its meaning for the present seems to slip away: 'And all glorified Zeus among the gods, but among men Nestor. That was I, among men, if it ever happened.'[64] In contrast to the definitiveness of a meaning assigned by the plan of Zeus in the conception of Allan or Murnaghan, and in contrast to the certainty Achilles had about his *kleos* before the death of Patroclus, these moments show the disconnection between the heroes' own past and the present in which they try to make that past meaningful again. Lynn-George writes:

> This phrase articulates distance, uncertainty and discontinuity in relation to a past which, in its remoteness, is situated on the blurred borders of the real and the realm of the imaginary, on the indeterminate threshold between history and fiction – a position which might be assigned to the epic itself in its constant movements between the constructions of 'it was' and 'it was as if'.[65]

The present which expresses this dissociated relationship with the past is not the living present of the first synthesis, and the past which loses its outline cannot be the all-encompassing form of the pure past we saw in relation to the second synthesis. With the phrase 'if it ever was', the heroes express what we might call the incommensurability of the past with the future, in that the meanings of the past no longer seem to offer a guide or context for future action. It is to this openness to the future that we will give more definition and a more precise structure.

'If it ever was' is an expression on the level of character speech. On the level of narrative form, a parallel function is served by the frequent occurrence of what Bruce Louden calls 'pivotal contrafactuals', those places in which the poem tells us that 'event X would have happened, had event Y not prevented it'.[66] In these cases, the event that was prevented, X, is usually something that would result in the violation of the received tradition. For instance, the Achaeans 'might have taken gate-towering Ilion under the hands of Patroklos' – prematurely, in the context of the tradition, which is rescued by event Y, Apollo repelling Patroclus' assault (XVI. 698–709). What is significant about these instances for Louden is their meaning for the present context in which they occur: 'The pivotal contrafactual is a sophisticated technique *to heighten a present moment* and immediately shift the course of the narrative in another direction.'[67] This is another expression of the living present, closest to Austin's interpretation of digressions discussed earlier. The contrafactual event in Louden performs the same function as the foil in Nagy.[68] The difference produced by the contrafactual is turned into an opposition to the 'real' event, with the goal of reasserting all the more strongly the fact and the self-identity of the latter. What we are interested in, in contrast, is the specificity of the form of the contrafactual, which is swallowed up in Louden's analysis. What does the contrafactual as a form mean?[69] In our context, we can see that the contrafactual event expresses dissent from the fixity of the tradition; it opens up the vista of other times and other possibilities, 'beyond fate [*hypermora*]' (II. 155). The contrafactual is thus the latest in a series of figures which express an overturning of fixed meaning or resistance to giving the pure past a definite content. The task that faces us now is to provide a structure in which these parallels can cohere.[70]

The notion that 'time is out of joint', which Deleuze proposes as a reply to the question of what the third synthesis means, will help us articulate what is at stake in these situations and connect them to the broader questions of meaning and the positions of Zeus and the poet. The most general way of characterizing the core of the upcoming argument is as a form of opposition to Aristotelianism, but let us first unpack the image of the 'joint'. Deleuze refers the joint to the hinge of a door:[71] 'Cardinal comes from *cardo*; *cardo* is precisely the hinge, the hinge around which the sphere of celestial bodies turns, and which makes them pass time and again through the so-called cardinal points, and we note their return: ah, there's the star again, it's time to move my sheep!'[72] Time in this conception is subordinated to an external *ratio*. Deleuze characterizes the 'classical philosophy' – to which he will oppose the idea that 'time is out of joint' – as the notion that time exists in order to measure 'something other than itself, such as, for example, astronomical movement':[73] 'I can say, going quickly, that the whole of ancient philosophy maintained a subordination of time to nature, even in its most complex forms; that classical philosophy, however complicated its conceptions of time were, never put into question this very very general principle. The famous definition: "time is the number of movement".'[74] Time which is still 'in joint' is thus time that is merely the measure or expression of something non-temporal. While the *locus classicus* of this classical philosophy of time is the 'moving image of eternity' of the *Timaeus* (37d), let us note two connections as points of reference for further discussion. First, the conception of time as expressing a prior, non-temporal content should remind us of the status of mythological history as expressing the will of Zeus, in the reading of Allan and, more directly, Murnaghan; the narratives of myth which unfold through time all express the non-temporal 'plot of mortality', the fact that mortals die and gods do not.[75] I choose Murnaghan as the example here only because her argument puts, in the most explicit way and without mincing words, the logic of all interpretations which derive propositional meaning from narrative. We are thus led to a second connection, which is that the most general structure for the operation of deriving meaning from narrative – of time 'in joint' – is offered by Aristotle, and thus time 'out of joint' becomes a form of resistance to Aristotelianism. Let us first extract the relevant aspect of Aristotle's approach to narrative from the *Poetics*, before relating it to Deleuze, in order to then return to the Homeric context.

For Aristotle, tragedy is identified with its plot, *muthos*, and the plot of a tragedy is a mimesis of an action, *praxis*.[76] We do not need to elaborate on Aristotle's well-known requirements for the unity of the plot, which must consist of events, *pragmata*, connected either through probability, *eikos*, or necessity, *anankaion*.[77] The criteria of probability and necessity also determines the plot as a unity, *holon*, beginning with what 'does not itself follow necessarily from something else, but after which a further event or process naturally occurs', and ending with 'that which itself naturally occurs, whether necessarily or usually, after a preceding event, but need not be followed by anything else'.[78] Aristotle thus conceives of the unity of the plot as a unity which presents itself to the understanding and independent from the unity or lack thereof of its characters – as in, to take Aristotle's examples, a potential *Heracleid* or a *Theseid* – or of a chronological period, as in the genre of history in his conception.[79] Aristotle uses a telling analogy for the requirements of the unity of the plot:

> For the beautiful consists in magnitude and order, whence neither could a very small animal be something beautiful . . . nor could a very great animal . . . so that, just as in the case of bodies and of animals they must have a magnitude, and this must be easily seen in a single glance (*eusynopton*), so also in the case of stories they must have a length, and this must be easily remembered.[80]

The analogy makes an equivalence between seeing and the experience of the plot, but what is at stake in this connection? The understanding of the plot and the activity of vision are mutually conditioning. On the one hand, seeing is here clearly a metaphor for understanding the logical connections of the plot, as probability or necessity, which are necessary in order to conceive of the plot as a pleasing whole. On the other hand, understanding is conceived on a model of vision in which everything seen is thought to present itself to the perceiver at once, a property is expressed in the key term, *eusynopton*, 'easily seen in a single glance'. Thus, what is at stake in modelling the understanding of plot through the categories of logical necessity and probability is the removal of time.[81] Events connected by probability or necessity are events which can be thought simultaneously, with one event set immediately next to another as its probable or necessary consequence. We can therefore think of Aristotle's theory of tragedy as an apparatus for turning the temporal unfolding of events into an atemporal image, explicating Plato's moving *eikōn* back into the atemporal eternity it is meant to express. The contrast Aristotle makes between tragedy and history re-emphasizes the atemporal nature of the perfection of the former against the messiness of the latter: because tragedy is composed of events distributed through time which had already been preselected to be logically connected, it is possible to see them in a single glance, whereas events in history are not preselected in this way.[82] The time of Aristotelian tragedy is thus fully 'in joint'.[83]

Deleuze's references on this point include Hamlet, Oedipus and Zarathustra. Of Hamlet, Deleuze claims that he is 'the first hero who truly needed time in order to act', and, through this condition, 'completes the emancipation of time'.[84] What does it mean that Hamlet 'truly needed' time to act, and how does needing time to act then lead to the emancipation of time? The clearest way to answer these questions and to connect to our discussions is through Deleuze's brief references to Harold Rosenberg, which are filled out by Henry Somers-Hall. Again, the question is of a conception of drama in which narrative is conceived as an expression of an atemporal principle, and the time of narrative becomes merely the measure of the unfolding of events predetermined according to some law or logic. Rosenberg calls this the form of 'old drama', in which '[the character's] emotions, his thoughts and his gestures' – the events which unfold – 'should correspond with and earn in every respect the fate prepared for him'.[85] Somers-Hall elaborates:

> In 'old drama', therefore, character is seen simply as a manifestation of the underlying unity provided by actions' relation to the law ... Rather than seeing the character as an entity that develops in time, we have a drama which is subordinated to the movement of the action. Similarly, the singularly human nature of action as relation to ethical structure reflects that what is being played out is something primarily atemporal. The duration of the play is simply the mode of expression of the underlying rational structure of the law of action.[86]

In contrast to 'old drama' in which action through time marches in congruence with a prior, atemporal law or logic, Hamlet cannot act even as he recognizes the set of actions that law prescribes for him; something prevents him from performing the prescribed actions (IV. iv): 'I do not know / Why yet I live to say "This thing's to do"; / Sith I have cause and will and strength and means / To do't.'[87] It would be possible to provide psychological explanations for Hamlet's hesitation, which would be an attempt to redeem the congruence of action and law by providing additional laws of psychology, thus rehabilitating the character's aberrant actions. Deleuze does not take this option, and instead sees 'a feeling of incongruence with the kind of rational cosmology put forward by the *Timaeus*'.[88] In this way, Hamlet's actions cannot be given all at once: they are not *eusynoptos*, 'seen in a single glance', but instead, Hamlet 'truly need[s]' time in order to act. This is an emancipation of time because the time that it takes for Hamlet to act is no longer merely the measure of an atemporal logic, but comes into its own through being freed from that subordination.

What we are drawing together is a nexus of connections between the eusynoptic Aristotelian tragedy and its expressions in drama, on the one hand, and a Deleuzian alternative to or escape from it, on the other hand, a time out of joint. Let us turn back to Homer. We have already seen that the Aristotelian position is represented by arguments like Murnaghan's, but is there an alternative, a Homeric out-of-joint-ness to compare with Hamlet's emancipation of time? It is at this moment in this ordered series of syntheses that the unknowability of *kleos*, with the consequent generalized division of time, finally finds its place. Let us recall the central example from chapter two: Achilles, like other heroes, assumes that the final meaning of their actions will come in the *kleos* they will gain in song. What marked Achilles' perspective is the fact that he thought, at the beginning of the *Iliad*, he could manipulate events so as to control the meaning of his *kleos*. This presupposes that *kleos* is knowable and certain, and thus *kleos* appears for Achilles at this point as an expression of the pure past, just as the plan of Zeus does for critics who see it as the rational ordering of mythological history. But when Achilles loses that certainty and recognizes that *kleos* is uncontrollable and unknowable, the meaning of every moment and of every action comes into question, that is, it comes to be split. In this way, each moment is freed from the meaning it appears to have in its present, because of its potential for change in an unforeseeable *kleos*. Each moment is thus accompanied by its pure difference from *kleos*, and time is emancipated from being a measure of the unfolding of some known *kleos* – be that the supremacy of Zeus or Achilles' status as the best of the Achaeans – becoming instead what Deleuze would call the 'pure and empty form of time' of the third synthesis, 'as though time had abandoned all mnemic content'.[89] It is the unknowability of *kleos* and the emptiness of time that is expressed by Helen, in two directions which reflect the same temporal form: towards the future, the unknowability of *kleos* is expressed in the inaccessible because indefinitely deferred song to come (VI. 357–8); and towards the past, the emptiness of time means that no meaningful link connects her history to her present and leads to the questioning of *ei pot' eēn ge*, 'if it ever was' (III. 180). All this we have discussed before in deriving the logic of *kleos* – so to speak, empirically – from the assemblage of Homeric poems and scholarship, though it is only here, in reconstructing these figures through Deleuze's philosophy of time, that they find their places in a conceptual order.[90]

So much for the reconstruction, but let us go a little way further and extend our discussions in one more direction. The potential fixity of *kleos* is associated with a particular, eusynoptic position, in the sense that a fixed *kleos* is *fixed by* the position of someone who can see it all in a single glance. Who can occupy this eusynoptic position and thereby fix *kleos*? We have already seen that Zeus is one candidate for the role of one who sees and controls all, but the *Iliad* resists that control. The power of Zeus and the sovereignty of the *Dios boulē* is challenged by, among other things, the *Dios apatē*, as Bergren points out. Another challenge to the power of Zeus appears in scenes of *kerostasia* in which Zeus weighs the dooms, *kēres*, of two fighting parties on a set of scales in order to determine who should die and who prevail; power seems paradoxically split between the god and fate.[91] James Morrison recognizes that the contradictions between the agency of fate and the will of Zeus has a metapoetic, formal significance. He observes parallel oppositions between freedom and fixity in a series of contrasting terms on three different levels: between the free will of the hero and superhuman influence; the free invention of the poet and the predestined story inherited from tradition; and the agency of fate and the power of the gods. Morrison highlights the same conflict between what is free to change and what is fixed and inevitable at all three levels of the heroic, the poetic and the divine:

> At some level Achilles seems to be free to leave Troy and return home to Greece, yet on the other side we find the idea that he is fated to die at Troy, being most short-lived of all mortals ... Even though he works within a tradition and the audience knows how the story will end, the poet, too, demonstrates a capacity to call the tradition itself into question [by teasing counterfactual events] ... [The gods] know the future, much as the poet and his audience do. Yet in spite of such providence, the gods also question the inevitability of preordained events.[92]

Morrison takes the first step in connecting these three levels of the poem by noting the parallels between them. This first step leads to the more pressing question of why. Why does this same tension recur in the human decisions within the plot, the narrative construction of the poem, and the paradox of omnipotent god and predestination? Morrison's argument stops at the generation of tension as a poetic technique: 'My main point is that this dynamism between fixedness and flexibility operates at three distinct levels: the heroic, the divine, and the poetic. The analogous polarities at these three levels mutually reinforce one another, allowing one to conclude with some confidence that this alternation is a deliberate effect of the storytelling technique of the *Iliad*'s poet.'[93] While Morrison leaves the threads here, what his discussion gives us is a whole series of figures which we can read as so many expressions of the formal structure of time in the poem. Morrison collects the evidence for the opposition to fixity in the

Iliad, of which the instance of fate, in the *kerostasia*, resists the power of Zeus who occupies the eusynoptic position.[94] But Morrison's discussion also reminds us that the eusynoptic position in the Homeric situation can be occupied not only by Zeus, but also by the poet. Can the will of the poet sustain the fixity of a pure past that the will of Zeus could not?[95]

It may be argued that the poet is an obsolete figure in the aftermath of oral theory, which disperses creative agency through the anonymity of the oral tradition. But the argument cannot be left there, since, even if the poet as a figure of creative origin is no longer available, the poet still exists as a discursive position within the poem; there is still the position of a voice that narrates, and that position can take on a range of properties. The question of whether a eusynoptic perspective exists, inflected for the position of the Homeric poet, becomes one of the poet's knowledge: is the poet supposed to know the definitive, final *kleos* as he confers it upon the heroes in his song? Can we identify the poem that is presented in oral performance with the song to come that had been anticipated in the heroic past? This point is particularly important as Egbert Bakker, on whose analyses of the split in the heroes' knowledge we have relied, argues that the poet *does* know that of which the heroes are ignorant. Let us recall that Bakker argues that the character who is *nēpios* 'is no more silly or out of touch than other humans': 'Rather his fundamental condition is that he is out of touch with poetic truth … [T]his means that he is explicitly presented as *not in the future*, and since he is not in the future, *he is no poet*.'[96] Bakker changes the stakes of the interpretation of the term *nēpios* from those of silliness as a persistent character trait and into a question of time, which we can fully endorse. But at the same time as making the stakes temporal, Bakker has also identified the time of the poet with a time of knowledge, in contrast to ignorance in the heroic past: 'When we shift from epic events themselves to the memory of epic events, the epic tradition, the contrast is not anymore between the event and its consequences in the future, but between the ignorance of the original experience [in the past] and the understanding of the present.'[97] The poet is here thought to be the one who is able to give meaning to the past event through his understanding, the one who is able to close the circle opened by the epic hero's projection of meaning into another time. But is this true? Is the poet able to occupy the eusynoptic position, most recently vacated by Zeus? Within the context of all of our discussions in which we have seen how *kleos* has resisted every attempt at fixation, does the figure of the poet – that most battered thing – return to hold everything in his hands again?

The question of the poet's knowledge is inseparable from his relationship to the muse and the contrast between the muses' knowledge and the poet's ignorance, as one of those who 'only hear the *kleos* and know nothing' (11. 486).⁹⁸ Although the heroes project the expectation that poets will provide narrative closure to their deeds and sufferings, the poets themselves project their song into a context in which the muses will provide the guarantee and the final meaning. The figure of the poet thus passes the role of occupying the eusynoptic position on again, to the muse.⁹⁹ But have we not simply regressed one step further and punted our problem down the line? After all, the real stakes of the question in the formal and temporal terms that we are considering here are not whether the poet in particular occupies the eusynoptic position, but whether *any* figure occupies that position and, by occupying it, fixes *kleos* and undoes the logic that would make it radically unknowable. Does the muse, then, perform the role of knowing and fixing?¹⁰⁰ We can escape from this regression by asking not whether the ultimate guarantor of meaning is the poet or muse or any other authority, but by seeing a response to the question of authority in the structured configuration of poet-and-muse. The *Iliad* presents the poet as calling upon the authority of the muse, but with the stipulation that – at the risk of stating the obvious – *the muse never sings*. The muse is thus a counterpart to the song to come: both are figures of the materialization of a final *kleos*, but only under the condition of never actually coming into being.¹⁰¹ Oral theory's vision of the perfect, instantaneous communication of an oral traditional performance finds its roots here, in the indefinitely deferred performance of the song to come when, at the end of history, the muse finally sings.

The displacement of the poet from the position of authority by the muse is a conceptual way of vacating the eusynoptic position. Let me finish with a second, poetic figure that evokes the same result. At the climactic point of the foot race around Ilium, as Hector flees from Achilles for his life, the narration resolves, unexpectedly and without precedence, into a question. The poet asks: 'How then could Hektor have escaped the death spirits, had not Apollo, for this last and uttermost time, stood by him close, and driven strength into him, and made his knees light?'¹⁰² The poet receives no reply. With this question, the poem relinquishes the fixity of authority and releases *kleos* into an indefinite, open future.

IV. Conclusion

Let us finish by looking back over the argument of this chapter and then of the book as a whole. Deleuze's three syntheses produce three different but connected forms of time. The logic and interrelations among these forms of time allow us to better understand the temporality of *kleos* as a locus of meaning constantly projected out of any given present and into another time. The first synthesis produces a living present and characterizes those conceptions of Homeric narrative in which the present forms an unbroken whole. These include readings which explain digressions of the distant past by the meanings they have in the narrative present, as well as readings which deny connections between different times by insisting that whatever is currently narrated is the only present. The living present is not, by itself, an adequate account of time because it cannot pass, in the sense that, even though the specific contents of the present can change, the living present cannot register that change. This parallels Nagy's account of the subjective perspective of a tradition that insists it is eternal and unchanging.

As we saw in chapter three, Nagy's alternative to this subjective perspective is the objective one of the scholar who can see from the outside what those within the tradition cannot not acknowledge: that the tradition changes. But the argument pursued throughout this book is that, for the Homeric tradition and for the *Iliad* in particular, there exist temporalities within these texts that exceed the eternity of the living present. Nagy himself provides a model for one of these possibilities in his conception of tradition in which the new can never exceed tradition, because even innovation is always already part of tradition. Even as something ostensibly new comes into being, it is already, at the point of its emergence, part of a prior tradition or an absolute and pure past. This corresponds to Deleuze's second synthesis. In the *Iliad*, the notion of an instance which orders and gives meaning to every event is expressed by the concept of *kleos* as well as the plan of Zeus, the *Dios boulē*. In examining different interpretations of the plan of Zeus, we were able to flesh out the function of the pure past in the *Iliad*.

The characterization of *kleos* as an instance which gives meaning to every event is still incomplete, because it leaves open the question of whether this ordering instance is fixed, accessible or knowable. Indeed, the interpretations of the *Dios boulē* discussed here interpret this ordering instance as rational and knowable. But the *Iliad* presents us with the possibility that the *Dios boulē* is not in complete control of all epic events and that *kleos* is fundamentally unknowable; the former is shown by the uncertainties regarding the power of fate and the *Dios apatē*, while the latter is a result of the arguments of chapter two in particular. These stipulations bring us to the third of Deleuze's syntheses, in which 'time is out of joint' and no longer follows any prior law or reason. The knowability of *kleos* is associated with the possibility of seeing the whole plot at once, or eusynoptically, in Aristotle's term. Thus, we then explored the possibility of Zeus, the poet or the muse occupying a position in which the whole plot is securely fixed and knowable, and I argued that the configuration of poet and muse provides a way of presenting *kleos* as an ordering instance but, in the same movement, taking away the possibility of knowing it. The poetics of the *Iliad* is thus an open one.

We are now in a position to better understand, or perhaps to repurpose, a challenging formulation found in Nagy. In a discussion of how we should conceive of the kind of repetition performed by a traditional singer, Nagy introduces a notion of re-enactment in which the performer *becomes* the archetype that he is re-enacting.[103] This conception is so far relatively familiar: the performer of epic poetry in some senses becomes 'Homer', his archetype, while he performs. The challenging part of Nagy's proposal is that it is not just the performer who re-enacts or repeats, but the archetype must do the same: 'But the paradox of mimesis is that the archetype to be re-enacted must re-enact, not just enact, in its own right.'[104] Nagy's archetype that repeats is paradoxical because repetition is usually conceived as the repetition of something that is chronologically before, but there can be nothing before an archetype if it is to remain an archetype. If an archetype is original, he cannot repeat, yet, for Nagy, both must be true. How can there be an *original* repetition? What can an original repetition repeat, if there is nothing before the repetition that is also a first time? Nagy provides a variety of instantiations of this paradoxical statement, but it remains unexplained. In the context of the discussions in this chapter, and in particular the image of performance resulting from the configuration of a poet who sings while relying on a muse who does not sing, we can offer an explanation: what does the original repetition repeat? *It repeats the future.* Deleuze writes: 'The present is the repeater, the past is repetition itself, but the future is that which is repeated.'[105] For us, this means that the performance of oral poetry happens in the living present, it presupposes a pure past as the site of meaning, but the archetypal performance of the song to come by the muse can only come in an indefinite future, even as it is adumbrated and repeated, *avant la lettre*, by actual, existing performances. The final, 'true' performance of the muse does not come until the end of time, but it is constituted by existing performances which repeat an archetypal performer, who himself repeats because he is already looking forward to the end.

How do the discussions of this chapter fit with the chapters which have come before? The persistent aim running through the book has been to connect figures in poetry and scholarship via the thread of temporality. Where the previous chapters have been organized thematically, following the contours and openings offered by the poems and their scholarship, this chapter uses Deleuze to present the various images of time in a structure that demonstrates their logical interrelations. Let us review the arguments of the previous chapters and connect them to the three syntheses of this chapter. The conceptual core of the book is the second chapter, which observed that *kleos* is projected out of the heroic present and into the elsewhere of a future song, and argued that *kleos* is unknowable and therefore inserts a potential or pure difference into every moment. The notion that *kleos* is a site of meaning in an absolutely other place, beyond every actual moment, is a form of the pure past of the second synthesis, while the unknowability of *kleos* that is always open and is constrained by no eternal law expresses the 'time out of joint' of the third synthesis. This last chapter therefore rederives 'philosophically' the concept of *kleos* previously reached 'empirically' through the *Iliad*.

Around the core concept are arranged the various figures of poetry and scholarship of the other chapters. Chapter one argued that we need a differential concept like *kleos* by demonstrating that the *sēmata* of the *Iliad*, in particular the Achaean wall, resist the ideals of continuity and self-identity of oral theory, as exemplified by Foley's traditional referentiality. The Achaean wall and the legendary *guslar* are, for the concept of *kleos*, what we might call objective correlatives, to misuse Eliot's phrase: they are figures which express a logic as yet unelaborated, or objects correlating to an undefined concept.[106] The need for a differential concept of *kleos* is the need to go beyond the living present of the first synthesis.

The structured connections between the syntheses of time also provide a way of reconceiving the relations between various schools of Homeric scholarship. Beyond the relatively crude opposition of writing and orality, which in any case had a tendency to become blurred, we saw in chapters two and three that there are differences in the images of time presupposed by neoanalysis and oral theory, and even further, there can be such differences between the various aspects of a single scholar's work. In this way, chapter three made the case that even as Nagy constructed a paradoxically synchronic diachrony drawn in a tension between the living present and a pure past, his concept of a rhapsode performing before a Panhellenic audience contained the potential for an open-ended process in which meanings remain unsettled.

Finally, chapter four further explored the poetic expressions of the core concept of *kleos*, exploring a variety of figures in which *kleos*, a formal structure, can appear in forms which turn it into graspable content, like the shadows of a three-dimensional object projected onto two-dimensional surfaces. In particular, the way in which *kleos* as the contentless form of future meaning can be given a content like 'Troy is doomed' represents a regression from the third to the second synthesis, fixing the openness of future meaning into a definite, predestined content of the pure past.

Over the course of this book, I hope to have shown the possibility of reading *kleos* as a concept of difference that complicates its role as the guarantor of identity and continuity through the epic tradition. But more than the narrow interpretation of the particular concept, I hope to have opened up the potential for a differential and temporal reading of *kleos* to connect seemingly distant figures and concepts across poetry and scholarship, demonstrating in the process some of the ways in which poetry can be a form of thought, just as Homeric scholarship can be a literary participant in the poetic tradition.

Notes

Introduction

1 I will use the term 'hero' as a convenient shorthand for 'characters in the epic past of the Homeric poems', including non-warriors like Helen. See also note 55 in chapter two.
2 We will soon discuss the connection with the alternative translation of *kleos*, as 'rumour'.
3 This means that my investigation will not explicitly treat classic questions like that status of *khronos* as an empty time of waiting, or whether the archaic imagination conceives of man as facing the future or the past, or if time is to be considered a duration or a point (these examples are drawn from Fränkel 1955, Treu 1953 and Accame 1961), although I will discuss these questions where they become relevant for my argument. See Theunissen's comments on the limitations of the lexical method of Fränkel and his successors and the necessity of a hermeneutic approach in order to reach Homer's 'pre-understanding' of time, which cannot be 'simply read off from linguistic expressions' (2000: 5 and 32). Translations from modern languages are my own, except where a published translation is cited or otherwise noted.
4 Purves 2010 charts something of the differences I see between the two poems in her distinction between a 'protocartographic' *Iliad* and a 'countercartographic' *Odyssey*, although, as it turns out, I am mostly interested in the converse association connecting 'countercartography' with the *Iliad*. Gazis 2018 outlines the revisionist attitude of the *Odyssey* with respect to the formal relation between heroic *kleos* and the different kinds of narratives, often more personal, that are made possible by Hades as a setting. Discussion of the *Odyssey* along the lines of the present study must for the most part be deferred to another occasion. (I make a start in my 2018 article.) My focus on the *Iliad* – and the separation of the *Iliad* and the *Odyssey* itself for the purposes of this study – can occasionally cause a mismatch when I discuss scholarship that speaks of 'the Homeric poems' en bloc, but I hope this will not cause too much confusion.
5 I will make this point most explicitly about neoanalysis, in chapter two: neoanalytic hypotheses which attempt to prove the existence of early fixed texts are driven by an interpretive need to respond to certain aspects of Homeric temporality.

6   Conversely, I do not wish to claim exclusive privilege or sole validity for my own readings. Just as I try to put scholarship and poetry in new combinations, this book hopes to contribute new elements for the *combinatoire*, new colours for the palette.
7   See Martindale 1993 and now in particular Butler 2016.
8   Butler 2016: 32–3.
9   Ibid. 33–4.
10 A general aside: I frequently use the term 'express' as in 'X expresses Y' or 'X is an expression of Y'. This should not be taken as meaning X and Y are the same, or that Y strictly determines or causes X, nor is any intentionality implied (as in 'he expressed his displeasure'). Rather, I understand expression to be a connection over a boundary or across different conceptual regimes, as here, where something manifests across antiquity and modernity but cannot do so without necessarily changing.
11 Ibid. 34.
12 The analyses of these figures – in particular the first two – are recapitulated from Li 2018.
13 καί ποτέ τις εἴπῃσι καὶ ὀψιγόνων ἀνθρώπων / νηῒ πολυκληΐδι πλέων ἐπὶ οἴνοπα πόντον· / ἀνδρὸς μὲν τόδε σῆμα πάλαι κατατεθνηῶτος, / ὅν ποτ' ἀριστεύοντα κατέκτανε φαίδιμος Ἕκτωρ. / ὥς ποτέ τις ἐρέει· τὸ δ' ἐμὸν κλέος οὔ ποτ' ὀλεῖται (VII. 87–91). The Homeric poems are cited from the Oxford Classical Texts. Unless otherwise noted, translations are quoted from Lattimore (1951 and 1967), with occasional minor modifications which will generally go unremarked. I adhere to the convention whereby upper case Roman numerals refer to books of the *Iliad*, and lower case numerals to books of the *Odyssey*.
14 De Jong 1999: 258–73.
15 Ibid. 264.
16 Ibid.
17 Ibid. 269–70. All emphases in quoted passages are original unless otherwise noted.
18 Elmer 2005 places Hector's couplet considered here into the context of Homeric passages which have been called 'epigrammatic'. Although differing in the details of interpretation and in the routes through which they are reached, Elmer's conception of a distinction between the epigrammatic categories of *Aufschrift* and *Beischrift* – in which the latter designates a move away from the 'monumental' presence of a 'real, living speech situation' in the direction of the absence and deferral for which he succinctly refers us to Derrida's notion of a 'writing before the letter' (3–9) – agrees well with the structures of discontinuity and difference that will be developed through the course of this book. Elmer's article is valuable for drawing together, under the common heading of the 'destabilization of the monumental present' (18), previous conceptions of this structural distinction from a variety of different fields, including the shift away from 'egocentrism' in Svenbro 1993, Detienne's conception of the discovery of the artistic image (1996), and close readings of a range of archaic

and classical inscriptions. The discussions in this book will parallel less the specific paths taken in Elmer's argument, but rather something of its spirit.
19 Nagy 1979: 16.
20 ὑμεῖς γὰρ θεαί ἐστε πάρεστέ τε ἴστέ τε πάντα, / ἡμεῖς δὲ κλέος οἶον ἀκούομεν οὐδέ τι ἴδμεν (II. 485–6), quoted in Nagy's translation at ibid. 16.
21 Ibid. See now also Pucci 2018: 265–8. Compare Gazis' comment (2018: 27) on the invocation of the muse in the *Iliad*'s proem, which focalizes specifically 'a human perspective on epic composition and inspiration, and thus offers us an insight into the poet's own view of his subject'. See also Ahuvia Kahane's argument (2005: 3–65) that the figure of Homer maps the tension between knowledge and ignorance to that between fixity and openness.
22 The works of Milman Parry are collected in M. Parry 1971, but we will also cover this in more detail in later chapters.
23 I take the concepts 'series' and 'image [of thought]', as well as 'majority' and 'minority', from the general vicinity of Deleuze. Although the aspect of Deleuze's thought that I will engage with most explicitly in this book is his philosophy of time – in chapter five – let me acknowledge here the broader affinities which may become evident between his work and the approaches I have adopted here.
24 Foley 1999: 55.
25 Compare, for instance, the pre-understanding involved in urban legends, which are produced collectively and anonymously and yet still express a certain, recognizable logic.
26 To take a recent example, a work like Ready 2019 resonates with this study through its discussion of 'the preexistence of tales' and anticipatory intertextuality (28–31, 77), much more so than in its hypotheses about how oral poetry was recorded and collected.
27 See Nagy 1990b: 29 and 1996a: 215, and our discussions in chapter three.
28 See notes 17, 26 and 34 in chapter one.
29 It may help the reader to know that, retrospectively, what also strikes me about the scholars I engage with most closely is that they sought to build interpretive *systems*, interposed between the history of the poems and their meanings, regulating the possible relations between them. This goes some way towards explaining my closer attention to oral theory and neoanalysis as compared to dictation models.
30 Ford 1992: 153, taking the term 'antifuneral' from Redfield 1975: 167–9.
31 οἷσιν ἐπὶ Ζεὺς θῆκε κακὸν μόρον, ὡς καὶ ὀπίσσω / ἀνθρώποισι πελώμεθ' ἀοίδιμοι ἐσσομένοισι (VI. 357–8).
32 ἔσσεται ἢ ἠὼς ἢ δείλη ἢ μέσον ἦμαρ / ὁππότε τις καὶ ἐμεῖο Ἄρῃ ἐκ θυμὸν ἕληται / ἢ ὅ γε δουρὶ βαλὼν ἢ ἀπὸ νευρῆφιν ὀϊστῷ (XXI. 111–13).
33 Pestalozzi 1945.
34 Dowden 1996.

35 Nagy 1990b: 29.
36 In chapter two, we discuss the reduction of neoanalytic difference to oral theoretical identity in Kullmann 1984. See now also Rengakos 2020.
37 After Miller 1966.
38 εἷς οἰωνὸς ἄριστος ἀμύνεσθαι περὶ πάτρης (xii. 243).
39 ἀλλ' ἧμαι παρὰ νηυσὶν ἐτώσιον ἄχθος ἀρούρης (xviii. 104).
40 As a corollary to this section on objecthood, the analysis of breaks in meaning will be extended to two poetic figures associated with the death of minor warriors in the *Iliad*: the brief narrative vignettes of their lives and the similes which often accompany their deaths. Both vignette and simile, we will see, emphasize the break in meaning occasioned by death.
41 'There will come a day when sacred Ilion shall perish' (ἔσσεται ἦμαρ ὅτ' ἄν ποτ' ὀλώλῃ Ἴλιος ἱρή, iv. 164 = vi. 448).
42 I thus hope to highlight a less prominent aspect of this currently popular philosopher.

1 A Different Poet of the Same Name

1 Foley's use of this figure remains clear even if he may have overstated the elusiveness of one of the names cited as the legendary *guslar*, Ćor Huso. See Čolaković 2019: 7 note 34: 'Foley claims that Ćor Huso, like Homer, represented a legendary cultural idol and that neither was a historical person. He thus reveals that he is not aware of the recordings made by Parry and Vujnović, and the manuscripts from Bijelo Polje. Several of Parry's singers undoubtedly learned their songs from Ćor Huso, especially Vlahovljak, who learned most of his repertoire from him.'
2 For 'rigid designator', see Kripke 1980. Ahuvia Kahane offers a penetrating analysis of Homer's identity. Kahane proposes that ambivalence and uncertainty regarding the identity of Homer as a concrete individual are essential features of Homer as a poetic function; it is because Homer's identity is nothing much more substantial than his name that he is able to be a 'conduit for transcendental knowledge' (2005: 40). What I would add to this analysis is to extend the uncertainty of Homer's individual identity to that very knowledge or tradition itself for which he is the conduit. Could a continuous, self-identical tradition be delivered through such a shifting figure, or will we find tradition's self-conception resonating with the indefiniteness of its poet? I will argue in this chapter that the latter is the case by reading signs and memory in the *Iliad*. See also Kahane's discussion of signs (95–131), which focuses more on the *Odyssey*.
3 I allude to Nagy's use of the term *mouvance* as a vibratory variation of the oral tradition, though I will be interpreting the phenomenon it denotes differently. See Nagy 1996: 7–38 and 2004: 170–1, as well as Nagy's sources in Zumthor 1991.

4 On a personal note, this chapter is an attempt to work through my own experience with Foley's account of traditional referentiality: I have always been attracted by the charismatic conviction that shines through his work, but also always found myself held back from full acquiescence. My pursuit of the logic and contradictions in traditional referentiality comes from this amalgam of fascinated admiration.
5 The preceding points are extensively argued in M. Parry 1928, translated from the French and collected in M. Parry 1971: 1–190. In summarized form at M. Parry 1971: 266–79; the definition of the formula is cited from p. 272 of the same volume.
6 'Now no reader of the study, so far as I know, has failed to grant its main thesis' (M. Parry 1971: 266). Parry's demonstration of the extension and economy of Homeric language has since been challenged in Austin 1975 and Shive 1987.
7 M. Parry 1930 and 1932, collected in M. Parry 1971: 266–324, 325–64.
8 M. Parry 1971: 301–4.
9 Ibid. 156.
10 A forceful critique is found in Lynn-George 1988: 55–81. We will be reading Lynn-George more closely later.
11 Foley 1991: xii.
12 The debates surrounding Parry's theory of orality reflect, at a distance, the problems of structural linguistics itself. Parry, in developing the theory of orality, was immediately faced with the competing claims of, on the one hand, the structural linguistic system of traditional poetic language – the system of formulas, first and foremost – and, on the other hand, the poet or singer within this system. He decisively determined in favour of the scientificity of the system, while others would quickly champion the intention of the poet. At stake here is a version of the conflict between structure and subject within structuralism itself: what is the relation between the linguistic structures of Saussure and Benveniste or the social and mythological structures of Lévi-Strauss, and the subjects who are, variously, determined or produced by these structures, or in any case experience their world within or through them? In a very different scene from the Anglophone Homeric scholarship we are considering now, these problems were formulated explicitly in the psychoanalytic Marxism of the *Cahiers pour l'Analyse* (see now Hallward and Peden 2012a and b), and will remain in the background of this book's discussions.
13 Foley 1991: xii.
14 Ibid. 7.
15 See Danek 2002: 5–7.
16 Foley 1999: 6. This phrase – and its emphasis – will receive further discussion below.
17 For an example of this method at work in Foley, see his analysis of the last book of the *Iliad* in terms of its formulaic language, opening onto a set of traditional themes at work and in mutual interaction (1991: 135–89, 'Death, honor, and peace in *Iliad* 24'). The reauthorization of interpretation has been the aspect of Foley's work that

has been most productive in subsequent scholarship. See, for instance, Kelly's statement of principle (2007: 4): 'Interpretation should proceed from the realization that Homeric poetry is characterized on every level by an aesthetic of repetition, because it is constructed of a large but finite number of repeated units. Since the repetition of these units breeds an association which adds a connotative level of meaning to the denotative level represented by the story pattern, typical scene, action or expression itself, context becomes deeply significant.' It is worth pointing out, with Lynn-George, that these processes of repetition and connotation are not specific to oral poetry, but are rather processes of language as such (1988: 65).

18 Chapter 5, 'Songs and the Song', in Lord 1964: 99–123.
19 'What arouses public demand is totality; what resounds is the fragment' (Zumthor 1990: 42). Zumthor wrote on medieval literature and was a major figure in theorizing orality outside Homeric scholarship. Andrew Ford raises the same point and emphasizes the necessary absence of the entire, ideal song (1992: 87): 'The text constantly makes us aware of other stories that cannot be told ... but this whole must always be put outside the text, for the text cannot at once contain it and rely on it as basis and ground.'
20 We might see the Homer Multitext Project as a way of asymptotically approaching, in a hypertext, the hypothetical text of the total song.
21 See, for example, the discussion at Nagy 2003: 7–19.
22 '[T]he convention allows for much more than a preset, one-to-one allusiveness' (Foley 1991: 7).
23 Ibid. 7–8.
24 'The most important *sēma* is the register as a whole ... *Sēmata* signal the ambient tradition' (Foley 1999: 21). The *sēma* is one of the names for a traditional reference, as we will examine shortly.
25 Foley 1991: 47 (emphases added). The role of indeterminacy will be discussed later in this chapter.
26 Ibid. 138 and 7. Kelly faithfully preserves Foley's assumption that the experience of the Homeric poems should be the total reproduction of a prior ideal (2007: 6, emphases added): 'With this duality [between denotation and the connotation provided by traditional references], the modern audience comes *as close as it ever will* to the *fluency* or *experience* of an Archaic audience hearing the poetry unravelled before it. Without it, an understanding or reception of the text is necessarily *defective*, because the audience fails to hear *all* there is to hear.'
27 Foley 1991: 143.
28 On the lack of differentiation (Foley 1999: 6): '*Composition and reception are two sides of the same coin.*'
29 'These signs defer primarily ... to the immanent implication that each instance is licensed to bear by fiat' (Foley 1999: 21).

30 As in, for example, Nagy 1996b: 111–12.
31 Foley 1999: 55.
32 Cf. Zumthor 1990: 30 (emphases added): 'Listening ethnologically to oral "texts" ends up "folklorizing" them unless it *joins in* and *participates* (disinterested *to the point of irrationality*) in the very presuppositions of the discourse that the texts embody. Such listening occurs at *the deep level of pre- or translogical apprehension* where art communicates. / Whence the necessary subordination of analysis to *a general preliminary perception*; the subordination of argumentation to *the experience of its object*.'
33 Oral theory more broadly is a thoroughly structuralist phenomenon, rooted in Parry's work in Paris with Antoine Meillet, but it is one that has its own development, independent of structuralism and its continuations in French theory. (For Parry in Paris, see Vet 2005.) We can note one particularly telling difference in emphasis that distinguishes Foley's traditional referentiality from other strands of (post-)structuralism. For Foley, what guarantees the traditional meaning of a traditional reference is the presence of some invisible element that signals the traditionality of a phrase like 'swift-footed Achilles'. *Something* is added to the plain old phrase to make it a resonant traditional reference, but that something is not expressed in words. It is, instead, a zero-element that nevertheless carries immanent meaning ('ordinary phrase' + zero-element imbuing traditionality = 'traditional reference'). While Foley proposes a zero-element in which meaning as such exists, French structuralism considerably complicates the picture. We can consider here a first stage of this problematic, the classic concept of *mana* in Lévi-Strauss. Instead of mystical or religious interpretations, Lévi-Strauss interprets *mana* symbolically as a necessary consequence of signifying language as such. For Lévi-Strauss, *mana* is an expression of a 'floating signifier' or 'a symbol in its pure state', a *something* in the set of signifiers which does not have any specific signified, but has the pure function of soaking up any inadequation between the order of the signifier in general and that of the signified in general. In contrast to Foley's zero-element in which *exists* the *presence* of meaning, Lévi-Strauss identifies a signifier which makes visible and thinkable the *insistence* of an *absence*, or of the incommensurability of language and world. See Lévi-Strauss 1987: 59–63, as well as Žižek's discussion (2012: 147–68). We will continue to note the fertile ground of associations and contrasts between oral theory and structuralism, and, in some senses, we can think of *kleos* as a similar expression of incommensurability, though in different contexts and with different stakes.
34 '[E]inen Formen- oder Ideenhimmel' (Reinhardt 1961: 16). Kelly is helpful again in expressing explicitly the notion that the signifying or meaning-making resources of oral traditions form a prior totality, and that the work of the scholar is 'the reconstruction of the poetic thesaurus' (2007: 9). See also, in Justin Arft's

(forthcoming) mapping of this thesaurus for the phrase ἄνδρεσσι μελήσει, how meaning in oral tradition 'exists primarily in memory of performance, not in specific textual instances'. Haun Saussy noted this characteristic feature already in Parry (1996: 307, emphases added): 'For Parry sees orality as compensating for its temporal boundedness through the use of "formulae", set expressions and expressions modeled on them. An adequately complex oral tradition is an *archive* of linguistic resources together with the skill of unpacking and combining the *stored* materials as they are needed.' The oral tradition is here thought to be self-identical, eternalized in a perpetual living present. We will explicitly conceptualize the living present as a form of time in contrast to other forms of time in chapter five.

35 'The poetic tradition properly understood is not at all a limiting but rather a connotatively explosive medium, a touchstone or nexus of indication and reference wholly different from the medium at the disposal of the "non-traditional" artist' (Foley 1990: 2).

36 Foley 1999: 54.

37 What *is* ubiquitous and present everywhere is the *absence* of the legendary *guslar*. In the structuralist context discussed in note 33 above, *mana* as Lévi-Strauss's pure symbol preserves its dissonant core of incommensurability between signifier and signified. The development of structuralism through Althusser, Lacan and Jacques-Alain Miller proceeds only through grappling with this initial feature: the signifier which signifies the lack of the signifier, the representation of the inadequacy of representation or the metaphor of metaphor. While Foley does not follow the same development because he has, at the beginning of this path, already closed off the paradoxical figure of the *guslar* by assimilating his absence to a presence, we can nevertheless still follow the traces and potential links left unexplored.

38 Nagy makes the same gesture of turning absence to presence (1996b: 111–12): '[T]his envisioning of Homer in evolutionary terms may leave some of us with a sense of aching emptiness ... [But] the evolutionary model may even become a source of consolation: we may have lost a historical author whom we never knew anyway, but we have recovered in the process a mythical author who is more than just an author: he is *Hómēros*, cultural hero of Hellenism, a most cherished teacher of all Hellenes, who will come back to life with every new performance of his *Iliad* and *Odyssey*.'

39 Foley 1999: 21.

40 Ibid. 60. The 'emergent reality' is that of the pure meaningfulness of tradition.

41 Ibid. 56.

42 See, for example, Nagy 1990a: 208–12.

43 'Monotonous' is not a pejorative description. It refers to the specific quality of traditional art captured in Foley's epigraph to the first chapter of *Immanent Art*, from Lejeune 1954: 331: 'Les chansons de geste aux formes immuables sont "monotones" comme sont "monotones" les sculptures romanes – et même gothiques – de nos

cathédrales, avec leurs thèmes identiques: "Jugement dernier" ou "Annonciation" à leur portail.'

44 Porter 2011, edited from Porter 2005. Maitland 1999: 2–9 summarizes the problems and potential inconsistencies in the depiction of the wall. See further consideration at Grethlein 2006: 145–50, with further bibliography at note 341. Let me also note Elmer's consideration of the Achaean wall and its destruction as a reflection of local and Panhellenic poetic traditions, in which the wall is a Panhellenic innovation that needs to be reconciled – through its destruction – with a local tradition (2013: 211–14). This line of argument will become more relevant for our discussion of the Panhellenic synthesis in chapter three.

45 The effect of 'form' on 'content' that we see here is a version of the structuralist problematic discussed in note 33 above. A certain aspect of the symbolic 'form' comes to be expressed as an object – or kind of object – in the 'content', in the same way as the incommensurability of the signifying order to the signified is expressed as *mana*. The Lacanians would say that the signifier crosses the bar that divides signifier and signified, and passes into the order of the signified. In the present context, we have already observed that a certain resistance to formal identity and continuity – we have not yet defined precisely what this resistance is – comes to be expressed in the figure of the legendary *guslar*, though Foley covers this up as soon as it appears in his text. Similarly, we will ask what formal aspects of Homeric poetry are expressed through the *sēma* and the Achaean wall in particular.

46 Porter 2011: 5.

47 Ibid. 2 (emphasis added).

48 Letters in brackets are printed in original but should be deleted.

49 Ibid. 32.

50 'Homer is nothing other than the modern idea of what is ancient about antiquity' (Porter 2004: 341, a reworking of Porter 2002).

51 Porter 2011: 33. Another such sublime object might be found in Hector's clothes, which Andromache declares she will burn on his death (XXII. 512). Canevaro initially interprets the burning as 'epitomiz[ing] this transience of objects' (2018: 183), but later observes that these clothes are 'unmade' in the same sense as Porter describes the wall (237–8). Can we not take the next step and say that, rather than exemplifying the transience or *temporariness* of objects, these sublime objects attest to a more complex *temporality* in which the failure to persist itself persists as a form of time? 'There is becoming, change, passage. But the form of what changes does not itself change, does not pass on. This is time, time itself, "a little time in its pure state": a direct time-image, which gives what changes the unchanging form in which the change is produced' (Deleuze 1989: 17). In the next chapter, I will argue that the name for this failure is *kleos*.

52 We must save for another occasion consideration of Porter's further discussions of the sublime in the major works 2010 and 2016.

53 Žižek 2008: 229–31 (including the quotations in the preceding sentences).
54 Porter 2011: 33.
55 Ibid. 25.
56 Ibid. 5. (emphases moved).
57 Ibid. 26.
58 Of course, other approaches are possible. Ruth Scodel (1982), for instance, takes a step back from interpretation and makes it the sign of the influence on epic tradition by the tradition of a myth of destruction.
59 '[G]iven the insecurities of the tradition, doubts touching the very existence of *Homer himself* are inevitable' (Porter 2011: 30).
60 This desire for presence correlates with Foley's evident fondness for Lord's description of the recordings he and Parry made on their field trips, as a 'half-ton of epic'. This phrase, like traditional referentiality itself, lends a certain physical materiality to a conceptualization of poetry that looms in its epiphanic presence. See Foley 1999: 51 and 288 note 43.
61 Ford 1992 makes the case that the wall is an image of the poem itself (147–57).
62 ἦμος δ' οὔτ' ἄρ πω ἠώς, ἔτι δ' ἀμφιλύκη νύξ, / τῆμος ἄρ' ἀμφὶ πυρὴν κριτὸς ἔγρετο λαὸς Ἀχαιῶν, / τύμβον δ' ἀμφ' αὐτὴν ἕνα ποίεον ἐξαγαγόντες / ἄκριτον ἐκ πεδίου, ποτὶ δ' αὐτὸν τεῖχος ἔδειμαν / πύργους ὑψηλούς, εἶλαρ νηῶν τε καὶ αὐτῶν (vii. 433–7).
63 ἀμφ' αὐτοῖσι δ' ἔπειτα μέγαν καὶ ἀμύμονα τύμβον / χεύαμεν Ἀργείων ἱερὸς στρατὸς αἰχμητάων / ἀκτῇ ἔπι προὐχούσῃ, ἐπὶ πλατεῖ Ἑλλησπόντῳ, / ὥς κεν τηλεφανὴς ἐκ ποντόφιν ἀνδράσιν εἴη / τοῖς οἳ νῦν γεγάασι καὶ οἳ μετόπισθεν ἔσονται. See also Nagy 1979: 340 ff.
64 Kirk 1990 *ad* vii. 334–5. It is possible for the bones to be gathered from the pyre and separated before the wall is built on top, but nothing of this is mentioned where this is narrated at vii. 431–41.
65 Ibid.
66 The same failure of commemoration is suggested, pointedly if less dramatically, by the *sēma* that was designated as the turning post for the chariot race at Patroclus' funeral games: 'Either it is the grave marker of someone who died long ago, or was set as a racing goal by men who lived before our time' (ἤ τευ σῆμα βροτοῖο πάλαι κατατεθνηῶτος, / ἢ τό γε νύσσα τέτυκτο ἐπὶ προτέρων ἀνθρώπων, xxiii. 331–2). See also Purves's discussion of the *sēma* in the context of the *Odyssey*, in particular the semantic instabilities of Odysseus' oar or winnowing fan and the precarious fixity of Odysseus' bed (2010: 80–4).
67 πέρθετο δὲ Πριάμοιο πόλις δεκάτῳ ἐνιαυτῷ, / Ἀργεῖοι δ' ἐν νηυσὶ φίλην ἐς πατρίδ' ἔβησαν, / δὴ τότε μητιόωντο Ποσειδάων καὶ Ἀπόλλων / τεῖχος ἀμαλδῦναι ποταμῶν μένος εἰσαγαγόντες. / ὅσσοι ἀπ' Ἰδαίων ὀρέων ἅλαδε προρέουσι.
68 οὔτε τὰ τεύχεα καλά, τά που μάλα νειόθι λίμνης / κείσεθ' ὑπ' ἰλύος κεκαλυμμένα· κὰδ δέ μιν αὐτὸν / εἰλύσω ψαμάθοισιν ἅλις χέραδος περιχεύας / μυρίον, οὐδέ οἱ

ὀστέ' ἐπιστήσονται Ἀχαιοὶ / ἀλλέξαι· τόσσην οἱ ἄσιν καθύπερθε καλύψω. / αὐτοῦ οἱ καὶ σῆμα τετεύξεται, οὐδέ τί μιν χρεὼ / ἔσται τυμβοχόης, ὅτε μιν θάπτωσιν Ἀχαιοί (XXI. 317–23). Ford 1992: 153, citing Redfield 1975: 167–9, 251. Note the play of negations implicit in the notion of an 'antifuneral' here: burial by mud and slime removes the possibility of heaping up a mound (τυμβοχόης), and yet this is precisely what will constitute a paradoxical *sēma* (αὐτοῦ οἱ καὶ σῆμα τετεύξεται). The *sēma*-as-commemoration becomes indiscernible from its opposite, *sēma*-as-obliteration. Conversely, while the Achaean wall itself is never explicitly called a *sēma*, it is the ghost of a *sēma* by its position atop a τύμβον; it is an anti-*sēma* – and thus a *sēma*.

69 Porter 2011: 19. Another account of the Achaean wall which emphasizes its impermanence is found in Garcia 2013: 97–110. Garcia's discussion takes place in the context of a certain interpretation of Heidegger, and argues for impermanence as an essential property of Homeric epic's self-conception. Our discussions differ in that we hope to place that impermanence within a broader context.

70 Karen Bassi's concept of the 'protoarchaeological' is similarly concerned with tracing the boundaries of continuity and interruption (2016: 2): 'Protoarchaeological narratives do two things. First, they activate a competition between the possibility (or promise) of seeing the past and the act of reading (about) it. Second, they activate a competition between the desire to preserve the past in visible or material form, on the one hand, and the past's susceptibility to destruction and decay, on the other.' Bassi, too, connects the interruption of tradition occasioned by the Achaean wall and Achilles' death-by-water (51) with 'the theoretical pitfalls of the scholarly faith in an idealized oral tradition, manifested in the power to turn readers into spectators of the epic events' (83). In linking the fate of material *sēmata* like walls and grave markers to the possibility of commemoration in oral tradition, I am suggesting an alternative to the interpretation that the perishability of material objects is meant as a foil to the durability and superiority of poetic tradition. For example, Ford 1992: 'Hector should not expect to find his undying glory in that *sēma* he bargained for; only in the poet's song will his burial be remembered' (146); Grethlein 2008: 'The fragility and ambiguity of material relics and the eternity of the poetic tradition highlight each other in their discrepancy' (35); Canevaro 2018: 'What we really need is reputation, rumour, *kleos*: things which can be transmitted orally after our death' (194; she nuances the discussion by distinguishing between 'oral memory linked to material triggers ... and the oral memory of the bard', 201). I do not wish to argue against this interpretation so much as shift the terms of the discussion: In the following chapters, I will make the case that all meaning and memory in the *Iliad* is marked by interruption, a form of meaning that embraces both oral and objective memory.

71 It is not unusual to see Parry's successors reacting strongly but implicitly against his positions while professing to be in wholehearted support of them.

72 Nägele 1991: 83.
73 Nägele 1987: 15.
74 Foley 1991, chapter two.
75 Ibid. 40–1.
76 Iser 1971: 13–14, quoted at Foley 1991: 41.
77 Ibid. 47. The latter half of the passage has already been cited above.
78 Ibid. 54. We will further consider, in chapter three, the notion of an audience's complete knowledge of the 'poetic thesaurus' (Kelly 2007: 9) and its implications for the possibilities of interpretation. For now, let us simply note the possibilities of a Homeric poetics that presupposes the audience's lack of knowledge as an irreducible part of its meaning. Scodel has explored the pragmatic uses to which this ignorance can be put (1997: 216, with a prefiguring echo at Andersen 1990: 43–4 note 30): 'The poet invites the audience to pretend to know everything already, which leaves no position from which they can distinguish what they could have known, but happened not to know, and what they could not have known, because it was not previously part of the tradition.' But what else can be done with gaps in knowledge?
79 Foley 1999: 5.
80 Ibid. 6, 14, 32, 60, 86, 87, 90, 91, 101, 111, 118.
81 ὣς ἄρ' ἔμελλον ὄπισθε Ποσειδάων καὶ Ἀπόλλων / θησέμεναι· τότε δ' ἀμφὶ μάχη ἐνοπή τε δεδήει / τεῖχος ἐΰδμητον (xii. 34–6).
82 Porter 2011: 5, as quoted above.
83 Ibid. 6.
84 Scodel 1982: 48.
85 οὐδ' ἄρ' ἔμελλε / τάφρος ἔτι σχήσειν Δαναῶν ... τὸ καὶ οὔ τι πολὺν χρόνον ἔμπεδον ἦεν ... ὣς ἄρ' ἔμελλον ὄπισθε Ποσειδάων καὶ Ἀπόλλων / θησέμεναι· τότε δ' ἀμφὶ μάχη ἐνοπή τε δεδήει (xii. 3–4, 9, 34–5).
86 Kahane (forthcoming, section 2.1) reaches a similar conclusion from an argument based on contrasts in narrative timescales in the Homeric poems – the way that sometimes years are covered over a matter of verses, while a single day takes up books viii–xviii of the *Iliad*: 'The contrast creates a parallax-view, a dual optic which allows us to observe invisible time in a manner dependent on action and narrative but from two different angles.'

2 The Breaking of the Present

1 xxiii. 331–3 and Ford 1992: 144–5.
2 There is copious scholarship on time in Homeric and archaic Greek thought, prominently Fränkel 1955 (original publication 1931) and close successors (Onians 1951, Treu 1953 and Accame 1961; additionally, Theunissen 2000: 19–42; see now

also Kahane forthcoming, with bibliography). These writers sought an account of archaic Greek thinking about the concept of time (even when the conclusion was that there was a lack of the concept), focusing on close interpretation of linguistic terms and usage as evidence for modes of thought. Our approach will be different in that we do not seek, say, how an actual oral singer of the archaic period might have conceived of time. We are not after what 'time' was for archaic Greek thought. Instead, we will be exploring the way *kleos* as difference divides every present moment, so that the present is split between the now and some other time. Thus, what we are after is less the time-conception of a historically existing people (the possibility of which is in any case fraught), but more an image of time produced in the encounter of the Homeric poems and modern discourses. We will nevertheless note places where these writers have, within their own contexts, prefigured certain aspects of the argument to be made here. There are closer parallels here with Jonas Grethlein's project on the *Geschichtsbild* of the *Iliad*, which is far from the lexical approach of Fränkel and instead seeks an image of time and temporality produced in the encounter of the *Iliad* and Heideggerian reflections, in particular the way contingency (*Kontingenz*) divides expectation (*Erwartung*) from experience (*Erfahrung*). See Grethlein 2006, in particular 20–41. Also related is Garcia 2013. I will soon compare and differentiate my approach from those of Grethlein and Garcia.

3 The notion of an uncontrollable *kleos* that cannot be mastered can be seen as the obverse side of Theunissen's (2000) notion of a *Herrschaft* of time that will be transcended in Pindar. This notion itself reflects Fränkel's discussion of man's *ephēmeros* nature (1946); we are *ephēmeros* because we are subject to time's *Herrschaft*.

4 Looking ahead to the next chapter, we will compare the division of the present analysed here to the insistence on the unity and wholeness of the present in oral theory, with particular attention on the work of Gregory Nagy.

5 From Indo-European root *kleu-*, 'hear', cognate with words meaning 'fame' in a number of Indo-European languages. See *Lexikon des frühgriechischen Epos* 14 (*LfgrE*) and *Dictionnaire étymologique de la langue grecque* (Chantraine 1999), s.v. κλέος; West 2007: 396–410.

6 Instead of listing a myriad of related literature on *kleos*, let me sketch a background by citing those works which inform my sense of those aspects of the existing consensus important for my argument: Redfield 1975, Nagy 1979, Griffin 1980: 81–143, Segal 1983, Schein 1984, Goldhill 1991: 69–166, Pucci 1998: 31–48 and 179–230, Hardie 2012: 1–77. I am also indebted to Lynn-George 1988. Other, more pointedly relevant discussions will be introduced over the course of the chapter.

7 That there is a gap or discontinuity within *kleos* as a concept has been noted before, forming, in particular, the theme and title of Philip Hardie's *Rumour and Renown*,

which, although focused on later literatures, recognizes that 'the Homeric epics show an awareness of the ways in which the monumental *kleos* of outstanding heroes – undying, unquenchable, ever-flowing fame – is not separable from more transient uses of the word, often operating through the mouths of the nameless crowd' (2012: 67). Earlier, Pietro Pucci has cast the distinction with a Derridean colouring (1998: 48; original publication 1980): 'In concrete terms, the text denounces the inescapable risk of repetition, that is at once deadly and vital, effacing truth and revealing truth; the text suggests both the anxiety of being forced to accept the pattern of repetition and the assurance that repetition does not prevent a special, even somehow subjective voice. But the text, by failing to support the distinctions, intimates that both modes of *kleos*, that is to say *kleos* (rumor-ignorance) and *kleos* (voice-*mnêmê*), resound and echo together at each moment, while the whole rhetoric of the poet tries to separate this combined echo in order to isolate and exalt the note of a pure, living voice.' As might be expected from the deconstructive framework, Pucci ascribes to the poem an ideological preference for the voice of 'renown' over the repetition of 'rumour'. Our discussion will echo these distinction from a distance imposed by differences in material and emphasis.

8 De Jong's formulation can serve as a typical example (2006: 195): 'There is no denying that the prophecy voiced here by Helen [at vi. 357–8, that epic events will be the subject of song] is fulfilled by the *Iliad*.' Garcia repeats this logic, though with a slight twist of his own which we will address later (2013: 237): '[A]s a temporal object existing in mortal temporality, the durability of the *Iliad* itself can only last as long as the process of Achilles' κλέος ἄφθιτον – celebrating and listening to Achilles' fame so that it remains unwithered – is repeated.' A similar logic is often claimed for the *sēma*, for instance: 'As long as the deceased's memory lived on in the community, and the grave monument was identified as the index of his burial, its physical presence inevitably activated the memory of the deceased, in those who perceived it, and in this way it also fed the memory and contributed to its preservation' (Sourvinou-Inwood 1995: 118). Bakker begins with the logic of equivalence between epic, memory and performance, but takes it to its rigorous conclusion (Bakker 2002: 27, emphasis added): 'So when a Homeric hero proclaims that his *kleos* or that of the story he is in will be *aphthiton* or that it "will never perish" (e.g. 11. 2.325; 7.91; 9.413), he is not merely talking about the future. The very fact that he can utter these words is due to the epic performance of the present. Epic events happen not only "now" but also in the future. *Epic in its very functioning thus collapses the distinction between present and future*, the very space in which *khrónos* is active in destroying and (re)generating. That space is precisely the place where Simonides and Herodotus, in commemorating the heroic exploits of the recent past, have to locate *kleos*. They can only talk about *kleos* in the future, just like Homeric heroes, but without the protective, *khrónos*-proof shield provided by epic.' In contrast to the

notion that epic *collapses* the distinction between present and future, I will argue instead that epic *generalizes* that distinction.

9 'And some day one of the lateborn men will say, sailing in his benched ship on the wine-blue water: "This is the mound of a man who died long ago, one of the bravest, and glorious Hektor killed him." So will he speak some day, and my glory will never perish' (καί ποτέ τις εἴπῃσι καὶ ὀψιγόνων ἀνθρώπων / νηΐ πολυκληΐδι πλέων ἐπὶ οἴνοπα πόντον· / ἀνδρὸς μὲν τόδε σῆμα πάλαι κατατεθνηῶτος, / ὅν ποτ' ἀριστεύοντα κατέκτανε φαίδιμος Ἕκτωρ. / ὥς ποτέ τις ἐρέει· τὸ δ' ἐμὸν κλέος οὔ ποτ' ὀλεῖται, vii. 87–91).

10 Redfield clearly makes this distinction (1975: 34): 'To think of life as a story is different from thinking of it in terms of praise and blame. A story is more than that; it has a shape – a beginning, middle and end; in Homer a man may be conceived as a narrative, may conceive himself as a narrative.' Kahane (forthcoming, section 2.3) points out the necessity of distinguishing 'what *kind* of identity is preserved' from *whether* it is preserved. Goldhill is very close to this position when he reflects on the embassy, how the fact that 'this scene has led to one of most intense critical exchanges among the *Iliad*'s readers (as readers repeat *the process of evaluation of Achilles* and the embassy dramatized in the scene) shows how the poem of *kleos* inevitably involves its audience in the exchange that is narrative, the crisis – decisions – of criticism. Reading the *Iliad* is not merely to recite the *kleos* of Achilles, but to be an active part of the process of its *recovering*' (1991: 86, emphases added). Goldhill, too, connects *kleos* with a narrative content and the meaning of that narrative, but seems to veer away in the very last word insofar as 'recovering' implies the restoration of a reified glory as opposed to the open contest of evaluation earlier in the quoted passage. The tendency to reify *kleos* is concomitant with a blurring of the *narrative* nature of *kleos* to the *quantitative* magnitude of *timē*.

11 αἰσχρὸν γὰρ τόδε γ' ἐστὶ καὶ ἐσσομένοισι πυθέσθαι / μὰψ οὕτω τοιόνδε τοσόνδε τε λαὸν Ἀχαιῶν / ἄπρηκτον πόλεμον πολεμίζειν ἠδὲ μάχεσθαι (ii. 119–21).

12 While heroes obviously do affect their *kleos*, my point here follows rather the emphasis of what Redfield calls 'the epic distance', in which the epic song of *kleos* is 'excluded from the *Iliad*' and 'can only be hinted at and anticipated': '[E]pic describes the heroic world to an audience which itself inhabits another, ordinary, world' (Redfield 1975: 35–6). The bar between the heroes and epic song is in fact the expression of what Redfield derives from a reading of Aristotle's *Ethics* (ibid. 64): 'The actor commits himself to the future and thus never knows his own act; since the future is without limit, there is no moment when the returns are in.' I take this to be the force of the qualification 'strangely' when Kahane (forthcoming, section 2.5, emphasis added) notes that the heroes 'can nevertheless sometimes *strangely* choose' the manner of their death.

13 The connections between the unexpected and time have been extensively worked out in Grethlein 2006.

14 The conflation of *timē* and *kleos* in scholarship is no accident, because it is precisely what is dramatized in the *Iliad*. For an overview of these terms, see the entries on 'glory', 'honor' and '*kleos*' in Finkelberg 2011.
15 Segal 1983: 22. I am thus resistant to the notion that *timē* confers *kleos* in any straightforward manner in the *Iliad*, for instance in Schein's formulation (1984: 71): 'Those who win such tangible honors also receive honor conceived abstractly; from this comes their *kleos*, "glory and reputation," what is said about them near and far, even when they are dead.'
16 τοὺς δὲ κατὰ πρύμνας τε καὶ ἀμφ' ἅλα ἔλσαι Ἀχαιοὺς / κτεινομένους, ἵνα πάντες ἐπαύρωνται βασιλῆος, / γνῷ δὲ καὶ Ἀτρεΐδης εὐρὺ κρείων Ἀγαμέμνων / ἣν ἄτην ὅτ' ἄριστον Ἀχαιῶν οὐδὲν ἔτισεν (1. 409–12). τίνω and τιμή are connected etymologically through PIE **kʷei-*, but see also the collocation (τίσωσιν . . . τιμῇ) in the next quotation.
17 ἀλλὰ σύ πέρ μιν τῖσον Ὀλύμπιε μητίετα Ζεῦ· / τόφρα δ' ἐπὶ Τρώεσσι τίθει κράτος ὄφρ' ἂν Ἀχαιοὶ / υἱὸν ἐμὸν τίσωσιν ὀφέλλωσίν τέ ἑ τιμῇ (1. 508–10).
18 τί νύ σ' ἔτρεφον αἰνὰ τεκοῦσα; / αἴθ' ὄφελες παρὰ νηυσὶν ἀδάκρυτος καὶ ἀπήμων / ἦσθαι, ἐπεί νύ τοι αἶσα μίνυνθά περ οὔ τι μάλα δήν· / νῦν δ' ἅμα τ' ὠκύμορος καὶ ὀϊζυρὸς περὶ πάντων / ἔπλεο· τώ σε κακῇ αἴσῃ τέκον ἐν μεγάροισι (1. 414–18; translation modified).
19 I use 'history' here to indicate the series of events that contribute to judgement or meaning at the site of *kleos*, as opposed to events which do not. Compare the position that Macbeth tries to take up with respect to the murder of Duncan. In hoping that 'If chance will have me king, why, chance may crown me without my stir' (I. iii), Macbeth wishes that his guilty desire may come to pass without a guilty act on his part becoming recorded as part of the judgement on his life. And in declaring that 'strange things I have in head that will to hand, which must be acted ere they may be scann'd' (III. iv), Macbeth hopes that if a guilty act can pass without hesitation or examination – 'be scann'd' – from conception to execution – from 'in head' to 'hand' – the lack of scansion will somehow hide the guilty act from the eye of history, like a child who imagines that he turns invisible when he closes his eyes.
20 Achilles will never fully acknowledge his responsibility in *asking for* the death of the Achaeans (κτεινομένους, 1. 410) – which resulted in the death of Patroclus – not even to himself in his dream of Patroclus' ghost. His self-blame in book XVIII focuses on his passive failure to protect (ἐμεῖο δὲ δῆσεν ἀρῆς ἀλκτῆρα γενέσθαι, 100) rather than his active request to Zeus, although it is possible to understand a more active force in τὸν ἀπώλεσα (82) – 'I have killed him' rather than 'I have lost him' (see Coray 2018 and Rutherford 2019 *ad loc.*). Buchan argues for Achilles' self-delusion on this point as 'the tragedy of Achilles' in a chapter of the same name (2012: 29–52).
21 μήτηρ γάρ τέ μέ φησι θεὰ Θέτις ἀργυρόπεζα / διχθαδίας κῆρας φερέμεν θανάτοιο τέλοσδε. / εἰ μέν κ' αὖθι μένων Τρώων πόλιν ἀμφιμάχωμαι, / ὤλετο μέν μοι νόστος,

ἀτὰρ κλέος ἄφθιτον ἔσται· / εἰ δέ κεν οἴκαδ' ἵκωμι φίλην ἐς πατρίδα γαῖαν, / ὤλετό μοι κλέος ἐσθλόν, ἐπὶ δηρὸν δέ μοι αἰὼν / ἔσσεται, οὐδέ κέ μ' ὦκα τέλος θανάτοιο κιχείη (ιx. 410–16).

22 We will soon elaborate the connection between death and *kleos*, but see for now Edwards 1985: 71–93. The connection between death and *kleos* is perhaps most memorably made in Sarpedon's reflections at xii. 322–8.
23 On this inconsistency see Morrison 1992: 101 and Burgess 2009: 50–2.
24 Achilles pre-assigned the narrative meaning of his re-entry into battle in his initial withdrawal (i. 240–4). Before the death of Patroclus, action for Achilles is the re-enactment of predetermined meaning.
25 Buchan 2012: 25.
26 This is a significant point of difference between my reading and those in which Achilles actually *makes* the 'choice of Achilles' from book ix. Goldhill, for instance, refers to Achilles' 'commitment to *kleos*' (1991: 75), his 'privileged position' in which '[h]e has a specific choice' (76) and 'actively chooses *kleos* and death over *nostos*' (105 note 120). A whole passage of narrative time is elided if we claim that Achilles chooses *kleos aphthiton* over long life according to the terms set out in book ix; we lose the whole content of Achilles' career and his tragedy. The statement of the choice itself (ix. 410–16) arises in the context of Achilles on the point of *leaving* and advising others to leave (καὶ δ' ἂν τοῖς ἄλλοισιν ἐγὼ παραμυθησαίμην / οἴκαδ' ἀποπλείειν, 417–18). Achilles retreats from the idea of leaving over the course of the Embassy, but he does not choose *kleos* over long life; he vacillates. Neither does he choose in book xi, nor in book xvi, and by the time he 'willingly proceeds to a certain death' (80), the choice had been made *for him* by the loss of Patroclus.
27 Further emphasis, if it were needed, of the distinction between caring *that* one's *kleos* endures and imagining *what* endures as one's *kleos*.
28 αὐτίκα γάρ τοι ἔπειτα μεθ' Ἕκτορα πότμος ἑτοῖμος (xviii. 96); αὐτίκα τεθναίην, ἐπεὶ οὐκ ἄρ' ἔμελλον ἑτάιρῳ / κτεινομένῳ ἐπαμῦναι (xviii. 98–9). To anticipate later discussions, the whiplash effect of the choice of Achilles which turned in an instant – though we cannot pinpoint which instant – from indefinitely deferred in the future to always already past is an effect of Deleuze's third synthesis, the 'pure empty form of time', which he also calls Aion, in contrast to Chronos: 'In accordance with Aion, only the past and future inhere or subsist in time. Instead of a present which absorbs this past and future, a future and past divide this present at every instant and subdivide it ad infinitum into past and future, in both directions at once' (Deleuze 1990: 164).
29 In anticipation of the focus of chapter four, we can note that, in book xi, Achilles uses Patroclus as a formal device – as his access to the plot or story – but Patroclus' journey turns out to be part of the content.
30 We had previously noted that the futurity of *kleos* is indexed by the word *essomenoisi*. In this context, Max Treu's observations on this word foreshadow the

connection from *essomenoisi* to the inaccessibility of *kleos* (1955: 132): 'Equally objective and abstracted from the subject is the Homeric term for the "afterworld", ἐσσόμενοι ... It is not the spatial conception of "after" or "before" transferred to the temporal ... There is no continuity here, one way nor another, towards those to come: not here, whereas it was clearly evident towards the earlier generations.' It will be possible, after the discussion in chapter five, to clarify Treu's thesis that the early Greek consciousness was strongly continuous with the past and less connected to the future; it combines in one hybrid expression the three forms of temporality we will analyse there. See also Theunissen's critique at 2000: 35–41.

31 See the discussion of Heidegger in the Homeric context at Garcia 2013: 31–42, with reservations in Grethlein's review at 2014: 483–4.
32 οὐχ ὁράᾳς οἷος καγὼ καλός τε μέγας τε; / πατρὸς δ' εἴμ' ἀγαθοῖο, θεὰ δέ με γείνατο μήτηρ· / ἀλλ' ἔπι τοι καὶ ἐμοὶ θάνατος καὶ μοῖρα κραταιή· / ἔσσεται ἢ ἠὼς ἢ δείλη ἢ μέσον ἦμαρ / ὁππότε τις καὶ ἐμεῖο Ἄρη ἐκ θυμὸν ἕληται / ἢ ὅ γε δουρὶ βαλὼν ἢ ἀπὸ νευρῆφιν ὀϊστῷ (XXI. 108–13).
33 Soph. *OT*. 1080.
34 For the specificity of morning, noon and afternoon in this passage, see Austin 1975: 86–7.
35 The hero, faced with unknowable *kleos*, can be compared to the jealous man in Deleuze's reading of Proust (2000: 52, emphasis added): '[M]emory always comes too late in relation to the signs to be deciphered. The jealous man's memory tries to retain everything because the slightest detail may turn out to be a sign or a symptom of deception, so that the intelligence will have the material requisite to its forthcoming interpretations. Hence there is something sublime in the jealous man's memory; it confronts its own limits and, straining toward the future, seeks to transcend them. *But it comes too late, for it cannot distinguish within the moment that phrase that should be retained, that gesture that it could not yet know would assume a certain meaning.*'
36 Ricoeur uses the term 'cosmological' for what I have been calling 'chronological', but I will retain the latter term for consistency.
37 See Ricoeur 1984: 5–87 and 1988: 12–22.
38 Ricoeur 1988: 120 and 86. See also Nankov 2014: 246 note 2.
39 See Ricoeur 1988: 23–59.
40 See ibid. 60–96 and Heidegger 1962. Grethlein 2006 is essential in this connection, and I will have further comment later.
41 For Grethlein, see note 2 above. What we reconceive as an escape from or breaking out of ordinary, chronological time is prefigured in earlier studies. The (in)famous *Indifferenzthese* of Fränkel's seminal 1931 study, which describes the 'carefree wandering into the emptiness' of a world still unhampered by any 'fixed temporal frame [*festen zeitlichen Rahmen*]', is in many ways a rejection not of time as such, but

of fixed and sequential chronological time (1955: 2 and 6). Indeed, despite his unsustainable contention that the 'steady course' of epic is 'never interrupted by a standstill or by turning back', Fränkel is perfectly well aware of non-chronological temporalities, as in his observations on the semantics of the 'day' (ibid. 3–5). The changeability and contingency that forms the link between Grethlein's thesis and our discussions here is foreshadowed in Fränkel's companion piece on *ephēmeros*: 'Just as, for instance, *epiphthonos* is "exposed and subject to envy", so *ephēmeros* is "exposed and subject to every actuality as it arises", and the term implies that man is moulded and remoulded by changing events and circumstances' (Fränkel 1946: 133 = 1955: 25). For Fränkel, however, this insight does not apply to the *Iliad*, which for him represented a past that was 'set and fixed forevermore', 'based on the idea of stability' (ibid. 140). There has been a distinct tendency to oversimplify various aspects of the *Iliad*, often in order to sharpen a contrast with the *Odyssey* or later works.

42 Kahane (forthcoming) presents a penetrating and wide-ranging exploration of Homeric temporality through Ricoeur's Heideggerian framework; it would have been invaluable for my argument if it had appeared before this book was substantially completed.
43 Bergson 1920: 164.
44 Ibid. 165.
45 Ibid. 166.
46 Ibid. 165. Bassi's reading of the *teichoscopia* describes exactly the split caused by the simultaneous existence of perception and memory (2016: 82, emphases added): 'But unlike the wall, this hypothetical past is not so overtly defined in terms of a continuum from visibility to invisibility. Rather, it emerges from a kind of *double vision* in which what Helen sees from the Trojan wall in the present moment of the poem (the scene on the plain below) is, in effect, *memorialized or fixed as a scene from the past* (the scene on the tapestry).'
47 This has implications for the position of the poet: does the poet in fact fulfil the heroes' expectations about *kleos* in epic song? We will explore this question in chapter five.
48 It is important to note that the conceptualization of the present at this point of the discussion still needs to clarify the nature and properties of this 'present'. For now, let us note that it is specifically a *divided* or *split* present, a notion that will be sharpened, in the next chapter, through a contrast with a *whole* and *self-sufficient* present. In chapter five, we will be able to assign these different versions of the present their specific places as part of a dynamic temporal structure.
49 Grethlein 2006: 135–6: 'Die Erfahrung von Schicksalskontingenz, die Patroklos' Tod für ihn darstellt, wird der Anlaß, sich dem Zufall in seiner schärfsten Form auszusetzen. Zudem wird der heroische Einsatz für Achill zur Möglichkeit,

Schicksalskontingenz zu überwinden. Als Lohn für seinen Einsatz erhält er κλέος ἄφθιτον. Die Unvergänglichkeit, die »der beste der Achaier« mit seinem frühen Tod erlangt, hebt die Macht des Zufalls auf und ermöglicht ein Leben jenseits von Kontingenz.' I have opted to translate *aufheben* as 'supersede' instead of a word that preserves a more Hegelian sense of 'sublation', and this is because of the closely connected uses of *überwinden*.

50 Kahane (forthcoming, section 2.3) also recognizes that what is *aphthiton* does not overcome mortality: 'But *kleos aphthiton* is not an imperishable modality of mortal *life*, it is, rather, precisely the preservation in memory and recollection of finite mortality that only emerges from the recognition of finitude.' I would only want to push this one step further: if Achilles' *kleos* is indeed to be *aphthiton*, what is *aphthiton* about that *kleos*, what persists and echoes, is precisely change and contingency. Similarly, in Kahane's evocative description (section 2.2) of the way the repetition of time descriptions like 'rosy fingered Dawn' 'invoke an anonymous image of natural time' with 'cosmological and theological dimensions', such repetition does not imply the passing of an eternally uniform time. 'The conventional, repeated epic formulae that describe quotidian time thus never simply mark the homogenous ticking of nature's indifferent clock.' They are alive with the potential for difference. The broader implication for the repetition of Homeric language and, in particular, epithets, is clear, and Kahane addresses this at section 2.6. I am tempted to read Foley's recuperation of the term 'monotonous' (see chapter one, note 43) as a highly compressed expression of an argument that identically repeated formulas are *not* monotonous because they invite potential comparisons (as, for instance, in the well-known repetition of 'man-killing', ἀνδροφόνους/ἀνδροφόνοιο at XXIV. 479, 509). Along these lines, see Ward 2019 for an analysis of how the epithet κοῖλος, used of ships, belies any simple self-identical reading of its literal meaning 'hollow' by carrying the tension between the empty hollows of the ships and the potential for them to be filled.

51 Let us also compare the discussions here with those of Garcia 2013 on the time of the Homeric poems. Garcia, too, is interested in describing an image of Homeric time, and the concept of time towards which he orients his argument is one of time that passes, ephemerality, *Vergänglichkeit*, in contrast to the *Unvergänglichkeit* so much insisted upon on behalf of *kleos*. It is this interest that leads him to interpret the *aphthiton* of *kleos aphthiton* as 'not yet withered' instead of the more common 'unwithering' or 'impossible to wither' (with valiant linguistic demonstrations at Garcia 2013: 9–14). In comparison to our concerns, Garcia is interested in a more chronological understanding of time as a sequence of presents that pass, and in his chapters, he demonstrates a wide range of phenomena – men, built structures, memorials, even the gods – in the Homeric poems as passing. (See also, in relation to gods, Purves 2006.) In contrast, we have tried to demonstrate how *kleos* produces a distinct structure of time as the difference that divides every present moment.

52 The assertion of the primacy of difference with respect to identity of course recalls a major theme of Deleuze 1994. I do not wish to 'apply' Deleuze to the Homeric context in the way that a 'theory' is 'applied' to a text, which becomes its object; such a method would be alien to Deleuze's thought about the relation of art and philosophy. Instead, what we are doing here can be thought of as extracting the concepts – concepts of difference and time – already expressed by the Homeric poems and scholarship, in this combination and in their own ways, and making them explicit.

53 οἷσιν ἐπὶ Ζεὺς θῆκε κακὸν μόρον, ὡς καὶ ὀπίσσω / ἀνθρώποισι πελώμεθ' ἀοίδιμοι ἐσσομένοισι (VI. 357–8). There is uncertainty regarding whether οἷσιν ('us') refers to only Helen and Paris or if it also includes Hector, the addressee of the speech (see Graziosi and Haubold 2010 *ad loc.*). This uncertainty is not urgent for my purpose here, as I am using it as emblematic of the heroic attitude in general.

54 To capture the implied judgement, ἀοίδιμοι is better rendered 'worthy of song' (Graziosi and Haubold 2010 *ad loc.*) – *wert, besungen zu werden* (*LfgrE* s.v. ἀοίδιμος) – as opposed to merely the *object* of song (also *LfgrE*: *Gegenstand eines Liedes*). What is distinguished here is, again, the difference between *that* one gains *kleos* and *what kind* of *kleos* is gained.

55 In this analysis of Helen's words, I am aware of making two generalizations. The less problematic of the two is the way I have generalized this statement to all Iliadic characters, when strictly speaking Helen has in mind herself and either Hector or Paris, or both. The more problematic may be the way I have assimilated Helen, a woman, into the markedly masculine framework of epic *kleos*. Both of these generalizations can be justified to some extent by the fact that the sentiment Helen gives voice to here is paralleled by Alcinous in the *Odyssey* (viii. 579–80): 'The gods did this, and spun the destruction of peoples, so that there would be a song for those to come' (τὸν δὲ θεοὶ μὲν τεῦξαν, ἐπεκλώσαντο δ' ὄλεθρον / ἀνθρώποισ', ἵνα ἦσι καὶ ἐσσομένοισιν ἀοιδή). Both Helen and Alcinous express the temporality of meaning I am describing. But my elision of gendered differences in the economy of epic fame also brings out an important qualification of my use of *kleos* as a concept more broadly: I emphasize *kleos* as the emblematic expression of the Iliadic temporality of meaning at the expense of its other aspects – what I propose is precisely not an *economy* of *kleos*, if we take 'economy' to imply an account of the quantifiable or commensurable. My account is therefore not mutually exclusive with those that bring out other facets of this important concept. For a form of *kleos* specific to women inspired by Helen's gift of a robe as a 'monument [*mnēma*] to the hands of Helen' (xv. 126), see Mueller 2010; there is an opportunity to connect women's weaving with the weaving of fate (ἐπεκλώσαντο, viii. 579). For the gendered conjunction of time and *kleos*, see Canevaro 2018; I will return to her account in chapter four.

56 See chapter one, notes 33, 37 and 45.
57 φίλε κασίγνητε θάνατόν νύ τοι ὅρκι' ἔταμνον / οἷον προστήσας πρὸ Ἀχαιῶν Τρωσὶ μάχεσθαι, / ὥς σ' ἔβαλον Τρῶες, κατὰ δ' ὅρκια πιστὰ πάτησαν (IV. 155-7).
58 The syntax is striking in giving ἔταμνον a double object in ὅρκια, oaths, and θάνατόν, death: 'I concluded [literally, 'cut'] oaths, death, as it turns out [νύ], to you.'
59 If there is such a thing as mere rhetoric.
60 ἆ δειλοὶ Δαναῶν ἡγήτορες ἠδὲ μέδοντες / ὡς ἄρ' ἐμέλλετε τῆλε φίλων καὶ πατρίδος αἴης / ἄσειν ἐν Τροίῃ ταχέας κύνας ἀργέτι δημῷ (XI. 816-18), quoted from Bakker 2005: 99-100 in his translation.
61 Ibid. 100.
62 Bakker's rejection of a 'purely temporal' interpretation of *emellete* does not put him at odds with our emphasis on an image of time, since what he rejects in the phrase 'purely temporal' is precisely the chronological understanding of time as a sequence of indifferent presents.
63 ὣς φάτο λισσόμενος μέγα νήπιος· ἦ γὰρ ἔμελλεν / οἷ αὐτῷ θάνατόν τε κακὸν καὶ κῆρα λιτέσθαι (XVI. 46-7), quoted from ibid. 108 in Bakker's translation.
64 Ibid. 112. This interpretation of *nēpios* in its temporal significance supplements rather than replaces broader analyses like Edmunds 1990.
65 The future song thus exhibits what Kahane (forthcoming, section 2.5) calls a 'stochastic unity', one that is also retrospective: 'The "unity" of such events is as much a matter of memory as it is of cosmic order – both of which are processes, not objects, and not fully calculable.'
66 It might be asked: if all moments are divided in a generalized division, why do we still maintain the category of a merely local division? Two reasons come to mind. First, the instances of local division perform a role in the derivation and presentation of the splitting of the present. Because we are accustomed to thinking chronologically about time, the concrete *sēma* that Hector imagines in book VII, for instance, allows us to understand the logic of splitting before making it a formal principle that applies generally. Second, they reveal the way that formal conditions – that meaning arrives elsewhere, on another stage – can find echoes in the content of the narrative. Without taking note of such narrative echoes, our discussion here would lean more towards the philosophical mode rather than the literary. These echoes let us argue that the *Iliad* is preoccupied with its temporality, rather than simply determined by it.
67 This is a consequence of my own methodological gambit in putting poetry and scholarship on the same plane, as opposed to judging scholarship as a scientistic discourse of which the poetry is the object. See my comments about this and about the temporalities of reception in the introduction.
68 For an overview, see now Tsagalis 2020 (especially 152-62).
69 Neoanalytic scholarship has also historically differed from oral theoretical approaches by presupposing the use of writing, although this has become less salient

as more recent neoanalytic scholars have aimed for compatibility with orality. In any case, I will argue the orality versus writing distinction is often and more significantly a proxy for interpretive decisions.

70 Contemporary scholars who work with or take into account the neoanalytic tradition often distance themselves from the notion of intertextuality, because intertextuality implies the existence of distinct, fixed and recognizable poetic texts (and further the implication of written texts rather than oral performance traditions), while these scholars prefer to think of the poetic tradition as composed of identifiable but relatively fluid narratives and motifs. See in particular Burgess 2012: 169–71, and more generally Tsagalis 2008. Bakker's reflections on what he calls 'interformularity' argue that there is no hard boundary between a fluid store of narrative motifs – Reinhardt's 'universal pantry' (1961: 11) – and the particularity of fixed texts, but rather a scale in which repetitions may bring to mind more or less specific allusions (Bakker 2013: 157–69). In contrast to the reservations of contemporary neoanalytic-influenced scholarship, we will focus more on the *unreasonable* and the *less likely* notion of allusion between fixed texts. It is precisely the unreasonableness of Homeric allusion that demands a literary connection. This is why the following discussion may seem to emphasize earlier neoanalytic scholars at the expense of more recent ones. It may be desirable to distinguish 'allusion' – unidirectional reference by one text to a specific other text – as a species of 'intertextuality', which would also include other forms of relations between texts, such as the quintessential oral theoretical notion of different performances drawing on a common store of traditional language, but this convention is often not adhered to. Bruno Currie offers an overview of the difficulties and possibilities of allusion in the Homeric context (2016: 1–38) that is clear and thorough, even if we do not accept his specific readings and judgements. Indeed, my objective here is not to decide which form of intertextuality – the neoanalytic or the oral theoretical – is more suitable, but rather the distinguish them by the image of time that they express.

71 For discussion of the pre-Homeric tradition, see Griffin 1977 and Burgess 2001.
72 Combellack 1962: 194, review of Kullmann 1960.
73 On the charge of circularity, see Currie 2016: 32–3.
74 Combellack 1962: 195.
75 Wilamowitz-Moellendorff 1916. The extent to which Wilamowitz's work can be called strictly 'analytic' may be disputed, but the approximation will suffice for present purposes.
76 Ibid. 11 and 21.
77 For a brief overview of analytic scholarship, see Heubeck 1974: 1–7.
78 '[A]us einer Art von allgemeiner Vorratskammer mündlicher Überlieferung' (Reinhardt 1961: 11).
79 It is possible to see that what is rejected in oral theory's image of writing is the possibility of memory as the record of a specific event in history, such as the

use of a phrase in a poem. These problems will be further discussed in the next chapter.

80 Kullmann 1992: 69, originally published as Kullmann 1981, in which the cited passage is found on 7–8. Recent reconsideration of neoanalytic interpretations and their validity can be found in Currie 2016: 55–72 and Davies 2016 (chapter 1). My interests here do not lie in that direction: I am less interested in how likely specific interpretations or assertions about the historical priorities of various texts are to be valid, and much more interested in how the method used to make those interpretations can be connected to our themes of temporality. Nevertheless, it is worth engaging briefly with Kelly's strong challenge of the neoanalytic reading of the mourning of Thetis on the occasion of Patroclus' death and its allusion – on the neoanalytic reading – to another scene, the death of Achilles (Kelly 2012: 221–65). Kelly demonstrates that there are multiple scenes of what he calls 'prospective lamentation' in the Homeric poems, and argues on this basis that the mourning of Thetis is not out of place and does not require reference to the other scene of the death of Achilles (250): 'Thetis could naturally be depicted in a semi-permanent state of mourning for her son well before his actual death.' Kelly's argument seems to re-establish an unblemished, continuous surface of the Homeric text, one which does not require the disjunction caused by an allusion from one scene to another, but it in fact only naturalizes that disjunction as part of Thetis' character. We need to ask *why* Thetis is 'naturally ... in a semi-permanent state of mourning', or what it means that Thetis is a figure who so often brings to the poem the double vision of the present of action and the other scene of Achilles' death. Thetis' natural state of mourning is therefore precisely the split that needs to be explained. From a methodological perspective, Kelly's argument displaces a split from the *form* of the Homeric poem – the neoanalytic need for seeing another poem beyond the present one – to the side of *content* – Thetis simply *is* that way. But the boundary between form and content does not go without being constructed and policed.

81 Pestalozzi 1945: 34.

82 Schadewaldt 1951: 157–8; see also 174 ('Die Memnonis war längst kein "Lied" mehr, sondern ein in Hexametern geschriebenes episches Gedicht.').

83 For what it is worth, I am myself less convinced, as a matter of empirical history, by the neoanalytic assertion of fixed, pre-*Iliad* texts in the Homeric tradition than by the oral theoretical conceptions, which are closer to Kullmann's tales.

84 The title of a 1991 article (collected in Kullmann 1992: 100–34) on the occasion of Kakridis' 90th birthday, 'Ergebnisse der motivgeschichtlichen Forschung zu Homer (Neoanalyse)'. 'Neoanalysis, in contrast, is mainly concerned with the history of motifs' (Kullmann 1984: 309).

85 Schadewaldt 1951: 172.

86 It must be recognized that it is Kullmann's approach which has been more productive in subsequent scholarship, helped by its greater compatibility with oral

theory. See Rengakos 2020 for a succinct statement of the rationale for this form of 'Oral, Intertextual Neoanalysis' (46).
87 αὐτὸς δ' ἐν κονίῃσι μέγας μεγαλωστὶ τανυσθείς (ad hoc translation).
88 See Schadewaldt 1951: 168, following Eva Sachs, Kakridis and Pestalozzi.
89 Aside from Davies 2016 and Kelly 2012: 221–65, see also Currie 2016 and Fantuzzi and Tsagalis 2015.
90 Dowden 1996: 53 and 54. *Faktenkanon* is Kullmann's term for the canonical sequence of events in a total tradition.
91 Ibid. 53. Dowden's formulation is the clearest for my purposes here, although hints of this thought can be found already in Griffin 1977 and, in restricted form, as 'Monro's law' (see Nagy 1979: 20–1). Slatkin's statement is also helpful (1991: 4): 'The epic audience's knowledge of the alternative possibilities allows the poet to build his narrative by deriving meaning not only from what the poem includes but from what it conspicuously excludes.' See also Kahane (forthcoming), section 2.1, which points out that 'what is directly told' in the Homeric poems must be supplemented by 'what is essential but not directly told'. If these are 'known knowns' and 'known unknowns', what I am pointing out here is the effect of 'unknown unknowns'.
92 Ibid. 52. Along these lines, Øivind Andersen has observed that 'often there is nothing "behind" a reference in terms of tradition' (1990: 37). This, however, is not a fact conclusively in favour of a 'law' of the 'primacy of the present' that he sees in the *Iliad* (42). Chapter five will continue this chain of thought, but for now, let us point out Michael Theunissen's counterarguments at Theunissen 2000: 32–42.
93 The argument here is not the rather tautological observation that we do not know what we do not know, but rather that not-knowing is incorporated into the method of neoanalysis in a specific way that repeats and resonates with the temporality of the Homeric poems themselves. What I am arguing can also be thought of as an extension of what Benjamin Sammons suggests (2010: 209), that 'wherever the poet seems to evoke another poem, he *must be doing so*, in the sense that the poem once evoked already exists as a *possible* poem'.
94 A parallel can be made with the 'mobile' or 'paradoxical' element in Deleuze's essay, 'How do we recognize structuralism?' (collected in Deleuze 2004: 170–92, in particular 184–9).

3 The Dream of the Instant

1 Contemporary acceptance of Nagy's work can vary greatly, particularly on the topic of the evolutionary theory. What interest might this chapter hold for those readers for whom Nagy has already become marginal? Two points are relevant here. First, this chapter is not intended to be another critique of Nagy which may be felt

superfluous. Instead, I am interested in exploring the temporality of reading and interpretation that is implicit in Nagy's conceptions, which thereby allows us to understand their connections to the forms of time we have already encountered in the *Iliad* and its scholarship. Second, these explorations can help us perceive the pervasiveness of the influence that Nagy's revision of oral theory has achieved, even in approaches which do not explicitly depend on his work.

2 Nagy 1990b: 29.
3 The following account draws principally upon Nagy 1996b, especially 29–63.
4 If not the literal moment of performance, then *as if* in performance, i.e. informed by the performance context.
5 Nagy 1996b: 25.
6 Steven Lowenstam complains in his dismissive review (1990) of Lynn-George 1988 that the book does not address the fact that the theses of oral theory 'have been developed, honed, and refined in extensive critical discussions'. What follows, by examining some of the products of those 'extensive critical discussions', hopes to shed some light on the extent to which the crossfire of criticism in each direction is justified.
7 Lynn-George 1988: 195.
8 Saussure 1974: 120, cited at Lynn-George 1988: 57–8.
9 The self-identity of Parry's epithets leads in a direct line to Foley's traditional referentiality. Because each formulaic epithet–noun combination for Parry is supposed to be identical to the noun – for instance, 'swift-footed Achilles' simply means 'Achilles' – the question then arises: what does the epithet add? Foley's answer is that the epithet, along with all traditional linguistic elements, adds the pure force of traditionality, the assertion that 'this idea is traditional'. As we saw in the first chapter of this book, when the entire poetic register of the epic *Kunstsprache* becomes traditional for Foley, every word bears with it its aura, and epic becomes a paean to the epiphanic presence of tradition.
10 M. Parry 1971: 154 and 241, cited in Lynn-George 1988: 59.
11 Lynn-George 1988: 60, citing M. Parry 1971: 272.
12 In chapter one, we had opposed Foley and Parry. This is because Foley's conception of what was whole is filled with the meaning of great art, in contrast to Parry, whose critics accuse him of creating a mechanical system emptied of meaning.
13 Recall from chapter one again that the difference between Parry and Foley does not rest on the need for a metalanguage, but on how to judge what comprises it. Parry's rule was that the metalanguage should connect formulas with what 'instantly and easily come to mind' (Parry 1971: 156), while Foley historicized the metalanguage by recognizing that what comes easily to mind for a modern audience is not necessarily the same as what would have easily come to the mind of an ancient one.
14 The quest for identity continued to govern developments in linguistic studies of the oral formula, which has been driven by the question of how to conceive what is

allowed to change within formulaic language and what must remain identical. Thus, for instance, the concept of a 'structural formula' seeks identity at the level of both syntax and metrical localization: the phrases *alge' ethēke* ['made pains'], *kudos ethēke* ['made glory'], *kudos edōke* ['gave glory'], *eukhos edōke* ['granted object of prayer'] and *eukhos apēura* ['took away object of prayer'] are all identical at the level of their noun–verb syntactical structure and in their localization at the end of the hexameter verse (these examples are taken from Russo 1997: 245). Nagler pursued the distribution of the changeable and the identical even further, discarding strict requirements for identity in metre or meaning in favour of a preverbal *Gestalt* (see Nagler 1974). What matters for us here is not the various levels at which different scholars seek a solid base on which to found formulaic language, but the fact that the object of their research is the identical as such, something solid and unmoving under the shifting surface of formula.
15 Lynn-George 1988: 63.
16 Ibid. 64.
17 Ibid. 57, quoting Saussure 1974: 73 and 71.
18 Ibid. 65, quoting Lord 1964: 35.
19 Ibid. 73.
20 Ibid. 74, citing M. Parry 1971: 332.
21 Ibid. That the spoken word emerges as something of a villain here is an effect of Derrida's influence (such as in *Speech and Phenomena*, 1973). But the point can as well be made without this animus, as in Elmer 2005: 2–3.
22 Ibid. 73.
23 See, for example, Nagy 1990b, especially 85–262.
24 See Nagy 1974.
25 The role of repeated formulas in shaping poetic metre is summed up, with appropriate adjustments, in J. W. Du Bois's succinct dictum, 'Grammars code best what speakers do most' (cited in Bakker 2013: 157).
26 Nagy 1996b: 22–3.
27 Nagy 1979: 3.
28 Ibid. 73.
29 Nagy 1996b: 22–5 (emphases added).
30 We should note again a contrast between the harmony of (signifying) form and (signified) content here, and the incommensurability of the signifying and signified orders in structuralism. See chapter one, notes 33, 37 and 45.
31 Ibid. 25. But see also the more nuanced discussion in Nagy 1996a, especially 5–58, which will be examined more closely later.
32 Saussure 1974: 71, cited from Lynn-George 1988: 57, as quoted above.
33 Nagy 1990b: 8.
34 Ibid. 19.

35 Quoted in ibid. 10. Elsewhere, ritual is defined as 'a given set of formal actions that correspond to a given set of thought patterns that can take shape as a given myth' (Nagy 1990a: 117). This formulation makes explicit the thought–word dichotomy at work in the ritual–myth pair – that is, in the conception of cult.
36 Nagy 1990b: 10.
37 Nagy 1990a: 149.
38 Saussure 1974: 120.
39 Nagy 1979: 78–9.
40 Ibid. 78.
41 There are strong resonances with Foley's rhetoric of a 'good and faithful audience' (Foley 1991: 143).
42 Nagy 1996b: 17.
43 Ibid. 15.
44 González 2013 must be noted as the most extensive working out of the 'diachronic' aspect of epic performance among the scholarship that relies on Nagy. Regarding the notion of the 'diachronic' itself, there will in fact be little overlap between my interests here and González's discussion, in which the emphasis on the diachronic refers simply to the need for understanding the epic rhapsode within the evolving context of performance traditions in pre- and high-classical Greece. We will refer to González's work on the rhapsode (though again in *recusatio*) later in this chapter, and, more relevantly, to his discussion of 'notional fixity' in chapter five.
45 Lynn-George 1988: 75.
46 Ibid., quoting from M. Parry 1971: 406–7 (emphasis added).
47 Ibid., quoting M. Parry 1971: 441 (emphasis added). See also Schein 2016: 123–4 on how for Parry '[t]here also is only one reader, whom Parry anonymously calls "the reader" but who really is an idealized version of himself and his own reading habits'.
48 Ibid. 2–37, discussing Auerbach 1953: 3–23.
49 Auerbach 1953: 6.
50 Ibid. 4–5.
51 But this earliest moment is, for Auerbach, strategically chosen to avoid the 'subjectivistic-perspectivistic' linkage of two verses earlier, when the scar first occurred to the mind of Odysseus, as opposed to its current position, when the scar first appears in the present moment of the story. See ibid. 7.
52 Nietzsche 1983: 61, quoted in Lynn-George 1988: 35.
53 Nagy 1990b: 29.
54 Nagy 1996a: 215.
55 See Freud *SE* vol. 5: 488–508. In this context, secondary elaboration is also what founds the possibility of reception as discussed in the introduction.
56 Nagy 1990a: 21 note 18.

57 The notion of seeing 'in a single glance' is drawn from Purves's conception of the Iliadic plot (2010), with reference to Aristotle's *eusynoptos*. Chapter five will treat this notion in further detail.
58 This procedure – whereby a synchronic system is decided and historical events either register within that system and are inscribed as the system's diachronic dimension or fail to register and become lost as the flotsam of history – is what is countered by Nietzsche's parable of the eternal return, in which eternal repetition makes every part of history count and inscribes every event.
59 Similar accounts are presented in tabular form in Nagy 1996a: 110, Nagy 1996b: 42 and Nagy 2003: 2.
60 Nagy 1990a: 54.
61 Ibid. 55. On textuality without writing, see Ready 2019: 15–97.
62 Nagy 1990b: 43.
63 I will not pursue a fundamental objection to this conception of Panhellenic synthesis, one based on the grounds of the Greek religion that anchors Nagy's conception of epic tradition itself: while it may seem logical to us that the encounter of conflicting versions of myth provides the impetus for a self-consistent, unified synthesis, it is not obvious that this would have been the case for archaic Greek polytheism, a system of religion and ritual of which the first thing we learn is its striking tolerance of variation and contradiction. An account is needed of these 'monotheists' who demand self-consistent versions of epic.
64 See Svenbro 1976: 11–45.
65 The discussion of *aoidos* and rhapsode undertaken here aims, relatively narrowly, to reach the implicit temporalities expressed through these modes of performance as Nagy conceives them. We are therefore leaving aside the empirical questions of rhapsodic performance and treatments of this topic as in Ford 1988 and, more recently, González 2013 and Ready and Tsagalis (eds) 2018, which would challenge and nuance the distinctions being made here. Put another way, we are interested less in whether or not Nagy's distinction between *aoidos* and rhapsode is historically correct, but rather in how they can help us connect Nagy's conception of oral theory to the network of figures from scholarship and poetry we are creating through the question of the extent to which each figure, to borrow Elmer's phrase, 'destabilizes the *hic et nunc* of an utterance', which here is epic performance (2005: 2).
66 Nagy 1990a: 54.
67 Nagy 1990b: 42.
68 See Svenbro 1976: 16–35.
69 As Elmer puts it, with somewhat different intonations which do not mask the point, the Iliadic tradition seeks 'to *establish* a community of stakeholders to whom the poem and its tradition will belong' (2013: 224, emphasis added). He also eloquently

expresses the necessary openness of such an audience or stakeholder community, one which includes the poem's modern audience (ibid.): 'The solution to the *Iliad*'s crisis of exception emerges in the here and now of performance, as audiences engage in the construction of an evolving consensus that affirms the norms of an exceptional tradition. That consensus is still evolving today as we, the modern successors to so many generations of audiences and readers, continue to debate the meaning of this remarkable poem ... The constitution of an interpretive consensus is an open-ended, continuously unfolding process. This is what ensures that the experience of poetry – even poetry that sets solidarity and cohesion as its highest values – can never be reduced to a totalitarian prescriptiveness, a tyranny of the collective.'

70 This distinction between *aoidos* and rhapsodic audiences reflects Elmer's contrast between a Panhellenic framing of performance and a local one: 'In the case of a locally oriented event, the performance will be constrained by epichoric traditions, to the extent that these are known to performer and audience: a legitimate performance will have to conform to these traditions. In the case of a performance that is framed in a more ecumenical way (at which the audience is invited to suspend, to a certain extent, its local prejudices), the performance may be liberated to a greater or lesser degree from the requirements of local tradition – but it is nevertheless constrained by the knowledge, on the part of both performer and audience, of what Jim Marks has recently called the "synthetic narrative" of the Panhellenic "borderless text", that is, the emerging body of Panhellenic narratives about Troy' (2013: 209, citing Marks 2010). I also wish to extend Scodel's argument regarding the poet's performative assumption that the audience knows more about the mythological tradition than it might actually have known. While I fully agree with Scodel's argument that '[t]he assumption that a successful oral performance must be fully transparent all the time is simply wrong' (2002: 10), we differ in that, for her, the audience's lack of knowledge is no obstacle to the smooth enjoyment of Homeric narrative, the unity and coherence of which remain the goal – see the occasions on which the audience is enjoined to 'ignore' or 'avoid recalling' or 'forget' complicating material (e.g. 14, 41, 90; but see also the treatment of obscurity at 127–8). I seek a more positive role for ignorance within a more fractured experience of epic. Where Scodel sees the poet's assumption of the audience's knowledge as an invitation to 'reaffirm his authority' (1997: 217; see also 2002: 92), I propose that the audience is not hoodwinked by the poet's gesture, but rather participates fully in the 'borderless' differential context of Panhellenic performance. The audience knows that it does not know – *what then?*

71 Nagy 1996a: 56.
72 See Nagy 1990a: 17–81.
73 Nagy 1996a: 60–1.

74 Ibid. 55. 'This' refers to the act of mimesis – say, a poetic performance in the present – while 'that' is the original that present performance repeats. In the earlier, 'mythological' mode of mimesis, the origin is absolute or divine, and *therefore* can be re-enacted or made to epiphanically appear. While in the later, 'fallen' mode of mimesis, the original is no longer absolute and re-enactment is no longer possible, leaving only the possibility of mere copying.
75 Ibid.
76 Ibid. 60, 61.
77 Bloch 1988: 68, in a discussion of the work of the oral theorist Paul Zumthor. We have previously seen this semiotic utopia in the form of the natural signs that are Foley's traditional references.
78 Nagy 1990b: 43.
79 Lynn-George 1988: 74.
80 Nagy 1990a: 21 note 18.
81 Nagy 1990b: 29.
82 Nagy 1990a: 57 (emphasis added), citing Nagy 1982: 47–9 and 52 (recast as Nagy 1990b, chapter 3).
83 Nagy 1996a: 215.
84 Nagy 1996a: 66 and note 26.
85 Nagy 1990a: 57.
86 Ibid. 58. Compare Lynn-George's (1988: 35) quotation from Nietzsche above: 'Then the man says "I remember" and envies the animal, who at once forgets and for whom every moment really dies, sinks back into night and fog and is extinguished for ever.'
87 Ibid. 72.
88 Ibid. 73.
89 Nagy 1990a: 21 note 18.
90 Nagy 1990b: 47.
91 Ibid. and Nagy 1989: 6.
92 Bloch 1988: 63.
93 Nagy 1990b: 43.
94 Nagy 1979: 229. The context is a discussion of the beggar Iros in the *Odyssey*.
95 Ibid. 246, §4, note 3. The context is a discussion of Archilochus' Cologne Epode.
96 Reinhardt 1961: 23.
97 The language of fandom in contemporary popular culture feels appropriate here.
98 Nagy 1996: 31: 'If indeed a multitext format is needed for editing medieval texts like the songs of Jaufré Rudel, then perhaps the need is even greater in the case of ancient Greek drama and epic.'
99 Dué 2019: 83–104.
100 See now ibid. 17–54.

4 Sutures

1 Parry 1971: 156.
2 Another reason for the choice of the term picks up its significance for the history of structuralism, previously discussed in the context of *mana*, the signifier of the lack of the signifier. Suture is the term introduced by Jacques-Alain Miller to designate the relation between the subject, as a representation of this lack, and the signifying structure (Miller 2012: 93; originally Miller 1966): 'Suture names the relation of the subject to the chain of its discourse; we shall see that it figures there as the element which is lacking, in the form of a stand-in [*tenant-lieu*]. For, while there lacking, it is not purely and simply absent. Suture, by extension – the general relation of lack to the structure – of which it is an element, inasmuch as it implies the position of a taking-the-place-of [*tenant-lieu*].' It is not necessary here to take on board the details of Miller's mathematical derivation of the concept or the position of suture within its Lacanian context. We only need note that suture designates the act of meaning-making under the conditions of a constitutively lacking – interrupted, incomplete and incompletable – structure of meaning.
3 εἷς οἰωνὸς ἄριστος ἀμύνεσθαι περὶ πάτρης (xii. 243).
4 μὴ ἴομεν Δαναοῖσι μαχησόμενοι περὶ νηῶν. / ὧδε γὰρ ἐκτελέεσθαι ὀΐομαι, εἰ ἐτεόν γε / Τρωσὶν ὅδ᾽ ὄρνις ἐπῆλθε περησέμεναι μεμαῶσιν / αἰετὸς ὑψιπέτης ἐπ᾽ ἀριστερὰ λαὸν ἐέργων / φοινήεντα δράκοντα φέρων ὀνύχεσσι πέλωρον / ζωόν· ἄφαρ δ᾽ ἀφέηκε πάρος φίλα οἰκί᾽ ἱκέσθαι, / οὐδ᾽ ἐτέλεσσε φέρων δόμεναι τεκέεσσιν ἑοῖσιν. / ὣς ἡμεῖς, εἴ πέρ τε πύλας καὶ τεῖχος Ἀχαιῶν / ῥηξόμεθα σθένεϊ μεγάλῳ, εἴξωσι δ᾽ Ἀχαιοί, / οὐ κόσμῳ παρὰ ναῦφιν ἐλευσόμεθ᾽ αὐτὰ κέλευθα· / πολλοὺς γὰρ Τρώων καταλείψομεν, οὕς κεν Ἀχαιοὶ / χαλκῷ δῃώσωσιν ἀμυνόμενοι περὶ νηῶν. / ὧδέ χ᾽ ὑποκρίναιτο θεοπρόπος, ὃς σάφα θυμῷ / εἰδείη τεράων καί οἱ πειθοίατο λαοί (xii. 216–29).
5 Herodotus, of course, delights in staging this theme again and again.
6 τύνη δ᾽ οἰωνοῖσι τανυπτερύγεσσι κελεύεις / πείθεσθαι, τῶν οὔ τι μετατρέπομ᾽ οὐδ᾽ ἀλεγίζω / εἴτ᾽ ἐπὶ δεξί᾽ ἴωσι πρὸς ἠῶ τ᾽ ἠέλιόν τε, / εἴτ᾽ ἐπ᾽ ἀριστερὰ τοί γε ποτὶ ζόφον ἠερόεντα. / ἡμεῖς δὲ μεγάλοιο Διὸς πειθώμεθα βουλῇ, / ὃς πᾶσι θνητοῖσι καὶ ἀθανάτοισιν ἀνάσσει. / εἷς οἰωνὸς ἄριστος ἀμύνεσθαι περὶ πάτρης (xii. 237–43).
7 Succinct summaries of standard views in Willcock 1976 and Hainsworth 1993 *ad loc*. See also Bushnell 1982: 4–7, Heath 1999, Trampedach 2008 (§4) and Ceccarelli 2011: 35–43.
8 Bushnell is sensitive to the temporality of Hector's position, although, without the concept of a divided present, her argument could only see it as a timeless present (1982: 6): 'Hektor, however, imposes an absolute atemporality on temporal-atemporal writing when he takes Zeus's promise of favor not just for the moment but for all time ... He thus compresses two modes of discourse that are fundamentally

discontinuous, the divine and contextually specific with the human and general, the sacred *sēma* and the cultural norm.' The last quoted sentence – with its association of the divine with ephemerality and the human with a certain permanence, as well as the impermanence of the *sēma* – seems to gesture at the interrupted form of time that we have been exploring.

9 νήπιε μή μοι ἄποινα πιφαύσκεο μηδ' ἀγόρευε· / πρὶν μὲν γὰρ Πάτροκλον ἐπισπεῖν αἴσιμον ἦμαρ / τόφρά τί μοι πεφιδέσθαι ἐνὶ φρεσὶ φίλτερον ἦεν / Τρώων, καὶ πολλοὺς ζωοὺς ἕλον ἠδ' ἐπέρασσα· / νῦν δ' οὐκ ἔσθ' ὅς τις θάνατον φύγοι ὅν κε θεός γε / Ἰλίου προπάροιθεν ἐμῆς ἐν χερσὶ βάλῃσι / καὶ πάντων Τρώων, περὶ δ' αὖ Πριάμοιό γε παίδων (xxi. 99–105).

10 ἀλλὰ φίλος θάνε καὶ σύ· τίη ὀλοφύρεαι οὕτως; / κάτθανε καὶ Πάτροκλος, ὅ περ σέο πολλὸν ἀμείνων. / οὐχ ὁράας οἷος καγὼ καλός τε μέγας τε; / πατρὸς δ' εἴμ' ἀγαθοῖο, θεὰ δέ με γείνατο μήτηρ· / ἀλλ' ἔπι τοι καὶ ἐμοὶ θάνατος καὶ μοῖρα κραταιή (xxi. 106–10).

11 Redfield 1975: 99–103 presents an eloquent restatement in connection with Sarpedon's well-known reflections at xii. 310–28.

12 ἔσσεται ἢ ἠὼς ἢ δείλη ἢ μέσον ἦμαρ / ὁππότε τις καὶ ἐμεῖο Ἄρη ἐκ θυμὸν ἕληται / ἢ ὅ γε δουρὶ βαλὼν ἢ ἀπὸ νευρῆφιν ὀϊστῷ (xxi. 111–13).

13 The gradations displayed in this series should make us recognize that the form–content distinction is itself constructed or synthesized. This point deserves greater elaboration than can be provided here, but see, for a start, Hughes 2009: 106.

14 ἣ δὲ μέγαν ἱστὸν ὕφαινε / δίπλακα μαρμαρέην, πολέας δ' ἐνέπασσεν ἀέθλους / Τρώων θ' ἱπποδάμων καὶ Ἀχαιῶν χαλκοχιτώνων, / οὕς ἕθεν εἵνεκ' ἔπασχον ὑπ' Ἄρηος παλαμάων (iii. 125–8).

15 The metapoetic symbolism was already noted by the bT scholiast who called the weaving a 'worthy model of [the poet's] own craft' (ἀξιόχρεων ἀρχέτυπον ἀνέπλασεν ὁ ποιητὴς τῆς ἰδίας ποιήσεως, Erbse 1969 on iii. 126–7). See Slatkin 2011: 152, Nagy 1996a: 64–6 and 75–6, Elmer 2005: 23–4 and Bergren 2008: 46–7. Purves 2010: 11 notes the status of Helen's weaving as an object in which the narrative of the poem can be visualized at a glance. For connections between weaving and the term 'rhapsode', see González 2013: 331–431. See also Canevaro's discussion of textiles as forms of women's agency and communication (2018: 55–107).

16 The field further opens up into assemblage theory, which has become influential though not without complications of its own. See Buchanan 2015 and 2017.

17 Purves 2015 recognizes this distinction (78) but leaves us with a tantalizing analogy without more detailed analysis (80): 'The hexameter line thus works a bit like the dip or the sunlight on the Baltimore street; it surfaces the object, and changes the way we read the human in relation to it.' Canevaro 2018: 14–42 wrestles with this problem, but despite the salutary injunction to 'keep the question of representation always to the fore' (23), this dimension does not often make an appearance.

18 Purves 2015: 82. Compare also Holmes 2015 in the same issue. See Bennett 2010 for the most immediate philosophical inspiration.
19 Ibid. 83.
20 Bennett's most influential work (2010) has been controversial. For a succinct critique, see Bowden 2015: 63–8.
21 Grethlein 2019: 468–9, discussing Bielfeldt 2014.
22 Ibid. 473. This reflects a fundamental temptation, parsed by Martin Holbraad (2011), when trying to hear the significations of things 'for themselves', that of emancipating things only on the basis of an analogy with the human subject.
23 Canevaro 2018: 21–2, with reference to Gell 1998.
24 See ibid. 11–42.
25 Without hoping to resolve this question here, I would highlight the importance of Deleuze 1990, which elaborates an ontology of materiality and language in which their point of meeting is not a conjunction – the *correspondence* of word and thing, an ideal that limits all the options surveyed by Holbraad – but rather a disjunction, in the sense that language as an ongoing event is a continued *failure* to speak of things. See Collett 2016, summarized at 205. An alternative account of human and non-human agency based on the same Deleuze text can be found at Bowden 2015: 74–8.
26 Canevaro 2018: 21. It is possible to work out quite precisely how Canevaro modulates the flat ontology of New Materialism with the use of gender theory. The latter becomes prominent in her argument whenever agency is conceived quantitatively: a subject can have more or less agency, often depending on whether the subject is man or woman. But how do we define what is 'more' when it comes to agency? The quantification of agency depends on a subject–object dualism in which agency is conceived as the capacity of a subject to affect the objective world, socially or materially. It means that some acts – fighting, winning *kleos*, gaining recognition within existing social values – are coded as more effective or more 'objective' than others – weaving, memorializing others, resisting the dominant social values through one's way of life – and therefore attest to greater agency. Canevaro's book reveals an important emancipatory aspect in the way it implicitly complicates this initial dichotomy and its conception of agency, by demonstrating how Homeric women use objects to construct different – not lesser – forms of agency. See also Mueller 2010.
27 In framing my argument in this way, I recuse myself from directly addressing the question of objective agency, hence my earlier characterization of my engagement with this body of scholarship as 'oblique'. If it were necessary to engage less obliquely, I would point out the need for further reflection on the notion of 'agency' itself. In considering the possibility of agency for objects, it is often tempting to construct a dichotomy between the distributed and bodily agency favoured by New

Materialisms and the Cartesian subject, that well-worn philosophical punching bag (see Canevaro 13–14). What might result if we compare 'agency' not with the Cartesian 'rational cognitive subject' – which even Canevaro's 'primary agent' strongly resembles – but with other accounts, such as the psychoanalytic subject that is decidedly not transparent to itself? To mention one possible point of contact, the 'thing' that appears when an object separates itself from human intentions (such as the can that Grethlein imagines tripping over, 2019: 471) had a psychoanalytic existence, even prior to psychoanalysis proper, as the 'non-understood' part of a perception (see Freud's 1895 *Project for a Scientific Psychology*, SE vol. 1: 281–397, especially 327–35 and 383–4; quotation from 383; early Lacan returns to *das Ding*, as recognized in Bill Brown's seminal article, 2001: 5). As a final aside, when Grethlein talks about situations 'in which things interfere with our lives without realizing human intentions, sometimes even contrary to their intended use' (ibid.), it is difficult not to hear, in the Homeric context, the echo of debates over intention and traditional language. Never mind stumbling over a carelessly dropped can – we have been experiencing for the past century the agency of Homeric formulas dropped with or without intention.

28 Having said this, a connection between weaving and resistance to signification does emerge in connection with the shroud that Penelope weaves for Laertes in the *Odyssey*. It is possible, of course, to read into the unweaving of Penelope's stratagem an analogy for the undoing of *textus*, but a more cogent connection is possible through the striking brightness of the shroud's description in the second *nekyia*: 'Then she displayed the great piece of weaving that she had woven. She had washed it, and it shone like the sun or the moon' (εὖθ' ἡ φᾶρος ἔδειξεν, ὑφήνασα μέγαν ἱστόν, / πλύνασ', ἡελίῳ ἐναλίγκιον ἠὲ σελήνῃ, xiv. 147–8). The connection between brightness and resistance to signification will be discussed presently.

29 νῦν δ' ἐπεὶ οὐ νέομαί γε φίλην ἐς πατρίδα γαῖαν, / οὐδέ τι Πατρόκλῳ γενόμην φάος οὐδ' ἑτάροισι / τοῖς ἄλλοις, οἳ δὴ πολέες δάμεν Ἕκτορι δίῳ, / ἀλλ' ἧμαι παρὰ νηυσὶν ἐτώσιον ἄχθος ἀρούρης (XVIII. 101–4).

30 Four of its six occurrences in the Homeric poems refer to the notion of weight and the act of carrying (XII. 452, XX. 247, iii. 312, ix. 233). The other two occurrences, in the passage under discussion and at xx. 379, are in the phrase *akhthos arourēs*, to be discussed here. See *LfgrE* s.v. ἄχθος: 'physical burden', 'psychic burden'. Compare s.v. ἄχθομαι: 'physically or psychically weighed down'.

31 The phrase 'useless burden on the good land' itself has not generated much scholarly attention. It has been linked to the supposed reason for the Trojan war given in the *Cypria*, the overburdening of the earth (Murnaghan 1997: 28 and Slatkin 2011: 95). Plato quotes a variant of this line (Pl. *Apol.* 28d), which is discussed in the context of oral formulaic theory at Finkelberg 2012: 70. The common literary interpretation that the phrase indicates Achilles' feeling of being 'a deadweight that failed to defend

his friends in need' is given at Liebert 2017: 94. For verbal correspondences, see Edwards 1991 and Coray 2018 *ad loc.*

32 ὤ μοι τέκνον ἐμόν, τί νύ σ' ἔτρεφον αἰνὰ τεκοῦσα;/αἴθ' ὄφελες παρὰ νηυσὶν ἀδάκρυτος καὶ ἀπήμων / ἧσθαι, ἐπεί νύ τοι αἶσα μίνυνθά περ οὔ τι μάλα δήν· / νῦν δ' ἅμα τ' ὠκύμορος καὶ ὀϊζυρὸς περὶ πάντων / ἔπλεο (I. 414–18).

33 The most sophisticated account of recompense – among other themes – is found in Lynn-George 1988.

34 Vernant 1991: 51.

35 Ibid. 59.

36 ἐκ νηῶν ἐλάσας ἰέναι πάλιν· εἰ δέ κεν αὖ τοι / δώῃ κῦδος ἀρέσθαι ἐρίγδουπος πόσις Ἥρης, / μὴ σύ γ' ἄνευθεν ἐμεῖο λιλαίεσθαι πολεμίζειν / Τρωσὶ φιλοπτολέμοισιν· ἀτιμότερον δέ με θήσεις (XVI. 87–90).

37 Here are echoes, at several removes, of the well-known argument of A. Parry 1956.

38 IX. 630–8.

39 νηλεές, οὐκ ἄρα σοί γε πατὴρ ἦν ἱππότα Πηλεύς, / οὐδὲ Θέτις μήτηρ· γλαυκὴ δέ σ' ἔτικτε θάλασσα / πέτραι τ' ἠλίβατοι (XVI. 33–5).

40 For instance, Priam twice at XXIV. 205, 521.

41 This will be clearest in connection with the arms and shield of Achilles, to be discussed presently.

42 παμφαίνονθ' ὥς τ' ἀστέρ' ἐπεσσύμενον πεδίοιο, / ὅς ῥά τ' ὀπώρης εἶσιν, ἀρίζηλοι δέ οἱ αὐγαὶ / φαίνονται πολλοῖσι μετ' ἀστράσι νυκτὸς ἀμολγῷ, / ὅν τε κύν' Ὠρίωνος ἐπίκλησιν καλέουσι. / λαμπρότατος μὲν ὅ γ' ἐστί, κακὸν δέ τε σῆμα τέτυκται (XXII. 26–30). Achilles is not unique in being compared to a star; Diomedes and his arms are made to shine like the same star of the late summer, Sirius, at V. 5–6 (see Kirk *ad loc.*). This passage does not, then, provide strong support by itself for my argument – that the failure of meaning is expressed as unreadable objecthood in the connection of brightness and Achilles – but should be taken in conjunction with the other associations between Achilles and objecthood. Another connection between astronomical brightness and failure of meaning is found at xxiv. 147–8, where the shade of the suitor Amphimedon compares Penelope's shroud to 'the sun or moon' (ἠελίῳ ἐναλίγκιον ἠὲ σελήνῃ). Astronomical brightness here is overwhelming and expresses the fact that the shroud exceeds the suitors' meaning-making ability, either because – as Amphimedon understood it – it was part of an unforeseeable, diabolical plot that overtook them, or because the feminine realm of weaving exceeded the suitors' masculine understanding (see Mueller 2010: 4 and Canevaro 2018: 64–6). We can also see here – as Amphimedon weaves his conspiracy theory about Penelope – that the meaning-making function is omnivorous in incorporating whatever has escaped it, and, returning to Achilles-as-a-star, Priam's focalization precisely makes a meaning – 'an evil sign', κακὸν σῆμα – out of Achilles' shining. (I owe this point

43 Scully (2003: 35–6) has gathered these and other references to the bright *selas* of Achilles and his arms and notes the affinities between them.
44 ἀριζήλη φωνή, ὅτε τ' ἴαχε σάλπιγξ (xviii. 219).
45 Purves 2015: 82.
46 The 'meaning-making apparatus' might well be thought of as what the psychoanalytic idiom calls the 'ego'.
47 Hence, when we connected the function of objecthood with the narrative or the plot of the *Iliad*, we should add the caveat that the category of narrative or plot, as it is usually understood, is inadequate for our purposes. The point of connection is in fact with the place where narrative intersects with the 'theme' of *kleos*, but this theme states at the same time the inadequacy of any theme to sum up the meaning of the narrative.
48 Μυρμιδόνας δ' ἄρα πάντας ἕλε τρόμος, οὐδέ τις ἔτλη / ἄντην εἰσιδέειν, ἀλλ' ἔτρεσαν. αὐτὰρ Ἀχιλλεὺς / ὡς εἶδ', ὥς μιν μᾶλλον ἔδυ χόλος, ἐν δέ οἱ ὄσσε / δεινὸν ὑπὸ βλεφάρων ὡς εἰ σέλας ἐξεφάανθεν (xix. 14–17).
49 Scully 2003: 35–6. See also Purves 2010: 53–5.
50 Ibid. 41 and 43.
51 In what way is the shield aligned with the failure of meaning, aside from its brightness that humans cannot bear to look upon? The most relevant aspect of the shield of Achilles for us here is in the extended ekphrasis of the scenes worked upon it by Hephaestus. In discussions elaborated elsewhere, I argue that there is a connection between ekphrasis as such and the resistance to signification. In the interest of brevity, that thesis may be summed up in Paul Fry's proposal (1995: 87): 'What [ekphrastic poems] always see, confined by words within the inescapable meaningfulness of history, is the nature of reality unconditioned by intentional structures, entailing at once the death of self-consciousness and the corporeality of life.' For Fry, what ekphrasis as a form reaches after is an escape from meaning as such – a paradoxical escape from signification staged within the inescapably meaningful matter of language. More closely connected to our current context, Michael Squire's analysis of visual representations of the shield of Achilles presents an Attic black-figure neck-amphora of the sixth century that is especially pertinent to the nature of the material object of ekphrasis and of the shield of Achilles in particular as unreadable and as the negation of representational conceptualization (Squire 2013: 167, with illustration). This depiction of the shield of Achilles does not attempt to reproduce the Homeric description, but replaces it with the head of the Gorgon Medusa, which is a quintessential image of the unreadable: 'As Françoise Frontisi-Ducroux has shown, the Gorgon had long been conceptualized and depicted as "the representation of the non-visible"... [W]hat better emblem than the

Gorgon for signalling the limits of looking?' (ibid., quoting from Frontisi-Ducroux 1995: 69; there is a slippage here between visibility and readability which would need to be negotiated in a fuller version of this argument). For the figure of the Medusa as a site of ekphrastic theory, see Jacobs 1985.

52 υἱὸν δὲ Στροφίοιο Σκαμάνδριον αἴμονα θήρης / Ἀτρεΐδης Μενέλαος ἕλ' ἔγχεϊ ὀξυόεντι / ἐσθλὸν θηρητῆρα· δίδαξε γὰρ Ἄρτεμις αὐτὴ / βάλλειν ἄγρια πάντα, τά τε τρέφει οὔρεσιν ὕλη· / ἀλλ' οὔ οἱ τότε γε χραῖσμ' Ἄρτεμις ἰοχέαιρα, / οὐδὲ ἐκηβολίαι ᾗσιν τὸ πρίν γ' ἐκέκαστο· / ἀλλά μιν Ἀτρεΐδης δουρικλειτὸς Μενέλαος / πρόσθεν ἕθεν φεύγοντα μετάφρενον οὔτασε δουρί / ὤμων μεσσηγύς, διὰ δὲ στήθεσφιν ἔλασσεν, / ἤριπε δὲ πρηνής, ἀράβησε δὲ τεύχε' ἐπ' αὐτῷ (v. 49–58).

53 Death is also only an improper form of finality with respect to *kleos* because, in contrast to the Solonian wisdom that a man's happiness can be judged at his death, death only ends the story for an already constituted individual, but not the individualities which constitute that individual. When Solon pronounces Tellos the Athenian the happiest of mortals because he lived through the prosperity of his native city, for which he gave his life, that prosperity, which formed one part of Tellos' identity and of his happiness, was merely ephemeral, and we can only attribute a merely psychological happiness to Tellos if we call him happy for never knowing of Athenian decline: '[D]eath does not order anything, nor decide anything' (Zourabichvili 2012: 101).

54 '"Ein Mann, der mit fünfunddreißig stirbt," hat Moritz Heimann einmal gesagt, "ist auf jedem Punkt seines Lebens ein Mann, der mit fünfunddreißig stirbt." Nichts ist zweifelhafter als dieser Satz. Aber dies einzig und allein, weil er sich im Tempus vergreift. Ein Mann, so heißt die Wahrheit, die hier gemeint war, der mit fünfunddreißig Jahren gestorben ist, wird *dem Eingedenken* an jedem Punkte seines Lebens als ein Mann erscheinen, der mit fünfunddreißig Jahren stirbt' (Benjamin 1991: 456 [trans. 1969: 100]).

55 More remains to be said about the contrast between the divided time of *kleos* and the seemingly straightforward and unified present of the battle narrations. Let us leave this point for now with a reference to Ann Bergren's argument that, in fact, the time of the battle narrations are not as straightforwardly linear as they first appear, but, in their sheer excess and in the impression that 'the action of these five [battle] books is not conceivable in the afternoon allotted to them by the explicit time frame of the text', begin to break 'temporal verisimilitude' and approach figures like Helen's weaving or the Teichoscopia in the 'transcendence of linear time' (Bergren 2008: 46–7). Further afield, the transcendence of linear time in Bergren is a Homeric parallel of Deleuze's project in the *Cinema* books, in which what Bergren calls 'temporal verisimilitude' is one aspect of Deleuze's notion of the sensori-motor schema, that is, the schema formed by common-sense understandings of space and time. Deleuze traces the breakdown of the sensori-motor schema and the action-

56 πρὶν ἐλθεῖν υἷας Ἀχαιῶν (ιx. 403, xiii. 172, xxii. 156).
57 For Grethlein, see chapter two. On the expectations between parents and children, see Pratt 2007: 32–4. Let us emphasize the unfulfilment that inheres in each of her examples.
58 Of the large bibliography on Homeric similes, let me highlight Minchin 2001 as the most relevant to the discussion here (see also her references at notes 1 and 2). In particular, our discussion picks up on her readings of 'irrelevant material' and 'similes which overshoot the mark' (39–42, 44–9). Minchin finds technical and formal explanations for the apparent excesses in those similes which contain 'material which does not correspond to the target domain' (39). Such occasions, for Minchin, serve either to make the images more vivid or are distracting defects resulting from the oral nature of Homeric poetry, which produces narratives with ease and thus tempts the poet to excessively extend narratives in similes. Our discussion will, in line with the theme of this chapter, show how the formal excess of the similes can have thematic significance, and runs closest to Minchin's remarks about contrastive pathos (41).
59 ὡς δ' ὅτε τίς τ' ἐλέφαντα γυνὴ φοίνικι μιήνῃ / Μῃονὶς ἠὲ Κάειρα παρήϊον ἔμμεναι ἵππων· / κεῖται δ' ἐν θαλάμῳ, πολέες τέ μιν ἠρήσαντο / ἱππῆες φορέειν· βασιλῆϊ δὲ κεῖται ἄγαλμα, / ἀμφότερον κόσμός θ' ἵππῳ ἐλατῆρί τε κῦδος (ιv. 141–5).
60 ὃ δ' ἐν κονίῃσι χαμαὶ πέσεν αἴγειρος ὣς / ἥ ῥά τ' ἐν εἰαμενῇ ἕλεος μεγάλοιο πεφύκει / λείη, ἀτάρ τέ οἱ ὄζοι ἐπ' ἀκροτάτῃ πεφύασι· / τὴν μέν θ' ἁρματοπηγὸς ἀνὴρ αἴθωνι σιδήρῳ / ἐξέταμ', ὄφρα ἴτυν κάμψῃ περικαλλέϊ δίφρῳ· / ἣ μέν τ' ἀζομένη κεῖται ποταμοῖο παρ' ὄχθας (ιv. 482–7). On this simile, see Moulton 1977: 56–8. Moulton's analysis is not closely connected with mine, although his work is valuable preparation in clearing away the limitations of older approaches. See also Austin 1975: 115–18. On the figure of Simoeisios, see Schein 2016: 5–9 (originally 1976). My readings here extend his evocation of the 'sense of non-fulfilment' and the temporality of 'the rhythm of a normal, peaceful pastoral life' (7 and 8).
61 To briefly return to biographical vignettes, we can see that the mention of parentage itself constitutes an evocation of expectations to be overturned by contingency. Whereas we have focused on vignettes presenting re-visions of a single life, the mention of parents – their hopes for their children, the dalliances that produced a child in their lives – shows that the same disjunction works across generations. Compare note 53 above on the non-finality of death.
62 Σιμοείσιον, ὅν ποτε μήτηρ / Ἴδηθεν κατιοῦσα παρ' ὄχθῃσιν Σιμόεντος / γείνατ', ἐπεί ῥα τοκεῦσιν ἅμ' ἕσπετο μῆλα ἰδέσθαι· / τοὔνεκά μιν κάλεον Σιμοείσιον· οὐδὲ τοκεῦσι / θρέπτρα φίλοις ἀπέδωκε, μινυνθάδιος δέ οἱ αἰὼν (ιv. 474–8).
63 Weil 1965.

64 See Scott 1979: 5 and Canevaro 2018: 191–3.
65 For 'stochastic', see Kahane (forthcoming), section 2.5.
66 εὖ γὰρ ἐγὼ τόδε οἶδα κατὰ φρένα καὶ κατὰ θυμόν· / ἔσσεται ἦμαρ ὅτ' ἄν ποτ' ὀλώλῃ Ἴλιος ἱρὴ / καὶ Πρίαμος καὶ λαὸς ἐϋμμελίω Πριάμοιο (vi. 447–9 = iv. 163–5). The repetition in the mouth of Agamemnon in book iv, as well as the general context, shows that the destruction meant will come in the present war, as opposed to an indefinite future one.
67 Ζεῦ ἄλλοι τε θεοὶ δότε δὴ καὶ τόνδε γενέσθαι / παῖδ' ἐμὸν ὡς καὶ ἐγώ περ ἀριπρεπέα Τρώεσσιν, / ὧδε βίην τ' ἀγαθόν, καὶ Ἰλίου ἶφι ἀνάσσειν· / καί ποτέ τις εἴπῃσι πατρός δ' ὅ γε πολλὸν ἀμείνων / ἐκ πολέμου ἀνιόντα· φέροι δ' ἔναρα βροτόεντα / κτείνας δήϊον ἄνδρα, χαρείη δὲ φρένα μήτηρ (vi. 476–81).
68 Indeed, even the psychological explanation includes an implicit splitting. What prompts Hector's vision of his son's future prowess is the child's fear at the sight of Hector's helmet (vi. 466–73). What he sees in the child's reaction is therefore not his present fear, but the promise of growth and change. The meaning of the child's present fear for Hector thus includes its own difference from itself. In this way, the formal structure of the splitting of the present undergirds the thematic level (in this case, what commentators have noted as the tenderly observed sentimentality of the scene). See Pratt 2007: 28, who explains psychologically what we approach formally: 'For what Hektor markedly does not conclude from his son's tears is that Astyanax is by nature a coward who will never be a successful warrior; these tears are a natural and accepted part of Astyanax's childhood, out of which the child will presumably grow.' Again, our formal interests do not prejudice the significance of psychological or thematic interpretations; the latter lead, in Pratt's case, to productive contrasts between Hector's attitude to his child's weakness and the less charitable attitude of Sophocles' Ajax (ibid. 28 note 15). Our formal interests allow us to make other connections, though these will lead us elsewhere. The closest approach in recent scholarship to what I will propose here is the discussion in Gazis 2018 in which Hades is read as a site where conventionally epic values are suspended, thereby allowing a contrast between 'official' and public versions of stories with more personal and intimate ones. Gazis focuses the Iliadic part of his study on Achilles' dream encounter with the shade of Patroclus, since this is the only explicit encounter with the underworld in the *Iliad*. The less literal and more formal approach of the present argument will find other versions of this contrast.
69 ἀλλ' ἥ γε ξὺν παιδὶ καὶ ἀμφιπόλῳ ἐϋπέπλῳ / πύργῳ ἐφεστήκει γοόωσά τε μυρομένη τε (vi. 372–3).
70 οὕνεκ' ἄκουσε / τείρεσθαι Τρῶας, μέγα δὲ κράτος εἶναι Ἀχαιῶν. / ἣ μὲν δὴ πρὸς τεῖχος ἐπειγομένη ἀφικάνει / μαινομένῃ ἐϊκυῖα . . . (vi. 386–9).
71 'But the wife of Hektor had not yet heard: for no sure messenger had come to her and told her how her husband had held his ground there outside the gates; but she

was weaving a web in the inner room of the high house, a red folding robe, and inworking elaborate figures. She called out through the house to her lovely-haired handmaidens to set a great cauldron over the fire, so that there would be hot water for Hektor's bath as he came back out of the fighting; poor innocent, nor knew how, far from waters for bathing, Pallas Athene had cut him down at the hands of Achilleus' (ἄλοχος δ' οὔ πώ τι πέπυστο / Ἕκτορος· οὐ γάρ οἵ τις ἐτήτυμος ἄγγελος ἐλθὼν / ἤγγειλ᾽ ὅττί ῥά οἱ πόσις ἔκτοθι μίμνε πυλάων, / ἀλλ᾽ ἥ γ᾽ ἱστὸν ὕφαινε μυχῷ δόμου ὑψηλοῖο / δίπλακα πορφυρέην, ἐν δὲ θρόνα ποικίλ᾽ ἔπασσε. / κέκλετο δ᾽ ἀμφιπόλοισιν ἐϋπλοκάμοις κατὰ δῶμα / ἀμφὶ πυρὶ στῆσαι τρίποδα μέγαν, ὄφρα πέλοιτο / Ἕκτορι θερμὰ λοετρὰ μάχης ἐκ νοστήσαντι / νηπίη, οὐδ᾽ ἐνόησεν ὅ μιν μάλα τῆλε λοετρῶν / χερσὶν Ἀχιλλῆος δάμασε γλαυκῶπις Ἀθήνη, xxii. 437–47). Let us note that this moment is marked by the weaving of a robe which might be compared with Helen and Penelope's weaving in the context of our earlier discussion of the connection between weaving and the projection of meaning to a future song: the relevance of the future song for the context of Hector's death is that the projection of meaning to an inaccessible elsewhere necessarily entails that it is missed in the present moment.

72 Most pointedly too early at vi. 500: 'So they mourned Hektor in his house while he was still living' (αἳ μὲν ἔτι ζωὸν γόον Ἕκτορα ᾧ ἐνὶ οἴκῳ).

73 τὴν ἤτοι ἄνδρες Βατίειαν κικλήσκουσιν, / ἀθάνατοι δέ τε σῆμα πολυσκάρθμοιο Μυρίνης (ii. 813–14). Other Homeric notices of divine and human names are found at i. 403–4 (Briareos/Aigaion), xiv. 290–1 (a bird), xx. 74 (Skamandros/Xanthos), x. 305 (the plant 'moly') and xii. 61 (the clashing rocks).

74 Grethlein 2008: 31. This analysis of the *sēma* agrees well with our discussions in chapter one. See also Tsagalis 2012, chapter one. The temporal significance here does not easily generalize to other instances of divine versus mortal names, although I would argue that the same alienating effect is achieved through the contrast.

75 Scodel 1997's focus on what the audience does not know is relevant again: the ignorance of the audience bears richer meanings than as a mere tool for enforcing the poet's authority.

76 See, for instance, Dué 2019, chapter four.

77 εὖ γὰρ ἐγὼ τόδε οἶδα κατὰ φρένα καὶ κατὰ θυμόν· / ἔσσεται ἦμαρ ὅτ᾽ ἄν ποτ᾽ ὀλώλῃ Ἴλιος ἱρὴ / καὶ Πρίαμος καὶ λαὸς ἐϋμμελίω Πριάμοιο, / Ζεὺς δέ σφιν Κρονίδης ὑψίζυγος αἰθέρι ναίων / αὐτὸς ἐπισσείῃσιν ἐρεμνὴν αἰγίδα πᾶσι τῆσδ᾽ ἀπάτης κοτέων· τὰ μὲν ἔσσεται οὐκ ἀτέλεστα· / ἀλλά μοι αἰνὸν ἄχος σέθεν ἔσσεται ὦ Μενέλαε / αἴ κε θάνῃς καὶ μοῖραν ἀναπλήσῃς βιότοιο (iv. 163–70).

78 The relative insignificance of the actual *thematic content* of the doom of Troy – despite the emphatic gestures of verse 163 in εὖ γὰρ ἐγὼ τόδε οἶδα κατὰ φρένα καὶ κατὰ θυμόν – is all the more clearly brought out by the continuation of the speech that follows directly from the passage already cited, in which Agamemnon seems to

have already forgotten his certainty of Troy's fall. Instead, he imagines the expedition 'a venture that went unaccomplished [ἀτελευτήτῳ ἐπὶ ἔργῳ]' (175) and 'in vain [ἅλιον]' (179), going home 'with ships empty and leaving brave Menelaos behind [σὺν κεινῇσιν νηυσὶ λιπὼν ἀγαθὸν Μενέλαον]' (181). The commentators give a standard psychological explanation ('Agamemnon's grief often turns quickly to self-pity, as here', Kirk 1990 *ad* 171–5), while, again, we can note its formal bases. It is true that Agamemnon's self-pity rather spoils any sympathy he might have gained for his grief in the previous verses, but let us assume he is flighty rather than heartless.

79 ἀλλ' οὔ μοι Τρώων τόσσον μέλει ἄλγος ὀπίσσω, / οὔτ' αὐτῆς Ἑκάβης οὔτε Πριάμοιο ἄνακτος / οὔτε κασιγνήτων, οἵ κεν πολέες τε καὶ ἐσθλοὶ / ἐν κονίῃσι πέσοιεν ὑπ' ἀνδράσι δυσμενέεσσιν, / ὅσσον σεῖ' . . . (VI. 450–4).

80 It would perhaps be more precise to say that *kleos* is projected as meaning that *will have become* fixed, but that moment of fixation is infinitely deferred. Meanwhile, despite the anticipated fixity and because of the infinite deferral, the unknowability of *kleos* means that it *functions* in the heroic present as open. This is of course before any suturing operation.

81 Szondi 1978: 499.

82 Ibid. 502.

83 See Morrison 1997 for an analysis of the opposition between fixity and openness on the level of heroic action, in the confrontation of Zeus and fate, and for the possibility of the poet's freedom within a 'fixed' tradition. Chapter five will discuss this further.

84 In the final analysis, these two reasons are the same thing for a rigorous understanding of the term 'historical'.

85 ὃ δ' ἀπέσσυτο δώματος Ἕκτωρ / τὴν αὐτὴν ὁδὸν αὖτις ἐϋκτιμένας κατ' ἀγυιάς. / εὖτε πύλας ἵκανε διερχόμενος μέγα ἄστυ / Σκαιάς, τῇ ἄρ' ἔμελλε διεξίμεναι πεδίονδε (VI. 390–3).

86 This use of *mellō* in the imperfect in fact accounts for most occurrences of this verb in the *Iliad*. For instance, at II. 36, Agamemnon wakes from the deceptive dream, 'believing things in his heart that were not to be accomplished [τὰ οὐ τελέεσθαι ἔμελλε]'. Or, at V. 685–8, where Sarpedon, thinking that he is about to die, distinguishes the fated death from other plans he had which are now foreclosed: '[S]ince otherwise in your city my life must come to an end, since I could return no longer [οὐκ ἄρ' ἔμελλον ἔγωγε / νοστήσας] back to my own house and the land of my fathers, bringing joy to my own beloved wife and my son, still a baby.' The examples can be multiplied. Bakker's interpretation of this verb (2005: 92–113; see chapter two) as a sign of the belated realization of truth is a special case of the more general interpretation we offer here; the distinction indicated by *mellō* between the fixity of fate and the halo of foreclosed possibilities is expressed as a belated realization of the truth when it appears in character speech.

87 εὖτε πύλας ἵκανε διερχόμενος μέγα ἄστυ / Σκαιάς, τῇ ἄρ' ἔμελλε διεξίμεναι πεδίονδε / ἔνθ' ἄλοχος πολύδωρος ἐναντίη ἦλθε θέουσα / Ἀνδρομάχη . . . (vi. 392-5).
88 The unexpectedness was noted by the scholiast (bT 6.371): τῷ τείχει παραδόξως συντυγχάνει αὐτοῖς, 'Contrary to expectation, they happen to be on the walls' (quoted from Morrison 1992: 138 note 44, in his translation). Morrison also notes (67): 'Andromache finds him at the last moment.' Of other translators, Cowper (1791) reproduces both verse-initial emphases. Chapman (1615) expands upon the sense of an almost missed encounter: 'All the great city pass'd, and came where, seeing how blood was spilt, / Andromache might see him come: who made *as he would pass / The ports without saluting her, not knowing where she was.*' Fagles 1990, too, emphasizes that Andromache only just caught up to Hector: 'the Scaean Gates, / *the last point* he would pass to gain the field of battle'. Fitzgerald 1974 is less emphatic, though he brings out the imminence of Hector's departure: 'the Skaian Gates, whereby / *before long* he would issue on the field'. Finally, Alexander 2015 marks the contrast between missing and fulfilling the encounter with an understated anaphora: '[T]*here* where he intended to pass through to the plain, *there* his worthy wife came to meet him.'

5 Three Syntheses of Time

1 Deleuze 1994, 1986 and 1989.
2 See Deleuze 1994: 70-128. Secondary literature includes: Smith 1997: 137-93, Bryant 2008: 92-134, Hughes 2009, Williams 2011, Somers-Hall 2011 and 2013: 55-96, Zourabichvili 2012: 94-111 and Lapoujade 2017: 79-130.
3 Deleuze 1994: 70.
4 Ibid. 75. By 'contemplation', Deleuze means the relation between the 'little selves' which contract and that which they contract.
5 Zourabichvili 2012: 95.
6 Lynn-George 1988: 61. See our discussion in chapter three, in particular the first section.
7 See chapter one, in which we show how the traditional reference acts as carte blanche for reintroducing literary interpretation in place of Parry's stipulation for meanings that 'instantly and easily come to mind' (Parry 1971: 156).
8 Lynn-George 1988: 10, quoting from Auerbach 1953: 4.
9 Austin 1966.
10 Lynn-George 1988: 14.
11 Austin 1966: 296-7. In Austin's diagnosis of this aspect of the oral theoretical approach, we recognize the distinctive slippage in which salutary reminders that oral

poetry sustains *different* forms of thinking turn into injunctions against thinking *too much*. Digressions, under the condition of this slippage, simply *are* and should not have too much meaning foisted upon them.

12 Ibid. 303 (emphasis added), with reference to van Groningen 1953: 13.
13 Ibid. 312. We should pick up Austin's reference to drama and note a connection between dramatic form and the present (Szondi 1986: 9): 'Because the Drama is primary, its internal time is always the present. That in no way means that the Drama is static, only that time passes in a particular manner: the present passes and becomes the past, and, as such, can no longer be present on stage. As the present passes away, it produces change, a new present springs from its antithesis. In the Drama, time unfolds as an absolute, linear sequence in the present.'
14 Lynn-George 1988: 15.
15 Nagy 1996b: 15.
16 Austin 1966: 303.
17 Ibid.
18 The valorization of the present which appears in Austin as an interpretive principle becomes literal in Andersen 1990: 29 and 42: '[T]he past is made up [that is, *fabricated*] as a function of the present ... [T]*he present takes precedence over the past*.'
19 Lynn-George 1988: 10.
20 This is the reasoning behind Auerbach's assertion that a relation *would* have been possible if the story of the scar had been moved (1953: 7): '[A] connection with it through perspective would have been all the easier had the content been arranged with that end in view; if, that is, the entire story of the scar had been presented as a recollection which awakens in Odysseus' mind at this particular moment. It would have been perfectly easy to do; the story of the scar had only to be inserted two verses earlier, at the first mention of the word scar, where the motifs "Odysseus" and "recollection" were already at hand.' For Auerbach, the link between the past and the present *could* have been integrated as the memory of a subject, Odysseus, but the poem does not take that option.
21 Lynn-George 1988: 15.
22 Zourabichvili 2012: 96.
23 Ibid. 99.
24 We have seen how oral theory does not construct a vision of Homeric poetry which can account for change and difference. It is neoanalysis which has most systematically made difference meaningful, although other scholars writing counter to the oralist position have also made this a theme. Russo 1968 is still essential in this regard.
25 We have discussed this problem earlier, but let us now reposition it within the structure of a broader problem.
26 Austin 1966: 311.

27 Nagy 1979: 3.
28 Nagy 1996b: 25.
29 Put differently, this past is absolute because it is equally distance from every present, unlike a point in a chronological past that can be nearer or further away from other points in chronological time.
30 Both Nagy and Agamemnon – if the oddness of the couple may be excused – presuppose a site which determines or conditions the present. Do we not find the same structure already in Parry? Writing on principle of 'economy' in Parry's formulaic system that requires only one formula correspond to every name or sense to be expressed in each metrical situation, Lynn-George claims that 'Parry constructs systems of substitution to deny the possibility of substitution – and this is the fundamental paradox in these paradigms – substitution systems without any substitutes within them' (1988: 66). Where, for Lynn-George, Parry's system falls apart as a result of this contradiction, let us ask instead what desire is expressed in it. Why does Parry insist on the form or structure of *substitutability* even when there are no possible *substitutes*? What does the virtual potential of substitution do when no actual substitutions happen? Like the absolute past of tradition, it opens up the present to its dehiscence.
31 Deleuze 1994: 79.
32 Bryant 2008: 109.
33 Deleuze 1994: 81. Deleuze makes use of Bergson's argument about memory, which we saw in chapter two.
34 Ibid. 82.
35 Saussure 1974: 71.
36 Another reason for moving on from Nagy's version of the pure past is that it does not receive further development in Nagy, at least not in a direction that connects to temporality. As we saw in chapter three, Nagy's work is often fascinating from being animated by conflicting impulses. In this case, his solution to the potential clash of traditional language and the poet's intent leads us towards the pure past and away from the strong affinity, in oral theory, with the continuity of the living present, but it remains isolated and unacknowledged. Nagy's version of the pure past is thus used here in a somewhat opportunistic way, as a convenient and clear illustration.
37 This statement should be taken with the caveats about the degree to which performances represented in Homer reflect Homeric performance itself. See the previous chapter's discussion of the *Iliad*'s differences from *klea andrōn*. (My thanks to Matthew Ward for this salutary reminder.)
38 See Bakker 2005: 112–13 as well as our discussion in chapter two.
39 Strictly speaking, the form of memory involved in this particular argument is active memory, rather than the memory that is the topic of the second synthesis, which is passive ('active' here means performed by an already constituted subject, as opposed

to the 'passivity' of a synthesis prior to and constitutive of subjective agency). Nevertheless, we can still make use of this argument for two reasons. First, the conditions of the active form of memory mirrors those of the more fundamental, passive form; the former is a condensed version of what Deleuze calls the 'constitutive paradoxes' of the latter (see Deleuze 1994: 81–2). Second, Deleuze himself makes use of similar approximations in a pedagogical way, such as in *Cinema 2*, when he introduces the 'conventional, extrinsic device' of the flashback in Marcel Carné's *Daybreak* (*Le jour se lève*, 1939) en route to more essentially temporal forms of time image (Deleuze 1989: 48).

40 Deleuze 1994: 80 (emphasis added).
41 Ibid. 81.
42 See also previous discussion of this problem in chapter two, where the context was Bergson's conception of memory.
43 We can refer again to Agamemnon and Patroclus reassigning the meaning of events in light of new developments; the new developments do not lead to new *kleos*, but only to the belated realization of what *kleos* has always been.
44 Redfield 1979: 105–8.
45 Allan 2008: 212.
46 Ibid. 214. Note 42 here explicitly connects *Dios boulē* with *klea andrōn*.
47 Ibid. Burgess makes a parallel point (2004: 15–16): 'Epic poetry is intrinsically hardwired for such sequence because of the fundamental framework provided by traditional myth. Myth of gods and mortals was always larger and longer than any single poetic piece of it. This mythological "supertext" (Dowden 1996: 51) or "divinely superintended tale" (Ford 1992: 41) did not just provide raw material to be worked up into poetry, it actively organized it. If a gap resulted when rhapsodes jumped from one episode to another, the whole performance hung together because of the notional mythological cycle.'
48 Allan 2008: 212.
49 Ibid. 214.
50 Murnaghan 1997: 24.
51 Ibid.
52 Ibid. 28, 36.
53 Ibid. 42. See also Slatkin 1991.
54 Bergren 2008: 50–2.
55 ἴδμεν γάρ τοι πάνθ', ὅσ' ἐνὶ Τροίῃ εὐρείῃ / Ἀργεῖοι Τρῶές τε θεῶν ἰότητι μόγησαν (xii. 189–90).
56 See Pucci 1979, Segal 1983 and Schur 2014, with further bibliography. See also Blanchot 2003: 3–10.
57 Pucci speaks of the heroes' 'self-destructive nostalgia' and the 'memory of their splendid and grievous past' (1979: 126).

58 'Over all the generous earth we know everything that happens.' (ἴδμεν δ' ὅσσα γένηται ἐπὶ χθονὶ πουλυβοτείρῃ, xii. 189–91.) Purves' observations (2010: 21) on the sirens, 'who epitomize the kind of still death that would accompany truly synoptic and "all-seeing" song', connect them to the concept of the 'eusynoptic', which we will explore below.
59 It is often understood that Odysseus does hear more of the song than is presented in the *Odyssey*, but the text is ambiguous. Odysseus says that he wanted to listen, but his comrades simply tied him more tightly until they sailed out of range (xii. 192–200).
60 My 2018 article (108–14) argues that Kafka, in his rewriting of the encounter with the sirens ('Das Schweigen der Sirenen', 1917), understood these aspects of the sirens' song in much the same way.
61 With the proviso that a whole range of 'improper' suturing operations connects the force of *kleos* to a series of thematic contents.
62 The other occurrences are in the speech of Nestor on his past prowess (xi. 762), and Priam on Hector (xxiv. 426) in the *Iliad*, as well as that of Penelope (xix. 315) and Laertes (xxiv. 289) in the *Odyssey*, both in recalling Odysseus.
63 Lynn-George 1988: 209.
64 πάντες δ' εὐχετόωντο θεῶν Διὶ Νέστορί τ' ἀνδρῶν. / ὣς ἔον, εἴ ποτ' ἔην γε, μετ' ἀνδράσιν (xi. 761–2).
65 Ibid. 36. The irreality of the past marked by the tag *ei pot' eēn ge* contrasts most strikingly with Treu's contention that attributes to the Homeric poems 'a strong consciousness of continuity with the past' as opposed to a 'low' continuity with the future (1955: 132–3). It marks precisely 'that deep gulf [*jene tiefe Kluft*]' between past and present – 'bridgeable only by memory, longing and dream' – that Treu wished to reserve for modernity (125). See Theunissen 2000: 39–40.
66 See Louden 1993, which also provides a list of all the instances at 183 note 5. See also Morrison's earlier discussion of 'A if not B' formulations (1992: 60).
67 Louden 1993: 198 (emphasis added).
68 See chapter three.
69 Or, as Deleuze might have put it, what is the function of *difference* here if it is not pushed into a *contradiction*, which is merely the other side of identity?
70 The figure which is expressed in the Homeric context as contrafactuals is pursued by Deleuze in a number of different forms. An important text for him is Jorge Luis Borges's 'Garden of Forking Paths', in which all possibilities – all contrafactuals – exist and are chosen simultaneously (see Deleuze 1994: 115–17). Deleuze thus pushes the literary notion to the level of ontology, and connections can be made with both Deleuze's use of and his dissent from Stoic philosophy and Leibniz. Both the Stoics and Leibniz, in Deleuze's reading, propose potentially divergent or forking events, only to reintegrate them under the unity of Zeus in the case of the Stoics or the pre-established harmony of God for Leibniz. See the discussion throughout

Deleuze 1990, as well as Bowden 2011: 15–94. (On the power of Zeus as a unifying agent – Homeric rather than Stoic – we will soon have more to say.) By gesturing towards divergent events only as contrafactuals, the Homeric poems do not reach the ontological level at which Deleuze situates his eventual argument, and this is one of the reasons that we can only use motifs from the third synthesis in this section, rather than argue for a closer connection. In remaining on the level of 'hermeneutics', the Homeric poems are perhaps closer to the films of Joseph Mankiewicz in the analysis Deleuze offers in *Cinema 2* (1989: 47–55); there, Mankiewicz's films present forks of time in which the meaning of events are overturned in interpretation.

71 The French is 'le temps est hors de ses gonds' (Deleuze 1968: 119, from the Shakespeare translation of Yves Bonnefoy).

72 Unpublished lecture 'Sur Kant: synthèse et temps' (14 March 1978), translated by Melissa McMahon.

73 Ibid.

74 Ibid.

75 Murnaghan 1997: 24.

76 ἔστιν οὖν τραγῳδία μίμησις πράξεως ... ἔστιν δὲ τῆς μὲν πράξεως ὁ μῦθος ἡ μίμησις ('Tragedy, then, is the mimesis of an action ... the plot is the mimesis of the action', Arist. *Poet.* 1449b 24 and 1450a 4; translation from Halliwell 1995).

77 See Arist. *Poet.* 1450b–1451a.

78 ἀρχὴ δέ ἐστιν ὃ αὐτὸ μὲν μὴ ἐξ ἀνάγκης μετ' ἄλλο ἐστίν, μετ' ἐκεῖνο δ' ἕτερον πέφυκεν εἶναι ἢ γίνεσθαι· τελευτὴ δὲ τοὐναντίον ὃ αὐτὸ μὲν μετ' ἄλλο πέφυκεν εἶναι ἢ ἐξ ἀνάγκης ἢ ὡς ἐπὶ τὸ πολύ, μετὰ δὲ τοῦτο ἄλλο οὐδέν (1450b 26–30).

79 1451a 20 and 1459a 17–24.

80 τὸ γὰρ καλὸν ἐν μεγέθει καὶ τάξει ἐστίν, διὸ οὔτε πάμμικρον ἄν τι γένοιτο καλὸν ζῷον ... οὔτε παμμέγεθες ... ὥστε δεῖ καθάπερ ἐπὶ τῶν σωμάτων καὶ ἐπὶ τῶν ζῴων ἔχειν μὲν μέγεθος, τοῦτο δὲ εὐσύνοπτον εἶναι, οὕτω καὶ ἐπὶ τῶν μύθων ἔχειν μὲν μῆκος, τοῦτο δὲ εὐμνημόνευτον εἶναι (1450b 36–1451a 6). Quoted from Purves 2010: 31 in the translation of Benardete and Davis 2002. My discussion of the Aristotelian concept of the eusynoptic presupposes Purves analysis (2010: 24–64), although I have a different view of how it applies to the *Iliad*.

81 Aristotle specifically extends the property of the eusynoptic to Homeric epic (1459a 30–4; quoted from Purves 2010: 25): 'Just as we said before, Homer would appear to speak in a divine way compared to the rest, in that he did not attempt to make the war a whole, even though it had a beginning and an end. For the plot would otherwise have been too large and not easily seen at one time [*ouk eusynoptos*], or, if scaled down in length, too closely woven with detail' (διὸ ὥσπερ εἴπομεν ἤδη καὶ ταύτῃ θεσπέσιος ἂν φανείη Ὅμηρος παρὰ τοὺς ἄλλους, τῷ μηδὲ τὸν πόλεμον καίπερ ἔχοντα ἀρχὴν καὶ τέλος ἐπιχειρῆσαι ποιεῖν ὅλον· λίαν γὰρ ἂν μέγας καὶ οὐκ εὐσύνοπτος ἔμελλεν ἔσεσθαι ὁ μῦθος, ἢ τῷ μεγέθει μετριάζοντα καταπεπλεγμένον

τῇ ποικιλίᾳ). Purves notes (2010: 36, emphases added): 'Aristotle's example suggests that what is read or heard in a narrative *over time* can be recollected *as a space or picture in the mind's eye*.'

82 Compare the parallel distinction in Nagy's concept of diachrony as opposed to history, discussed in chapter three.

83 This summary of Aristotle does not take into account applications to actual tragedies, or even the temporality of Aristotle's own conceptions of *peripeteia* and *anagnōrisis*.

84 Deleuze 1997: 28.

85 Rosenberg 1959: 139.

86 Somers-Hall 2011: 66–7.

87 Ibid. 69: 'Now, as these lines makes clear, Hamlet is very much aware of what he should do, but he is simply not able to do it. To this extent, we have an odd dramatic structure since, if characters are understood in terms of the relations of acts to the judgement of the law as they would be in classical drama, then Hamlet's various speeches, and use of speech in the first half of the play, are simply irrelevant to the structure of his role.'

88 Ibid. 68.

89 Deleuze 1994: 110–11.

90 Let us note here that the sequence of syntheses is not a one-way street: the operation of suture is precisely what makes it run backwards by giving the pure and empty form of *kleos* content again.

91 For instance, at VIII. 69–74: 'Then the father balanced his golden scales, and in them he set two fateful portions of death [*kēre*], which lays men prostrate, for Trojans, breakers of horses, and bronze-armoured Achaians, and balanced it by the middle. The Achaians' death-day was heaviest. There the fates [*kēres*] of the Achaians settled down towards the bountiful earth, while those of the Trojans were lifted into the wide sky' (καὶ τότε δὴ χρύσεια πατὴρ ἐτίταινε τάλαντα· / ἐν δ' ἐτίθει δύο κῆρε τανηλεγέος θανάτοιο / Τρώων θ' ἱπποδάμων καὶ Ἀχαιῶν χαλκοχιτώνων, / ἕλκε δὲ μέσσα λαβών· ῥέπε δ' αἴσιμον ἦμαρ Ἀχαιῶν. / αἳ μὲν Ἀχαιῶν κῆρες ἐπὶ χθονὶ πουλυβοτείρῃ / ἑζέσθην, Τρώων δὲ πρὸς οὐρανὸν εὐρὺν ἄερθεν).

92 Morrison 1997: 280, 284 and 286.

93 Ibid. 275.

94 The key point about fate here is that it is not known and exceeds intentionality.

95 What follows develops a conclusion that Morrison reaches via different lines (1992: 105): 'In the end, the audience finds that all perspectives – human or divine, looking to the heroic past with the narrator or to the future with the seer – are fallible.'

96 Bakker 2005: 112.

97 Ibid.

98 The following argument is further developed in my 2018 article.
99 The passing on of authority, as an enactment of the resistance to fixity that marks the logic of *kleos* in the third synthesis, is also what we saw in the figure of the legendary *guslar* of the South Slavic tradition back in chapter one. The legendary *guslar*, who is everywhere else identified as the origin of the songs of the oral tradition, nevertheless does not fully assume this role. By replying that he learnt his songs 'from Isak' – his own name – the legendary *guslar* divides his own identity and thereby preserves the resistance to fixity.
100 The regression can continue: from whom does the muse herself obtain her knowledge and authority? Hesiod would return us to the power of Zeus and Memory, their parents, but is this a position that could be endorsed by the *Iliad*, which has resisted the notion of Zeus as all-knowing and staging the failure of memory?
101 The poet–muse configuration also parallels the situation of the siren song: the possibility of knowing all and telling all is held out and withdrawn in the same gesture. It is instructive to compare González's conception of the poet–muse relation (2011: chapter 7; compare Jonathan Ready's discussion of the 'preexistence of tales' at 2019: 28–31). My reading parallels that of González insofar as I concur that there is a place for a 'notional fixity' in epic. For González, this means that despite any actual variations across different performances, the epic remains notionally the same, while I would connect this notional fixity with the pure past of the *Dios boulē*. We diverge on how to relate this notional fixity to the poet–muse relation: for González, the muse guarantees the notional fixity of the poem insofar as the poet relies on the 'infallible autopsy' derived from her supernatural authority (209). In contrast, I read for the logic that must be at work in this configuration since, as the Homeric poets must have known better than we do, the muse never actually tells them anything. Notional fixity is thus an expression of the pure past of the second synthesis, while the poet–muse configuration is a figure of the third. If it is tempting to object that scepticism regarding the existence of the muses is a modern anachronism – perhaps the Homeric poets did 'really believe' they were divinely inspired – it is only to punt the real problem down the line: what did the Homeric poets *express as* the belief in divine inspiration? The interpretation that the muse is *actually* able to guarantee fixity is obliged to answer that what is expressed as the belief in divine inspiration is *actual* divine inspiration. In contrast, I argue that that belief ought to be considered in the context of the whole structure of time we have been considering: what is primary is not a belief in divine inspiration, but a poet–muse configuration that expresses the nature of *kleos* as that which can only be given as withheld.
102 πῶς δέ κεν Ἕκτωρ κῆρας ὑπεξέφυγεν θανάτοιο, / εἰ μή οἱ πύματόν τε καὶ ὕστατον ἤντετ' Ἀπόλλων / ἐγγύθεν, ὅς οἱ ἐπῶρσε μένος λαιψηρά τε γοῦνα; (xxii. 202–4). I

quote these lines as an emblem or evocation, rather than as substitute for the arguments that have led to this point.
103 See Nagy 1996a: 39–58.
104 Nagy 1996a: 57.
105 Deleuze 1994: 94.
106 Eliot's use of the term correlated objects to an *emotion* (1950: 100–1).

Bibliography

Accame, S. (1961), 'La concezione del tempo nell'età omerica ed arcaica', *Rivista di Filologia e di Istruzione Classica* 39: 359-94.

Alexander, C. (2015), *The Iliad*, New York, NY.

Allan, W. (2008), 'Performing the Will of Zeus: The Διὸς βουλή and the Scope of Early Greek Epic', in M. Revermann and P. Wilson (eds), *Performance, Iconography, Reception: Studies in Honour of Oliver Taplin*, 204-16, Oxford.

Andersen, Ø. (1990), 'The Making of the Past in the *Iliad*', *Harvard Studies in Classical Philology* 93: 25-45.

Andersen, Ø. and D. Haug, eds (2012), *Relative Chronology in Early Greek Epic Poetry*, Cambridge.

Arft, J. T. (forthcoming), 'Repetition or Recurrence? A Traditional Use for ἄνδρεσσι μελήσει in Archaic Greek Poetry', in D. Beck (ed.), *Repetition, Communication, and Meaning in the Ancient World*, Leiden.

Auerbach, E. (1953), *Mimesis: The Representation of Reality in Western Literature*, trans. W. R. Trask, Princeton, NJ.

Austin, N. (1966), 'The Function of Digressions in the *Iliad*', *Greek, Roman, and Byzantine Studies* 7: 295-312.

Austin, N. (1975), *Archery at the Dark of the Moon: Poetic Problems in Homer's Odyssey*, Berkeley, CA.

Bakker, E. J. (2002), 'Khrónos, kléos, and Ideology', in M. Reichel and A. Rengakos (eds), *Epea pteroenta: Beitäge zur Homerforschung*, 324-43, Stuttgart.

Bakker, E. J. (2005), *Pointing at the Past: From Formula to Performance in Homeric Poetics*, Washington, DC.

Bakker, E. J. (2013), *The Meaning of Meat and the Structure of the Odyssey*, Cambridge.

Bassi, K. (2016), *Traces of the Past: Classics between History and Archaeology*, Ann Arbor, MI.

Benardete, S. and Davis, M. (2002), *Aristotle On poetics*, South Bend, IN.

Benjamin, W. (1969), *Illuminations: Essays and Reflections*, ed. H. Arendt, trans. H. Zohn, New York, NY.

Benjamin, W. (1991), *Gesammelte Schriften*, vol. 2, Frankfurt am Main.

Bennett, J. (2010), *Vibrant Matter: A Political Ecology of Things*, Durham, NC.

Bergren, A. (2008), *Weaving Truth: Essays on Language and the Female in Greek Thought*, Washington, DC.

Bergson, H. (1920), *Mind-Energy, Lectures and Essays*, New York, NY.

Bielfeldt, R. (2014), *Ding und Mensch in der Antike*, Heidelberg.

Blanchot, M. (2003), *The Book to Come*, trans. C. Mandell, Stanford, CA.
Bowden, S. (2011), *Priority of Events: Deleuze's Logic of Sense*, Edinburgh.
Bowden, S. (2015), 'Human and Nonhuman Agency in Deleuze', in J. Roffe and H. Stark (eds), *Deleuze and the non/human*, 60–80, Basingstoke.
Brown, B. (2001), 'Thing Theory', *Critical Inquiry* 28: 1–22.
Bryant, L. R. (2008), *Difference and Givenness: Deleuze's Transcendental Empiricism and the Ontology of Immanence*, Evanston, IL.
Buchan, M. (2012), *Perfidy and Passion: Reintroducing the Iliad*, Madison, WI.
Buchanan, I. (2015), 'Assemblage Theory and Its Discontents', *Deleuze Studies* 9: 382–92.
Buchanan, I. (2017), 'Assemblage Theory, or, the Future of an Illusion', *Deleuze Studies* 11: 457–74.
Burgess, J. S. (2001), *The Tradition of the Trojan War in Homer and the Epic Cycle*, Baltimore, MD.
Burgess, J. S. (2004), 'Performance and the Epic Cycle', *Classical Journal* 100: 1–23.
Burgess, J. S. (2009), *The Death and Afterlife of Achilles*, Baltimore, MD.
Burgess, J. S. (2012), 'Intertextuality without Text in Early Greek Epic', in Ø. Andersen and D. Haug (eds), *Relative Chronology in Early Greek Epic Poetry*, 168–83, Cambridge.
Bushnell, R. W. (1982), 'Reading "Winged Words": Homeric Bird Signs, Similes, and Epiphanies', *Helios* 9: 1–13.
Butler, S. (2016). 'Homer's Deep', in S. Butler (ed.), *Deep Classics: Rethinking Classical Reception*, 21–48, London.
Canevaro, L. G. (2018), *Women of Substance in Homeric Epic*, Oxford.
Ceccarelli, L. (2001), *L'eroe e il suo limite: responsabilità personale e valutazione etica nell'Iliade*, Bari.
Chantraine, P. (1999), *Dictionnaire étymologique de la langue grecque*, Paris.
Čolaković, Z. (2019), 'Avdo Međedović's Post-Traditional Epics and Their Relevance to Homeric Studies', *Journal of Hellenic Studies* 139: 1–48.
Collett, G. (2016), *The Psychoanalysis of Sense: Deleuze and the Lacanian School*, Edinburgh.
Combellack, F. M. (1962), 'Review of Wolfgang Kullmann, *Die Quellen der Ilias* (Troischer Sagenkreis)', *American Journal of Philology* 83: 193–8.
Coray, M. (2018), *Homer's Iliad, Book XVIII*, ed. S. D. Olson, trans. B. Millis and S. Strack, Berlin.
Currie, B. (2016), *Homer's Allusive Art*, Oxford.
Danek, G. (2002), 'Traditional Referentiality and Homeric Intertextuality', in F. Montanari and P. Ascheri (eds), *Omero tremila anni dopo*, 3–19, Roma.
Davies, M. (2016), *The Aethiopis: Neo-Neoanalysis Reanalyzed*, Washington, DC.
Deleuze, G. (1986), *The Movement-Image*, trans. H. Tomlinson and B. Habberjam, Minneapolis, MN.
Deleuze, G. (1989), *The Time-Image*, trans. H. Tomlinson and R. Galeta, Minneapolis, MN.

Deleuze, G. (1990), *The Logic of Sense*, ed. C. Boundas, trans. M. Lester and C. Stivale, New York, NY.
Deleuze, G. (1994), *Difference and Repetition*, trans. P. Patton, New York, NY.
Deleuze, G. (1997), *Essays Critical and Clinical*, trans. D. W. Smith and M. A. Greco, Minneapolis, MN.
Deleuze, G. (2000), *Proust and Signs*, trans. R. Howard, Minneapolis, MN.
Deleuze, G. (2004), *Desert Islands and Other Texts, 1953-1974*, ed. D. Lapoujade, trans. M. Taormina, Cambridge, MA.
Derrida, J. (1973), *Speech and Phenomena, and Other Essays on Husserl's Theory of Signs*, trans. D. B. Allison, Evanston, IL.
Detienne, M. (1996), *The Masters of Truth in Archaic Greece*, New York, NY.
Dowden, K. (1996), 'Homer's Sense of Text', *Journal of Hellenic Studies* 116: 47–61.
Dué, C. (2019), *Achilles Unbound: Multiformity and Tradition in the Homeric Epics*, Washington, DC.
Edmunds, S. T. (1990), *Homeric nēpios*, New York, NY.
Edwards, A. T. (1985), *Achilles in the Odyssey*, Königstein im Taunus.
Edwards, M. W. (1991), *The Iliad: A Commentary*, vol. 5, Cambridge.
Eliot, T. S, 1950, *The Sacred Wood*, London.
Elmer, D. F. (2005), 'Helen Epigrammatopoios', *Classical Antiquity* 24: 1–39.
Elmer, D. F. (2013), *The Poetics of Consent: Collective Decision Making and the Iliad*, Baltimore, MD.
Erbse, H. (1969), *Scholia Graeca in Homeri Iliadem: scholia vetera*, Berolini.
Fagles, R. (1990), *The Iliad*, New York, NY.
Fantuzzi, M. and C. Tsagalis, eds (2015), *The Greek Epic Cycle and its Ancient Reception: A Companion*, Cambridge.
Finkelberg, M. (2011), *The Homer Encyclopedia*, Malden, MA.
Finkelberg, M. (2012), 'Oral Formulaic Theory and the Individual Poet', in F. Montanari, A. Rengakos and C. Tsagalis (eds), *Homeric Contexts. Neoanalysis and the Interpretation of Oral Poetry*, 73–82, Berlin.
Finnegan, R. H. (1977), *Oral Poetry: Its Nature, Significance, and Social Context*, Cambridge.
Fitzgerald, R. (1974), *The Iliad*, New York, NY.
Foley, J. M. (1991), *Immanent Art. From Structure to Meaning in Traditional Oral Epic*, Bloomington, IN.
Foley, J. M. (1999), *Homer's Traditional Art*, University Park, PA.
Ford, A. (1988), 'The Classical Definition of ΡΑΨΩΙΔΙΑ', *Classical Philology* 83: 300–7.
Ford, A. L. (1992), *Homer: The Poetry of the Past*, Ithaca, NY.
Fowler, R. L., ed. (2004), *The Cambridge Companion to Homer*, Cambridge.
Fränkel, H. (1946), 'Man's "Ephemeros" Nature According to Pindar and Others', *Transactions and Proceedings of the American Philological Association* 77: 131–45.

Fränkel, H. F. (1955), 'Die Zeitauffassung in der frühgriechischen Literatur', in F. Tietze (ed.), *Wege und Formen frühgriechischen Denkens: literarische und philosophiegeschichtliche Studien*, 1–23, Munich.

Freud, S. (1953), *The Standard Edition of the Complete Psychological Works of Sigmund Freud*, ed. J. Strachey, London.

Frontisi-Ducroux, F. (1995), *Du masque au visage: aspects de l'identité en Grèce ancienne*, Paris.

Fry, P. H. (1995), *A Defense of Poetry: Reflections on the Occasion of Writing*, Stanford, CA.

Garcia, L. F. (2013), *Homeric Durability: Telling Time in the Iliad*, Washington, DC.

Gazis, G. A. (2018), *Homer and the Poetics of Hades*, Oxford.

Gell, A. (1998), *Art and Agency*, Oxford.

Goldhill, S. (1991), *The Poet's Voice*, Cambridge.

González, J. M. (2013), *The Epic Rhapsode and His Craft: Homeric Performance in a Diachronic Perspective*, Washington, DC.

Graziosi, B. and J. Haubold, eds (2010), *Homer: Iliad Book VI*, Cambridge.

Grethlein, J. (2006), *Das Geschichtsbild der Ilias: eine Untersuchung aus phänomenologischer und narratologischer Perspektive*, Göttingen.

Grethlein, J. (2008), 'Memory and Material Objects in the *Iliad* and the *Odyssey*', *Journal of Hellenic Studies* 128: 27–51.

Grethlein, J. (2014), 'Homeric Durability: Telling Time in the *Iliad* by Lorenzo F. Garcia (review)', *American Journal of Philology* 135: 481–5.

Grethlein, J. (2019), 'Odysseus and His Bed: From Significant Objects to Thing Theory in Homer', *Classical Quarterly* 69: 467–82.

Griffin, J. (1977), 'The Epic Cycle and the Uniqueness of Homer', *Journal of Hellenic Studies* 97: 39–53.

Griffin, J. (1980), *Homer on Life and Death*, Oxford.

Groningen, B. A. van (1953), *In the Grip of the Past: Essay on an Aspect of Greek Thought*, Leiden.

Hainsworth, B. (1993), *The Iliad: A Commentary*, vol. 3, Cambridge.

Halliwell, S. (1995), *Poetics. Longinus: On the Sublime. Demetrius: On Style*, Cambridge, MA.

Hallward, P. and K. Peden, eds (2012a), *Concept and Form, Volume 1: Selections from the Cahiers pour l'Analyse*, London.

Hallward, P. and K. Peden, eds (2012b), *Concept and Form, Volume 2: Interviews and Essays on Cahiers pour l'Analyse*, London.

Hardie, P. R. (2012), *Rumour and Renown: Representations of* fama *in Western Literature*, Cambridge.

Heath, J. (1999), 'The Serpent and the Sparrows: Homer and the Parodos of Aeschylus' Agamemnon', *Classical Quarterly* 49: 396–407.

Heidegger, M. (1962), *Being and Time*, trans. J. Macquarrie and E. Robinson, New York, NY.

Heubeck, A. (1974), *Die homerische Frage*, Darmstadt.
Holbraad, M. (2011), 'Can the Thing Speak?', *OAC PRESS Working Papers* 7: 2–26.
Holmes, B. (2015), 'Situating Scamander: "natureculture" in the *Iliad*', *Ramus* 44: 29–51.
Hughes, J. (2009), *Deleuze's Difference and Repetition: A Reader's Guide*, London.
Iser, W. (1971), 'Indeterminacy and the Reader's Response in Prose Fiction', in J. H. Miller (ed.), *Aspects of Narrative: Selected Papers from the English Institute*, 1–46, New York, NY.
Jacobs, C. (1985), 'On Looking at Shelley's Medusa', *Yale French Studies* 163–79.
Jong, I. J. F. de, ed. (1999a), *Homer: Critical Assessments*, London.
Jong, I. J. F. de (1999b), 'The Voice of Anonymity: tis-Speeches in the *Iliad*', in I. J. F. de Jong (ed.), *Homer: Critical Assessments*, vol. 3: 258–73, London.
Jong, I. J. F. de (2006), 'The Homeric Narrator and His Own *kleos*', *Mnemosyne* 59: 188–207.
Kahane, A. (2005), *Diachronic Dialogues: Authority and Continuity in Homer and the Homeric Tradition*, Lanham, MD.
Kahane, A. (forthcoming), 'Homer and Ancient Narrative Time', *Classical Antiquity* 40.
Kelly, A. (2007), *A Referential Commentary and Lexicon to Iliad VIII*, Oxford.
Kelly, A. (2012), 'The Mourning of Thetis: "Allusion" and the Future in the *Iliad*', in F. Montanari, A. Rengakos and C. Tsagalis (eds), *Homeric Contexts: Neoanalysis and the Interpretation of Oral Poetry*, 221–65, Berlin.
Kennedy, G. A., ed. (1989), *The Cambridge History of Literary Criticism*, Cambridge.
Kirk, G. S. (1990), *The Iliad: A Commentary*, vol. 2, Cambridge.
Kripke, S. (1980), *Naming and Necessity*, Cambridge, MA.
Kullmann, W. (1960), *Die Quellen der Ilias (troischer Sagenkreis)*, Wiesbaden.
Kullmann, W. (1981), 'Zur Methode der Neoanalyse in der Homerforschung', *Wiener Studien* 15: 5–42.
Kullmann, W. (1984), 'Oral Poetry Theory and Neoanalysis in Homeric Research', *Greek, Roman, and Byzantine Studies* 25: 307–23.
Kullmann, W. (1992), *Homerische Motive: Beiträge zur Entstehung, Eigenart und Wirkung von Ilias und Odyssee*, Stuttgart.
Lapoujade, D. (2017), *Aberrant Movements: The Philosophy of Gilles Deleuze*, trans. J. D. Jordan, South Pasadena, CA.
Lattimore, R. (1951), *The Iliad of Homer*, Chicago, IL.
Lattimore, R. (1967), *The Odyssey of Homer*, New York, NY.
Lejeune, R. (1954), 'Technique formulaire et chansons de geste', *Le Moyen Âge* 60: 311–34.
Lévi-Strauss, C. (1987), *Introduction to the Work of Marcel Mauss*, London.
Li, Y. (2018), 'The Silence of the Muse', *Arethusa* 51: 91–115.
Liebert, R. S. (2017), *Tragic Pleasure from Homer to Plato*, Cambridge.
Lord, A. B. (1964), *The Singer of Tales*, Cambridge, MA.
Louden, B. (1993), 'Pivotal Contrafactuals in Homeric Epic', *Classical Antiquity* 12: 181–98.

Luce, T. J., ed. (1982), *Ancient Writers: Greece and Rome*, New York, NY.
Lynn-George, M. (1988), *Epos: Word, Narrative and the Iliad*, Basingstoke.
Maitland, J. (1999), 'Poseidon, Walls, and Narrative Complexity in the Homeric *Iliad*', *Classical Quarterly* 49: 1–13.
Marks, J. (2010), 'Context as Hypertext: Divine Rescue Scenes in the *Iliad*', *Trends in Classics* 2: 300–22.
Martindale, C. (1993), *Redeeming the Text: Latin Poetry and the Hermeneutics of Reception*, Cambridge.
Miller, J.-A. (1966), 'La Suture. Éléments de la logique du signifiant', *Cahiers pour l'analyse*, 1: 37–49.
Miller, J.-A. (2012), 'Suture (Elements of the Logic of the Signifier)', in P. Hallward and K. Peden (eds), *Concept and Form, Volume 1: Selections from the Cahiers pour l'Analyse*, 91–101, London.
Minchin, E. (2001), 'Similes in Homer: Image, Mind's Eye, and Memory', in J. Watson (ed.), *Speaking Volumes: Orality and Literacy in the Greek and Roman World*, 25–52, Leiden.
Montanari, F., A. Rengakos and C. Tsagalis, eds (2012), *Homeric Contexts: Neoanalysis and the Interpretation of Oral Poetry*, Berlin.
Morris, I. and B. B. Powell, eds (1997), *A New Companion to Homer*, New York, NY.
Morrison, J. V. (1992), *Homeric Misdirection: False Predictions in the Iliad*, Ann Arbor, MI.
Morrison, J. V. (1997), '*Kerostasia*, the Dictates of Fate, and the Will of Zeus in the *Iliad*', *Arethusa* 30: 276–96.
Moulton, C. (1977), *Similes in the Homeric Poems*, Göttingen.
Mueller, M. (2010), 'Helen's Hands: Weaving for *Kleos* in the *Odyssey*', *Helios* 37: 1–21.
Murnaghan, S. (1997), 'Equal Honor and Future Glory: The Plan of Zeus in the *Iliad*', in D. H. Roberts, F. M. Dunn and D. Fowler (eds), *Classical Closure: Reading the End in Greek and Latin Literature*, 23–42, Princeton, NJ.
Nägele, R. (1987), *Reading after Freud: Essays on Goethe, Hölderlin, Habermas, Nietzsche, Brecht, Celan, and Freud*, New York, NY.
Nägele, R. (1991), *Theater, Theory, Speculation: Walter Benjamin and the Scenes of Modernity*, Baltimore, MD.
Nagler, M. N. (1974), *Spontaneity and Tradition: A Study in the Oral Art of Homer*, Berkeley, CA.
Nagy, G. (1974), *Comparative Studies in Greek and Indic Meter*, Cambridge, MA.
Nagy, G. (1979), *The Best of the Achaeans: Concepts of the Hero in Archaic Greek Poetry*, Baltimore, MD.
Nagy, G. (1982), 'Hesiod', in T. J. Luce (ed.), *Ancient Writers: Greece and Rome*, 43–72, New York, NY.
Nagy, G. (1989), 'Early Greek Views of Poets and Poetry', in G. A. Kennedy (ed.), *Cambridge History of Literary Criticism*, vol. 1, 1–77, Cambridge.
Nagy, G. (1990a), *Pindar's Homer: The Lyric Possession of an Epic Past*, Baltimore, MD.

Nagy, G. (1990b), *Greek Mythology and Poetics*, Ithaca, NY.
Nagy, G. (1996a), *Poetry as Performance: Homer and Beyond*, Cambridge.
Nagy, G. (1996b), *Homeric Questions*, Austin, TX.
Nagy, G. (2003), *Homeric Responses*, Austin, TX.
Nagy, G. (2004), *Homer's Text and Language*, Urbana, IL.
Nankov, N. (2014), 'The Narrative of Ricoeur's Time and Narrative', *Comparatist* 38: 227–49.
Nietzsche, F. W. (1983), *Untimely Meditations*, trans. R. J. Hollingdale, Cambridge.
Onians, R. B. (1951), *The Origins of European Thought: About the Body, the Mind, the Soul, the World, Time, and Fate*, Cambridge.
Parry, A. (1956), 'The Language of Achilles', *Transactions and Proceedings of the American Philological Association* 87: 1–7.
Parry, M. (1928), *L'épithète traditionnelle dans Homère; essai sur un problème de style homérique*, Paris.
Parry, M. (1930), 'Studies in the Epic Technique of Oral Verse-making. I. Homer and Homeric Style', *Harvard Studies in Classical Philology* 41: 73–147.
Parry, M. (1932), 'Studies in the Epic Technique of Oral Verse-making. II. The Homeric Language as the Language of an Oral Poetry', *Harvard Studies in Classical Philology* 43: 1–50.
Parry, M. (1971), *The Making of Homeric Verse*, Oxford.
Pestalozzi, H. (1945), *Die Achilleis als Quelle der Ilias*, Zürich.
Porter, J. I. (2002), 'Homer: The Very Idea', *Arion* 10: 57–86.
Porter, J. I. (2004), 'Homer: The History of an Idea', in R. L. Fowler (ed.), *Cambridge Companion to Homer*, 324–43, Cambridge.
Porter, J. I. (2005), 'Making and Unmaking: The Achaean Wall and the Limits of Fictionality in Homeric Criticism', *Classics@* 3.
Porter, J. I. (2010), *The Origins of Aesthetic Thought in Ancient Greece: Matter, Sensation, and Experience*, Cambridge.
Porter, J. I. (2011), 'Making and Unmaking: The Achaean Wall and the Limits of Fictionality in Homeric Criticism', *Transactions and Proceedings of the American Philological Association* 141: 1–36.
Porter, J. I. (2016), *The Sublime in Antiquity*, Cambridge.
Pratt, L. (2007), 'The Parental Ethos of the *Iliad*', *Hesperia Supplements* 41: 25–40.
Pucci, P. (1979), 'The Song of the Sirens', *Arethusa* 12: 121–32.
Pucci, P. (1998), *The Song of the Sirens: Essays on Homer*, Lanham, MD.
Pucci, P. (2018), *The Iliad: the Poem of Zeus*, Berlin.
Purves, A. C. (2006), 'Falling into Time in Homer's *Iliad*', *Classical Antiquity* 25: 179–209.
Purves, A. C. (2010), *Space and Time in Ancient Greek Narrative*, Cambridge.
Purves, A. C. (2015), 'Ajax and Other Objects: Homer's Vibrant Materialism', *Ramus* 44: 75–94.
Ready, J. L. (2019), *Orality, Textuality, and the Homeric Epics: An Interdisciplinary Study of Oral Texts, Dictated, and Wild Texts*, Oxford.

Ready, J. L. and C. Tsagalis, eds (2018), *Homer in Performance: Rhapsodes, Narrators, and Characters*, Austin, TX.
Redfield, J. M. (1975), *Nature and Culture in the Iliad: The Tragedy of Hector*, Chicago, IL.
Redfield, J. M. (1979), 'The Proem of the *Iliad*: Homer's Art', *Classical Philology* 74: 95–110.
Reichel, M. and A. Rengakos, eds (2002), *Epea pteroenta: Beiträge zur Homerforschung*, Stuttgart.
Reinhardt, K. (1961), *Die Ilias und ihr Dichter*, Göttingen.
Rengakos, A. (2020), 'Neoanalysis and Oral Poetry: A Historic Compromise?', in A. Rengakos, P. Finglass and B. Zimmerman (eds), *More than Homer Knew – Studies on Homer and His Ancient Commentators*, 37–50, Berlin.
Ricœur, P. (1984), *Time and Narrative*, vol. 1, trans. K. McLaughlin and D. Pellauer, Chicago, IL.
Ricœur, P. (1988), *Time and Narrative*, vol. 3, trans. K. Blamey and D. Pellauer, Chicago, IL.
Roberts, D. H., F. M. Dunn and D. Fowler, eds (1997), *Classical Closure: Reading the End in Greek and Latin Literature*, Princeton, NJ.
Rosenberg, H. (1959), *The Tradition of the New*, New York, NY.
Russo, J. A. (1968), 'Homer against His Tradition', *Arion* 7: 275–95.
Russo, J. A. (1997), 'The Formula', in I. Morris and B. B. Powell (eds), *A New Companion to Homer*, 238–60, New York, NY.
Rutherford, R. B. (2019), *Homer: Iliad Book XVIII*, Cambridge.
Sammons, B. (2010), *The Art and Rhetoric of the Homeric Catalogue*, Oxford.
Saussure, F. de (1974), *Course in General Linguistics*, trans. C. Bally, A. Sechehaye and A. Riedlinger, London.
Saussy, H. (1996), 'Writing in the *Odyssey*: Eurykleia, Parry, Jousse, and the Opening of a Letter from Homer', *Arethusa* 29: 299–338.
Schadewaldt, W. (1951), *Von Homers Welt und Werk*, Stuttgart.
Schein, S. L. (1976), 'The Death of Simoeisios: *Iliad* 4.473–489', *Eranos* 74: 1–5.
Schein, S. L. (1984), *The Mortal Hero*, Berkeley, CA.
Schein, S. L. (2016), *Homeric Epic and Its Reception*, Oxford.
Scodel, R. (1982), 'The Achaean Wall and the Myth of Destruction', *Harvard Studies in Classical Philology* 86: 33–50.
Scodel, R. (1997), 'Pseudo-intimacy and the Prior Knowledge of the Homeric Audience', *Arethusa* 30: 201–19.
Scodel, R. (2002), *Listening to Homer*, Ann Arbor, MI.
Scott, M. (1979), 'Pity and Pathos in Homer', *Acta Classica* 22: 1–14.
Scully, S. (2003), 'Reading the Shield of Achilles: Terror, Anger, Delight', *Harvard Studies in Classical Philology* 101: 29–47.
Segal, C. (1983), '*Kleos* and Its Ironies in the *Odyssey*', *L'Antiquité Classique* 52: 22–47.
Shive, D. (1987), *Naming Achilles*, Oxford.
Slatkin, L. M. (1991), *The Power of Thetis*, Berkeley, CA.

Smith, D. W. (1997), 'Gilles Deleuze and the Philosophy of Difference: Toward a Transcendental Empiricism', PhD diss., University of Chicago, Chicago, IL.
Somers-Hall, H. (2011), 'Time Out of Joint: Hamlet and the Pure Form of Time', *Deleuze Studies* 5: 56–76.
Somers-Hall, H. (2013), *Deleuze's Difference and Repetition*, Edinburgh.
Sourvinou-Inwood, C. (1995), *'Reading' Greek Death: To the End of the Classical Period*, Oxford.
Squire, M. (2013), 'Ekphrasis at the Forge and the Forging of Ekphrasis: The "Shield of Achilles" in Graeco-Roman Word and Image', *Word & Image* 29: 157–91.
Svenbro, J. (1976), *La parole et le marbre: aux origines de la poétique grecque*, Lund.
Svenbro, J. (1993), *Phrasikleia: An Anthropology of Reading in Ancient Greece*, trans. J. Lloyd, Ithaca, NY.
Szondi, P. (1978), 'Hope in the Past: On Walter Benjamin', *Critical Inquiry* 4: 491–506.
Szondi, P. (1986), *Theory of the Modern Drama*, Minneapolis, MN.
Theunissen, M. (2000), *Pindar: Menschenlos und Wende der Zeit*, Munich.
Trampedach, K. (2008), 'Authority Disputed: The Seer in Homeric Epic', in B. Dignas and K. Trampedach (eds), *Practitioners of the Divine: Greek Priests and Religious Officials from Homer to Heliodorus*, 207–30, Washington, DC.
Treu, M. (1955), *Von Homer zur Lyrik: Wandlungen des griechischen Weltbildes im Spiegel der Sprache*, Munich.
Tsagalis, C. (2008), *The Oral Palimpsest: Exploring Intertextuality in the Homeric Epics*, Washington, DC.
Tsagalis, C. (2012), *From Listeners to Viewers: Space in the Iliad*, Washington, DC.
Tsagalis, C. (2020), 'The Homeric Question: A Historical Sketch', *Yearbook of Ancient Greek Epic* 4: 122–62.
Vernant, J.-P. (1991), 'A "Beautiful Death" and the Disfigured Corpse in Homeric Epic', in F. I. Zeitlin (ed.), *Mortals and Immortals: Collected Essays*, 50–74, Princeton, NJ.
Vet, T. de (2005), 'Parry in Paris: Structuralism, Historical Linguistics, and the Oral Theory', *Classical Antiquity* 24: 257–84.
Ward, M. (2019), 'Glory and Nostos: The Ship-epithet ΚΟΙΛΟΣ in the *Iliad*', *Classical Quarterly* 69: 23–34.
Weil, S. (1965), 'The *Iliad*, or the Poem of Force', *Chicago Review* 18: 5–30.
West, M. L. (2007), *Indo-European Poetry and Myth*, Oxford.
Wilamowitz-Moellendorff, U. von (1916), *Die Ilias und Homer*, Berlin.
Willcock, M. M. (1976), *A Companion to the Iliad: Based on the Translation by Richmond Lattimore*, Chicago, IL.
Williams, J. (2011), *Gilles Deleuze's Philosophy of Time: A Critical Introduction and Guide*, Edinburgh.
Žižek, S. (1989), *The Sublime Object of Ideology*, New York, NY.
Žižek, S. (2012), '"Suture," Forty Years Later', in P. Hallward and K. Peden (eds), *Concept and Form, Volume 2: Interviews and Essays on Cahiers pour l'Analyse*, 147–68, London.

Zourabichvili, F. (2012), *Deleuze: A Philosophy of the Event: Together with the Vocabulary of Deleuze*, ed. G. Lambert and D. W. Smith, trans. K. Aarons, Edinburgh.
Zumthor, P. (1972), *Essai de poétique médiévale*, Paris.
Zumthor, P. (1991), *Toward a Medieval Poetics*, trans. P. Bennett, Minneapolis, MN.

Index

Achaean wall 21, 30-40, 41-2, 52-5, 103-4, 171 n.44, 173 nn.68-70
Achilles 34-5, 45-55, 64-6, 98-9, 105-7, 110-15, 144-7, 154-5
  and Agamemnon 111
  and Patroclus 4-5, 66, 99
Agamemnon 44-5, 50-2, 56-60, 66-9, 116, 123-4, 204 n.86
Andromache 120-9, 171 n.51
Aristotle 48, 51, 82, 149-54, 177 n.12
Auerbach, Erich 85-6, 94-6, 132-41

Bakker, Egbert 57-9, 156, 176 n.8, 185 n.70, 200 n.86
Bergson, Henri 52-4
brightness (*selas*) 112-15, 197 n.28

content and form 26, 31, 44-5, 49, 56, 59-60, 74, 78-82, 101-7, 114, 117-20, 122-9, 134, 144-7, 154, 171 n.45, 184 n.66, 186 n.80

death 49-50, 54, 59-60, 66, 68, 95, 105-7, 115-17, 146-7
  of Achilles 46-50, 54, 66, 98, 99
  of Hector 121, 128
  of Menelaus 56-7, 124, 140-1
  of minor warriors 115-19, 127
  of Patroclus 48, 54, 58-9, 99, 106, 110-15, 178 n.70
Deleuze, Gilles 131-60, 171 n.51, 179 n.28, 180 n.35, 183 n.52, 187 n.94, 196 n.25, 200-1 n.55
diachrony 72, 78-83, 83-97, 190 n.44
  and history 83-97
  and synchrony 24, 46, 78, 81, 83-97
difference 5-8, 40-2, 55, 60-9, 74-5, 90-9, 117, 120, 122-3, 138-9, 202 n.68, 209 n.69
divination 103-5
double perspective 40, 47-8, 85-6, 95, 142-3, 181 n.46, 186 n.80

epic poet 7-8, 19-36, 43, 59, 72-95, 97, 116, 135, 138-9, 142-5, 155-7, 176 n.7, 187 n.91, 187 n.93, 195 n.15, 201 n.58, 203 n.75, 212 n.101
  aoidos and rhapsode 4-5, 89-97, 160, 191 n.65, 192 n.70, 195 n.15, 208 n.47
epithet 3, 8, 21-2, 74-5, 182 n.50, see also formula
eusynoptos, eusynoptic 145, 152-8, 209 n.58

fate 47, 121-8, 143, 150, 153, 155-6, 183 n.55, 204 n.86
foil 97-8, 150, 173 n.70
Foley, John Miles 9, 80-6, 102, 131-6, 182 n.50, 188 n.9, see also traditional referentiality
formula 3, 8, 22-4, 29, 36-8, 74-82, 136, 182 n.50, 185 n.70, 207 n.30
Freud, Sigmund 86-8, 197 n.27
future 1-2, 5-6, 43-60, 98-9, 103-7, 125-7, 133, 137-8, 143-4, 149-50, 154-61, 176 n.8, see also song to come

Grethlein, Jonas 52-4, 108-9, 117, 122, 173 n.70, 175 n.2
guslar 9, 20-1, 27-33, 39-40, 54

Hector 6-7, 44-5, 50-2, 66, 98, 103-8, 120-9, 157
Helen 55-6, 59, 107-8, 110, 115, 147-9, 154, 163 n.1, 181 n.46, 183 n.55, 195 n.15, 200 n.55, 203 n.71
history 3-4, 47, 63-5, 88-9, 93-7, 110, 144-8, 151-7, 178 n.19

ignorance 7-8, 49-50, 56, 107, 156, 165 n.21, 174 n.78, 192 n.70, 203 n.75

Index

kleos 7–8, 41–60, 66–9, 71–2, 101–29, 143–61, 169 n.33
   klea andrōn 122–9
   rumour 7–8, 43, 173 n.70, 175–6 n.7

Lykaon 50, 52, 105–7
Lynn-George, Michael 73–81, 84–6, 133–8, 149–50, 168 n.17, 193 n.86, 198 n.33, 207 n.30

mellein 40, 57–8, 128, 204 n.86
memory 1–3, 30–6, 40, 52–4, 63–4, 77, 95–6, 98–9, 122, 126, 134–6, 140–2, 176 n.8, 180 n.35, 184 n.65
Menelaus 56–60, 116, 118, 124, 204 n.78
minor warriors 115–20
muses 7–8, 92, 142, 145, 148, 156–9, *see also* sirens

Nagy, Gregory 7, 11, 30, 71–99, 136–46, 150, 158–9, 166 n.3, 170 n.38
neoanalysis 10–11, 60–9, 82–3, 88, 90–1, 97–9, 206 n.24
nēpios 58–9, 142, 156
Nietzsche, Friedrich 86, 191 n.58

objecthood 108–15, 118–20
Odysseus 109, 139, 172 n.66, 209 n.62
   scar 85–6, 134–7
   and sirens 148–9
Odyssey 2, 10, 24, 96, 109, 148–9, 163 n.4, 172 n.66, 181 n.41, 183 n.55, 197 n.28
Oedipus 50, 153
oral theory 2–3, 6–11, 19–27, 36, 61, 63–4, 71–99, 138, 145–6, 156–7, *see also* Foley, John Miles, Parry, Milman, Nagy, Gregory

Panhellenic synthesis 73, 89–97, 171 n.44
Parry, Milman 8, 21–9, 36, 72–86, 90, 93–7, 102, 132–6, 207 n.30
past 5, 7, 51–4, 57–9, 85–6, 98, 126–7, 133–51, 154–61, 173 n.70, 179 n.28, 179–80 n.30, 181 n.41, 181 n.46
   pure past 140–51, 154–61
Patroclus 4, 57–60, 66, 98–9, 105–6, 112, 116, 150, 172 n.66, 178 n.20, 179 n.29, 202 n.68, *see also under* Achilles, death

Penelope 197 n.28, 198 n.42, 209 n.62, *see also* weaving
performance 9, 19, 22–30, 39–40, 43–4, 54, 71–7, 80–99, 139, 142–5, 156–7, 159, 176 n.8, 185 n.70, 192 n.70
Polydamas 103–5
poet *see* epic poet
present 41–61, 66–9, 85–6, 95–9, 103–7, 123–7, 133–7, 140–3, 149–50, 157–9
   living present 132–41, 150, 158–60, 170 n.34
   instant/now 47, 51–2, 71–7, 82–9, 97–9, 133–8, 140–2

reception 4–5, 26, 37–8

Scamander 35, 203 n.73
sēma 19–21, 28–30, 33–40, 54–5, 122, 168 n.24, 176 n.8, 184 n.66, 195 n.8
short circuit 27–32, 97, *see also* suture
signification 9, 36–9, 56, 74, 77–81, 108–14, *see also* structuralism, *sēma*
simile 115–20
Simoeisios 118–19
singer *see* epic poet
sirens 148–9, 212 n.101
Skamandrios 115–17, 127
song to come 13, 44–59, 69–71, 91, 99, 103–8, 110, 114–6, 119–20, 123, 126, 147–8, 154–7, 159, 203 n.71
structuralism 27, 56, 74–6, 167 n.12, 169 n.33, 170 n.37, 171 n.45, 187 n.94, 189 n.30, 194 n.2
suture 101–29, 144, 147, 194 n.2, 211 n.90
synchrony 46, 63, *see also under* diachrony

tradition 1–3, 7–11, 19–44, 54–5, 61–3, 67, 71–99, 133–47, 150, 155–6, 158
traditional referentiality 19–30, 34, 36–8, 40, 66, 75, 97

vignette 115–20, 122, 127–8

weaving 107–8, 110, 183 n.55, 196 n.15, 197 n.28, 198 n.42, 200 n.55, 202 n.71
women 109, 183 n.55, 195 n.15, 196 n.26, *see also* Andromache, Helen, Penelope, weaving

www.ingramcontent.com/pod-product-compliance
Lightning Source LLC
Chambersburg PA
CBHW062217300426
44115CB00012BA/2099